DESIGN FOR EMBROIDERY

DESIGN FOR EMBROIDERY

AN EXPERIMENTAL APPROACH

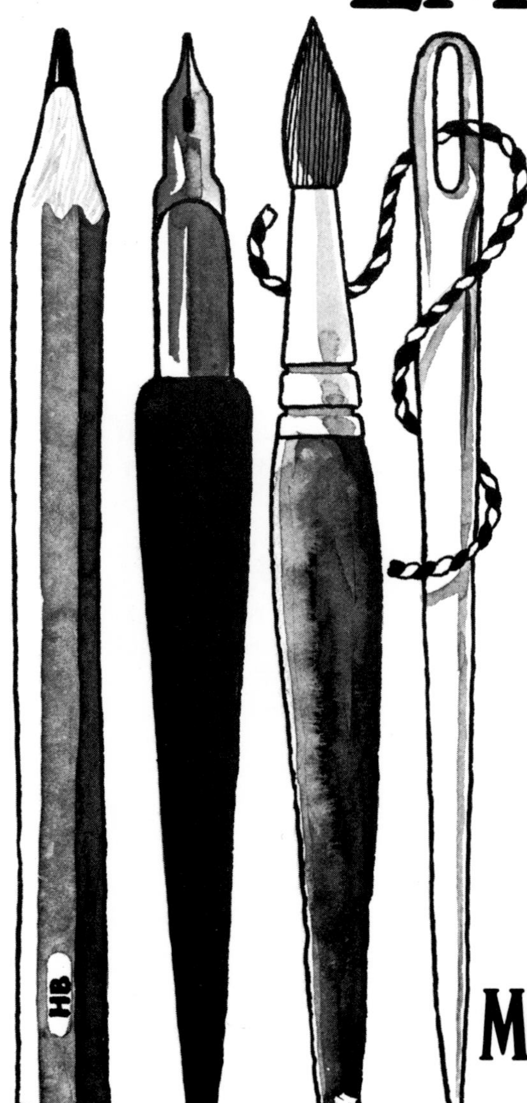

BETTY WHYATT
& JOAN OXLAND

MILLS & BOON Limited,
LONDON

TO our mothers, who first made us visually sensitive.

To those who by their teaching gave us the joy of creativity, and to our pupils and students who responded and shared our delights and enthusiasms.

First published in Great Britain 1975 by Mills & Boon Ltd, 17-19 Foley Street, London W1A 1DR.

ISBN 0 263 05893 X

Book designed by Alec Davis

Made and printed in Great Britain by Ebenezer Baylis and Son, Limited The Trinity Press, Worcester, and London.

Contents

ACKNOWLEDGEMENTS

We wish to thank all those who in any way have helped in the producing of this book. They are too many to mention all by name, but especially we thank Ann Rees, our advisor and mentor, without whose interest and encouragement it would never have started, and Joan Bryant, Executive Director of Mills and Boon Ltd, who together with Alec Davis, designer, saw its possibilities, received it with enthusiasm and so gave us the confidence to continue.

Keith Bowen and his wife Lois volunteered to be official photographers and we thank them for their time and skill so generously given, and also Margaret Routley who contributed some of the colour photography.

A book of this kind owes much to its illustrative content and we thank all who allowed their work to be included: past students of Glamorgan College of Education; past students of Llandaff College of Education; pupils of Llanedeyrn High School, Cardiff; Mrs Routley who provided us with leisure work.

Introduction

Man has always felt the need to be creative, but whereas primitive man had many outlets for his instinct to decorate and make things with his hands, civilised man is often deprived in this sphere. Contemporary educationalists are catering for this basic need by giving every pupil a taste of working creatively in a wide variety of media. As a result, a few may become professionals in a craft, many will find a satisfying leisure occupation to pursue in later life, and all will have a richer appreciation and greater enjoyment of the world around them. Nowadays creative work is included in the curriculum to balance the academic diet and make for a 'whole man'; adults – parents and teachers alike – envy the child and would have liked to have had such opportunities.

Creative work provides a satisfying way of using leisure time, and many people would like to express their ideas through some artistic medium but are at a loss to know how to get started. The reader may be artistic and wish to use this gift with fabrics, or she may well be a trained craftswoman looking for a fresh outlook and a better understanding of designing for needlecraft. We have written this book for such people – not for artists or designers. Each reader will know her own needs, but we hope that she will read *all* the chapters, at least once, before concentrating on the section that interests her most. Design for a craft needs to be considered as a whole.

We believe that anyone with the skill of a craft at their fingertips, given the right attitude of mind, devoid of rigidity and prejudice, can cast out forever the thought that creativity is beyond their reach. There is a real need to break down the superior attitude that the understanding of creativity is the prerogative of a chosen few.

We offer a course of study to encourage visual awareness and adventurous needlecraft. It is a way of working which we have tried with students and pupils of limited artistic experience and which seemed to succeed; a way of working – not the *only* way of working. Nearly all the illustrations shown are of work done by students and pupil designers during their course of study – no work of professional designers is included.

It is hoped that readers will start working practically as well as theoretically. No amount of theory alone will teach design for craft. Time is needed for experiment, for becoming involved and for enjoyment. In the early chapters we concentrate on what seem to us to be the priorities, namely design and experiment using freer techniques with the materials and tools. This is the grammar that must be acquired before ideas are expressed and finished works are attempted. We hope that those who read this book will be helped and inspired to try out the methods of working creatively, not copying the examples shown, but, by understanding and adapting the method of observation and experiment both with ideas and with materials, to find their own world of interests. Given this basic training – the sky is the limit.

1

DESIGN FOR CRAFT

Design is a plan, a purpose, contrived by man. It is artificial and although frequently inspired by nature, it is never found in natural form. Kenneth Clark writes in his book, *Landscape into Art,* that, 'Facts become Art through love, which unifies them and lifts them to a higher plane of reality'. He is talking of landscape painting, but what he says could just as well apply to design.

No two designers would arrive at the same result given the same object as inspiration. Each would make a personal comment in the final design after selecting and abstracting from the original inspiration. The design may be far removed from the original. Given a snail-shell, one designer might draw the spiral with mathematical order and accuracy, discarding the accidents of nature, while another might feel excitement in the movement and distort and exaggerate the ever-increasing size of the whirling form.

The designer must be excited, become involved with the subject, explore it, simplify it in some way in order to make this personal comment. The quality that appeals may be exaggerated, be it swinging curves or brittle angularity. Some aspect of the object contemplated may be presented larger than life, in order that the beholder of the design receives something of the exhilarating visual experience that the designer had when seeing the original source of inspiration. He interprets this vision. He abstracts from nature. (A similar problem of interpretation confronts the actor who on stage makes a gesture that is large enough to be significant for the gallery, moving in a way which he would not move in real life, and yet it is accepted as natural by the audience, and he communicates his meaning to them.

For his task of communication the designer uses his special vocabulary, the artist's language, the elements of basic design, colour, shape, line and texture. Learning a language is a long process, there is a lot of hard graft, but understanding comes with listening, reading and practising. Progress comes in fits and starts, then quite suddenly there arrives total understanding. This is equally true of learning the design process. The reader who is willing to get a real understanding of this basic vocabulary can acquire the art of designing.

Colour is a more important element in some crafts than others. It is absolutely vital in needlecraft. Shape, spatial relationships, line and texture we would think equally important in all crafts. This basic knowledge of design is at the back of the mind when things go well but must be brought to the front when the design does not succeed. Then it is necessary to analyse why it does not work and to put it right with knowledge.

The designer/craftsman works towards the solution of the problem understanding the basic elements of design and disciplined by the characteristics of the craft. Every craft has its characteristics and its limitations. These must be recognised, respected and never strained. Needlecraft is typically two-dimensional and decorative. The flat surface should be respected and the structural and textural quality of the craft should be exploited. A clearly defined warp and weft, for example, may inspire a design of vertical and horizontal shape and line. This very limitation may induce a closer look at things in the environment, such as architecture, which would be sympathetic to this basic geometric structure. Knowledge of the tools of the craft ensures the best selection of needle or scissors for the purpose and an awareness of the limitations of some tools. The sewing machine, designed for speed, requires a design that avoids frequent cutting of threads and instead accepts the limitation of a continuous line.

We would advise the needlewoman to cut or tear paper when designing rather than to draw with a pencil. A pair of scissors is already a familiar, skilled tool and she would probably cut shapes with more confidence, and therefore success, than she would draw them. But any design in pen and ink or cut paper is only a starting point to which the designer should not slavishly adhere. Once the general composition is established, then the materials 'take over' and the work proceeds within the discipline that the materials and the tools impose.

Design for needlecraft will plan for a decorative art in two dimensions, composed of shapes of cloth, lines of stitches and thread, textures of fabric, stitches, beads, sequins, combined with an appreciative use of colour. Once this has been achieved, then the language of design will have been applied to the medium of needlecraft to create work that should grow naturally from a sensitive use of the tools and materials of the craft.

Misdirected skill has often been a criticism levelled at needlecraft by designers in the past. The pendulum always swings too widely, and now there is a tendency to decry good craftsmanship in the cause of artistry. There must be a good marriage of design and craftsmanship if embroidery is to be considered as an art.

So, a word of warning. A good design deserves good finish–it is not good design without it. No amount of inspiration, however brilliant, can be allowed to be expressed on a puckered piece of ground fabric. Careful preparation is essential in tacking materials together with the grain of the weaves parallel and without stretching. Every fabric relaxes in a different way and must be tacked in a state of non-stress. This type of technical skill and knowledge distinguishes the professional from the amateur. All works of art are produced by a mixture of freedom and discipline, and for those who love their craft this discipline will be surmounted by their interest and they will not find it tedious.

2

COLOUR

Colour is one of the basic elements of design – the vocabulary that makes up the language of the designer. It is a very vital element in needlecraft, be it for colour in dress or creative embroidery. The needlewoman needs to feel confident when selecting colours to be put together, and she needs to choose with knowledge. There are some people born with an instinctive gift for arranging colour in a pleasing way, and a very small minority with real flair can choose the right amount of the most surprising colours, put them together, and get away with it brilliantly. If the reader is one of these, she may find this chapter tedious. On the other hand, she may be interested to study, in theory, what she is doing in practice, when choosing colours and assembling them. The vast majority of mortals do not have this confidence and will find it helpful to have some guide in the use of colour.

Nature often inspires the designer in the use of colour. Many designers use natural objects as a starting point for their colour schemes. Everyone will be familiar with tweed colourings which seem made to blend with the colouring of the moor, heather, bracken etc. A student of colour would do well from the outset to try to become more sensitive, more aware, of the colour in nature. Not vast landscapes, but small pieces of bark, stones, shells, leaves, lichen and suchlike, which can be carried home and studied at leisure.
It will be necessary to have some powder paint in order to make studies and experiments. We would advise the three primary colours and black and white. These are all the colours that are needed. True primary colours are essential – these are discussed later in this chapter.

ABSTRACTION OF COLOUR FROM NATURE

Select a natural object. Make a small frame in paper, 1″ × $\frac{3}{4}$″ (2·5cm × 2cm) approximately, hold it before one eye and look through it, examining different areas of the surface. Select a part of the colouring that pleases most, and place the frame over it (Fig. 1).

Perhaps the size and proportion of the frame will require some adjusting for this. Mix the colours as seen in the frame, study the proportions and juxtapositions of the colours. Paint them onto a sheet of paper on which has been prepared a network of rectangles, arranged to receive the colours in the proportions and juxtapositions found in the object. Let the rectangles of colour touch each other with no white paper between them just as the colours touch in the object (see colour plates 1 and 2).

Similarly, colour schemes may be selected from a study of part of a painting. It may be necessary to repeat the colours several times in order that all possible arrangements of juxtaposition are used. In doing

Fig. 1

this the designer will have selected and abstracted from nature. Now she can make a personal comment by highlighting the feature which attracted. This may require that the colour be made larger than life–pepped up, made more positive, more intense, more dramatic–by exaggerating the tone, the intensity, or the changes of colour temperature.

Fig. 2a

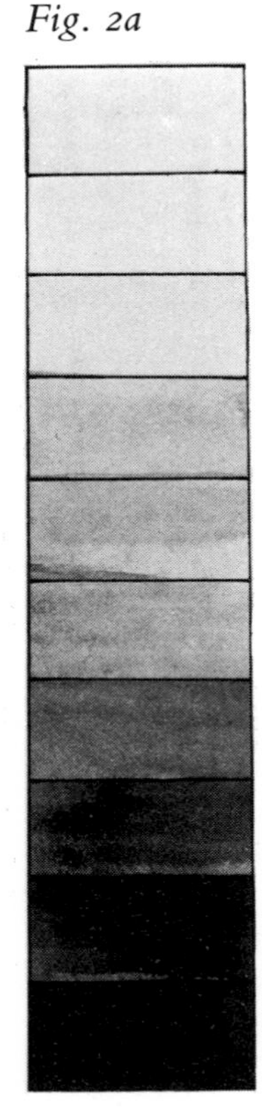

TONE

It is necessary to know exactly what is meant by tone. It may be visualised as a long musical scale with black as the lowest note, white as the highest, and limitless grey notes in between, ranging from those that are almost black, to mid-greys, to those that are almost white (Fig. 2a).

A design could be carried out to great effect using black, white and greys. The greatest impact would be seen when black and white are placed together, and

1 *Selecting a colour scheme from nature*

2 *Selecting a colour scheme from part of a painting*

3 *The colour circle and the family tree of colour*

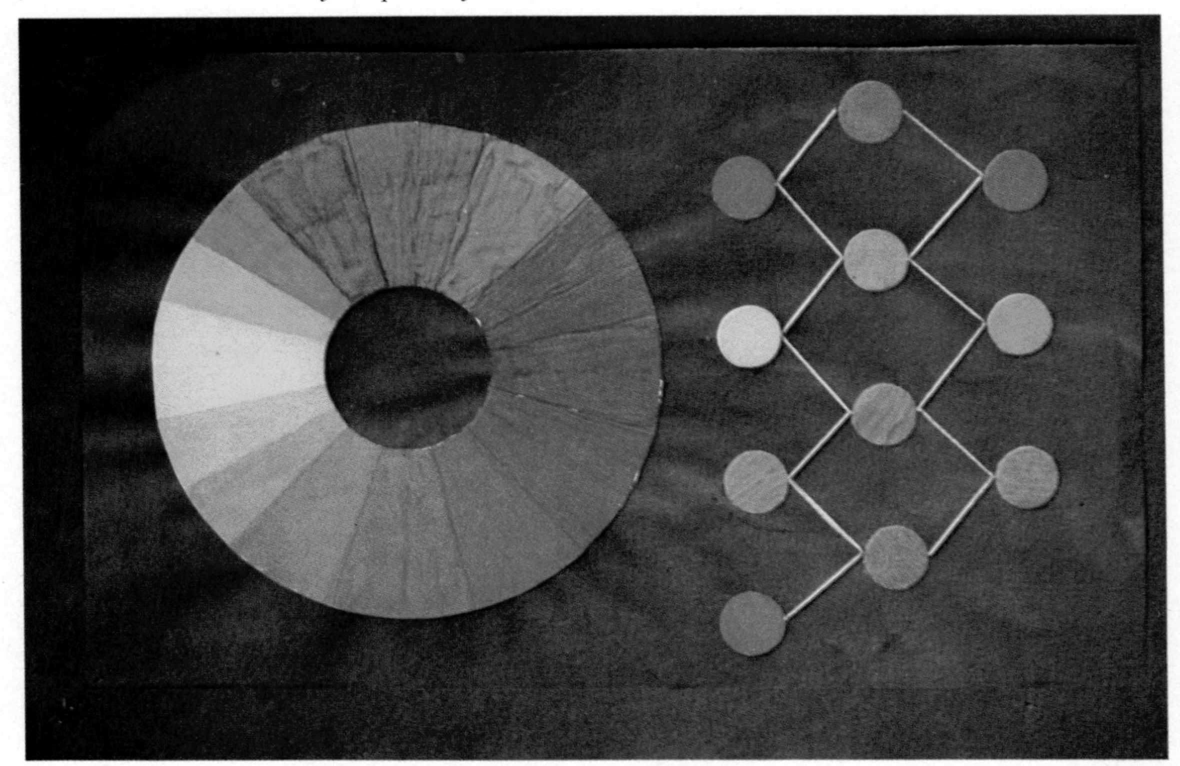

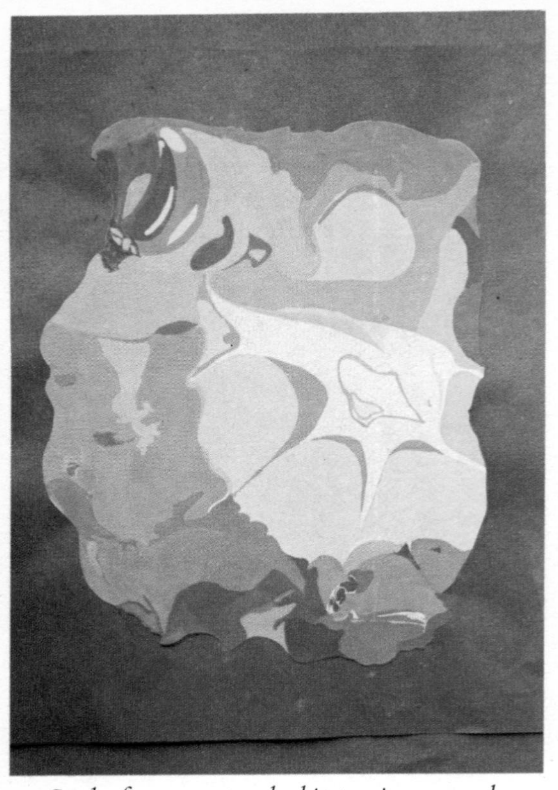

4 *Study from a natural object using monochrome*

5 *Study from a natural object using monochrome*

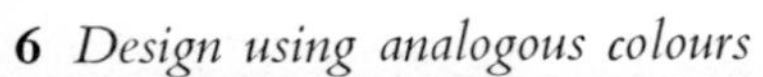

6 *Design using analogous colours*

7 *Appliqué collage based on exploded circle (Heulwen Parry Jones)*

8 *Pile of unrelated fabrics before dyeing*

9 *Same pile now dyed red and thus unified*

10 *Another pile of similarly unrelated fabrics dyed turquoise*

11 *Fabric collage makes use of an exciting variety of materials*

12 *Experimental weaving in two dimensions*

13 *Experimental weaving (Gillian Griffiths)*

14 *Experimental weaving in three dimensions (Sandra James)*

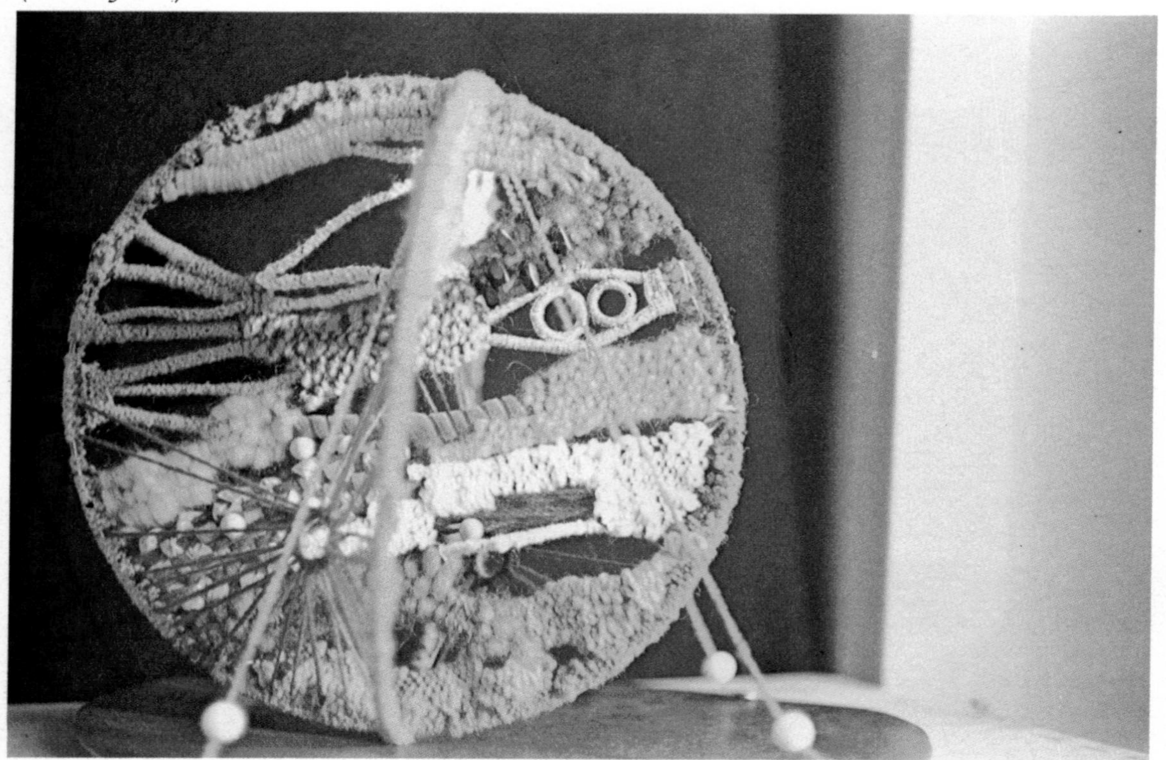

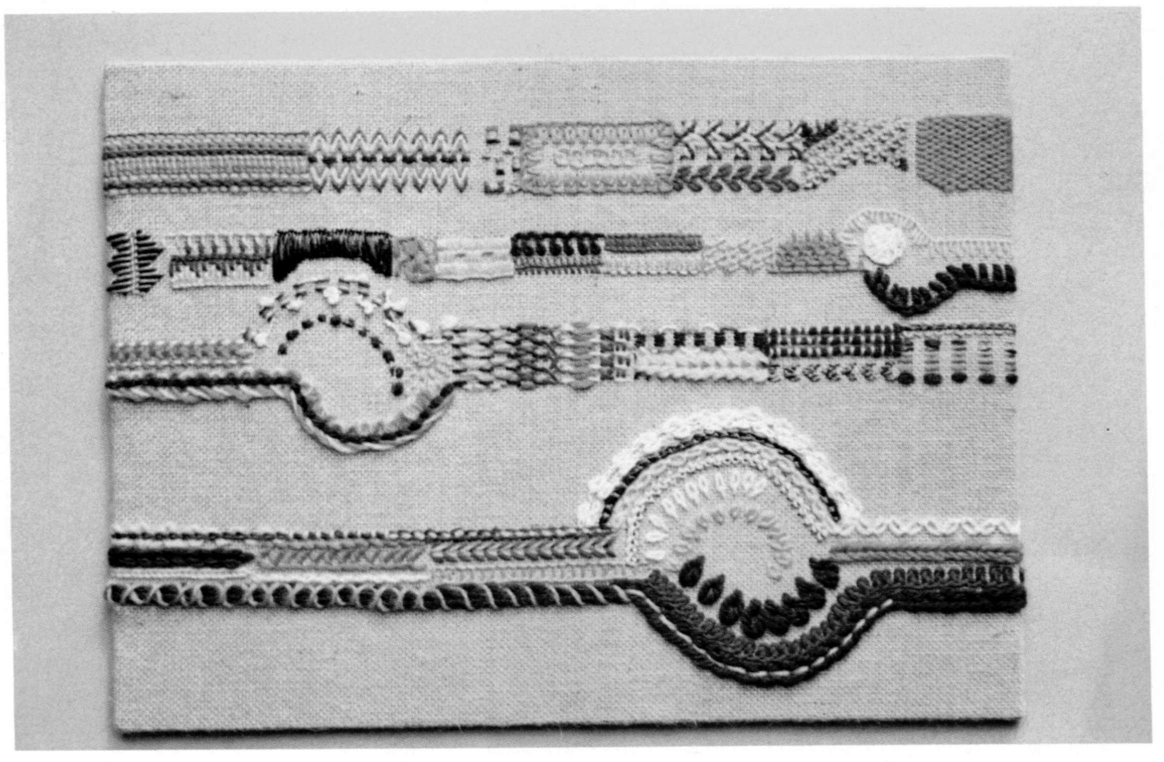

15 *Stitch exercises*

16 *This tie-dyed circle inspired . . .*

17 *. . . this piece of free weaving*

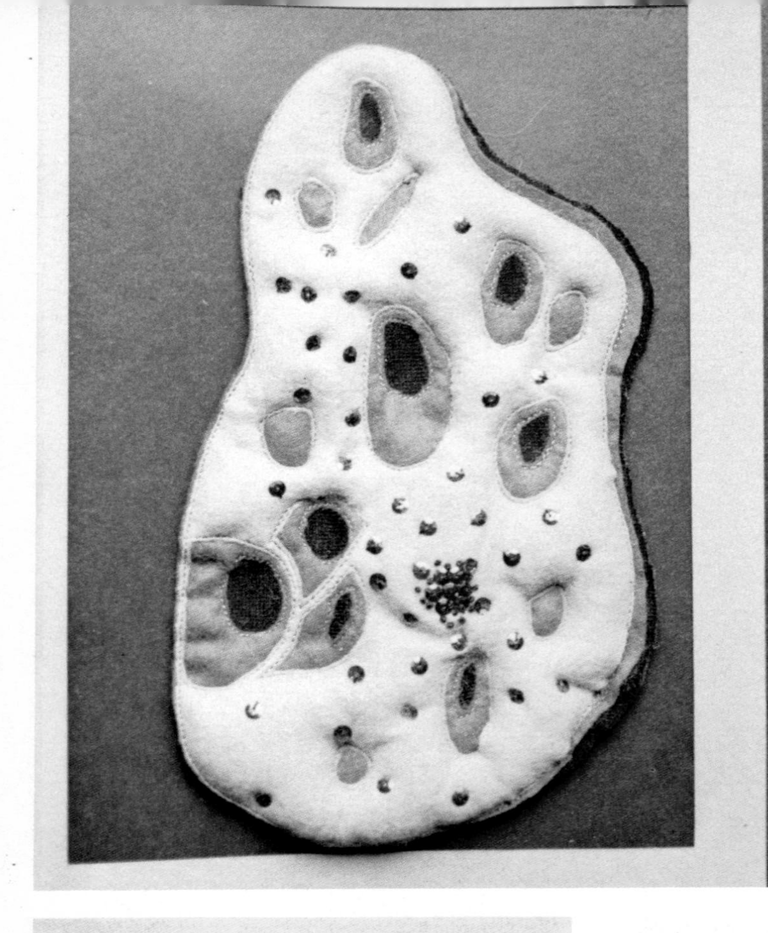

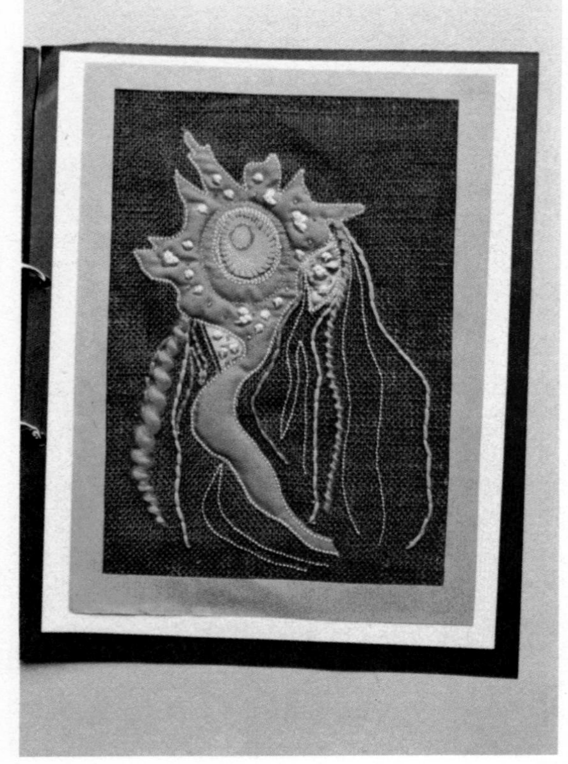

18 (*above*) *Appliqué collage based on drawing of limestone riddled with holes, Fig. 158*

19 (*left*) *Appliqué and stitchery based on seaweed drawing, Fig. 157*

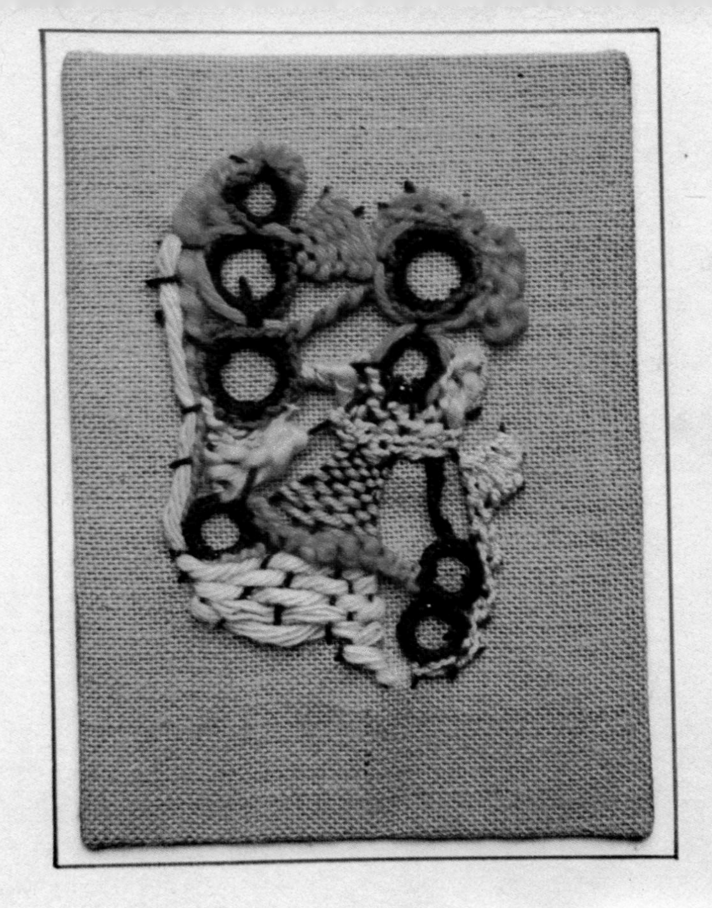

20 *and* **21**
Experimental weaving interpretations based on pebble embedded in concrete, Fig. 160

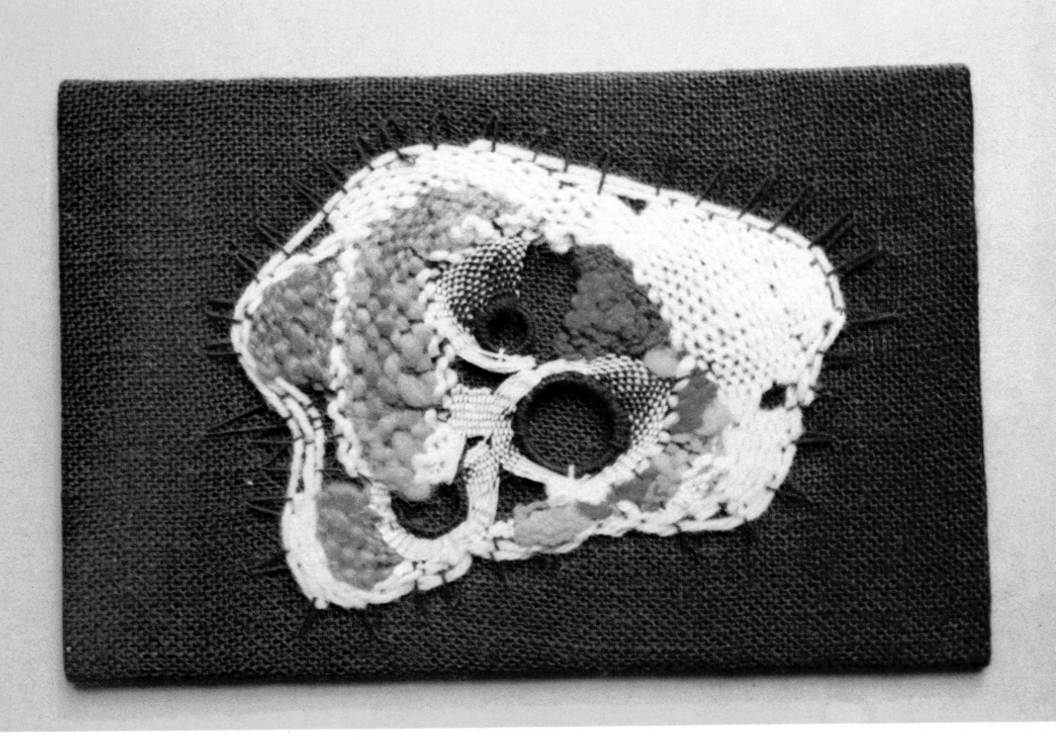

22 *and* **23** *Stages in the development collage based on bark drawing, Fig. 1 (Susan Rogers)*

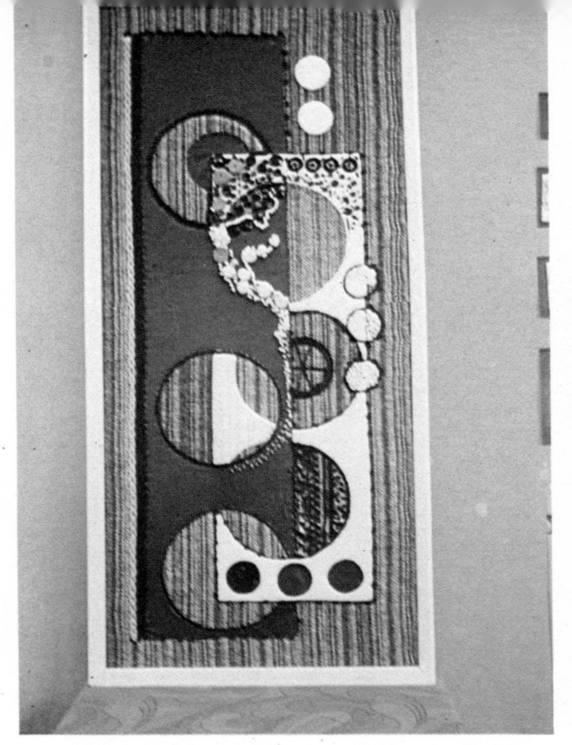

24 *Collage using circles and the rectangle from which they were cut (Shân Humphrey Thomas)*

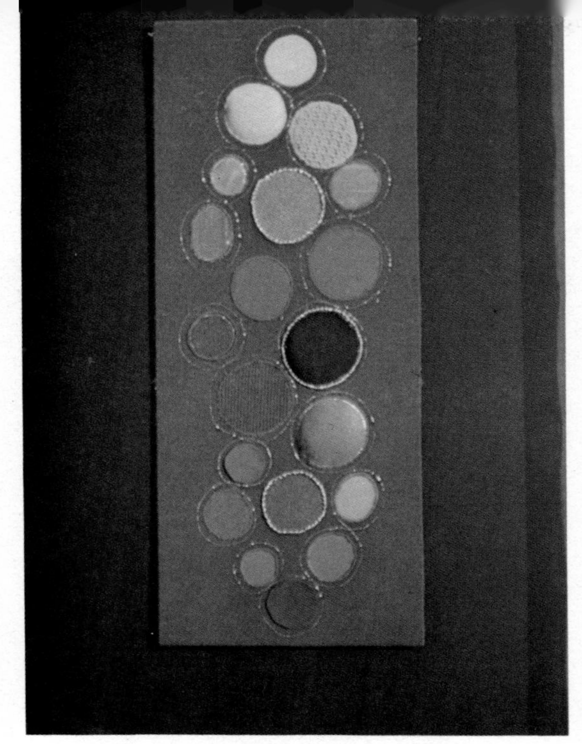

25 *Appliqué collage using colours from one third of the colour circle arranged in natural order (Sandra James)*

26 *Design based on section through a gourd (Christine Perry)*

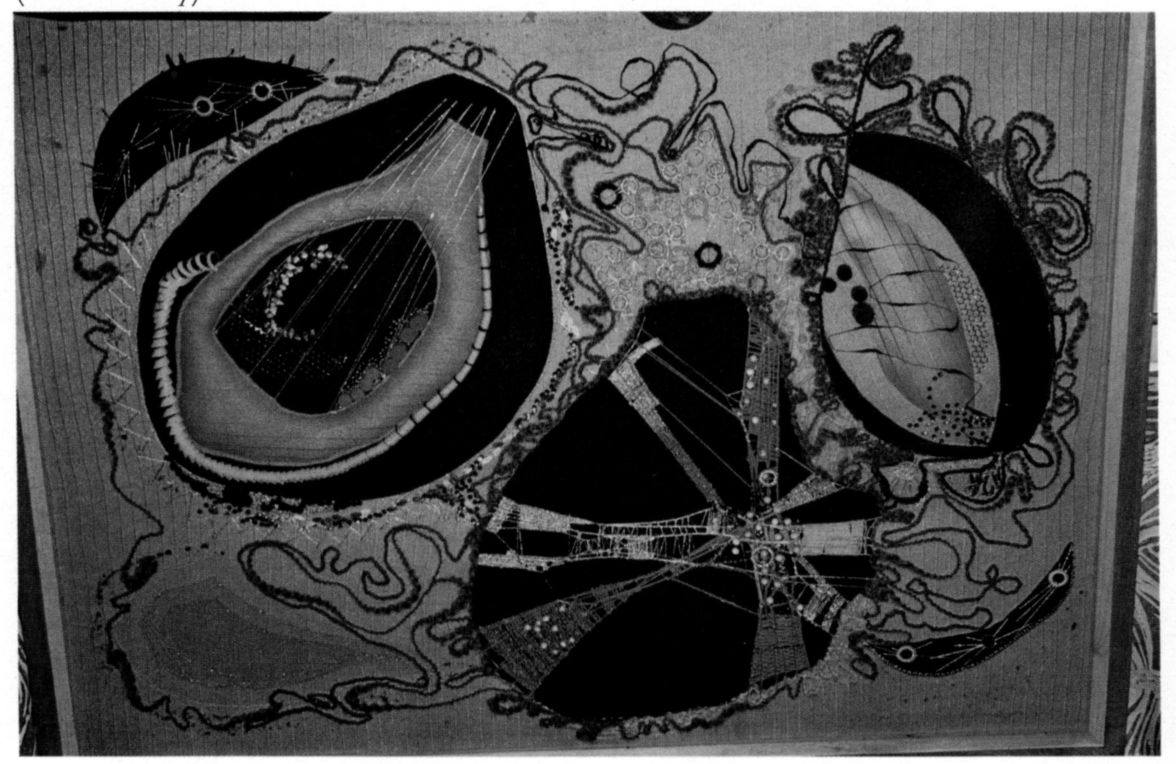

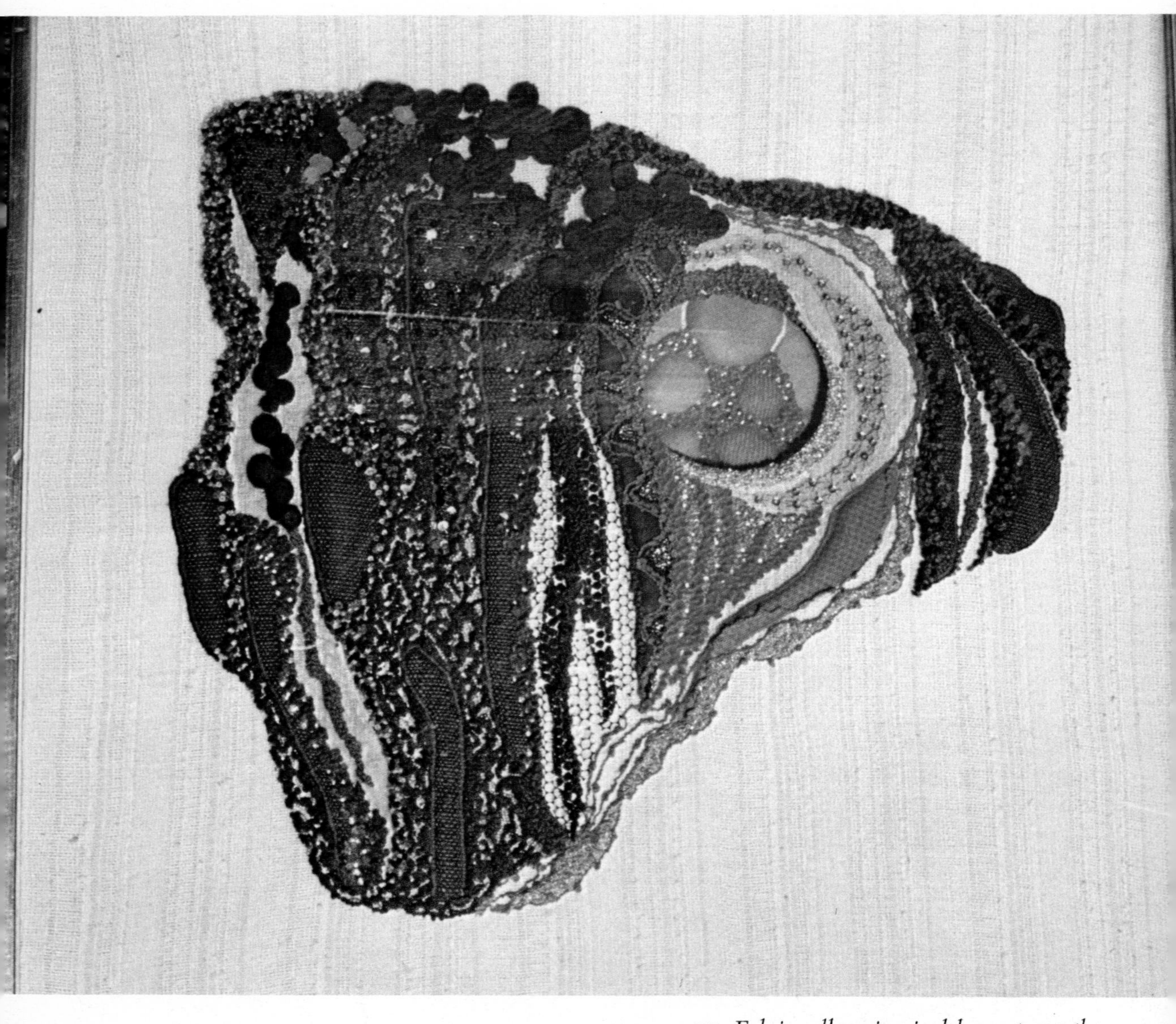

27 *Fabric collage inspired by a stone; the appliqué is systematically covered with beadwork and couched thread (Irene Clarke)*

28 *Three interpretations of cellular shape unified by the colour scheme (Angela Burt)*

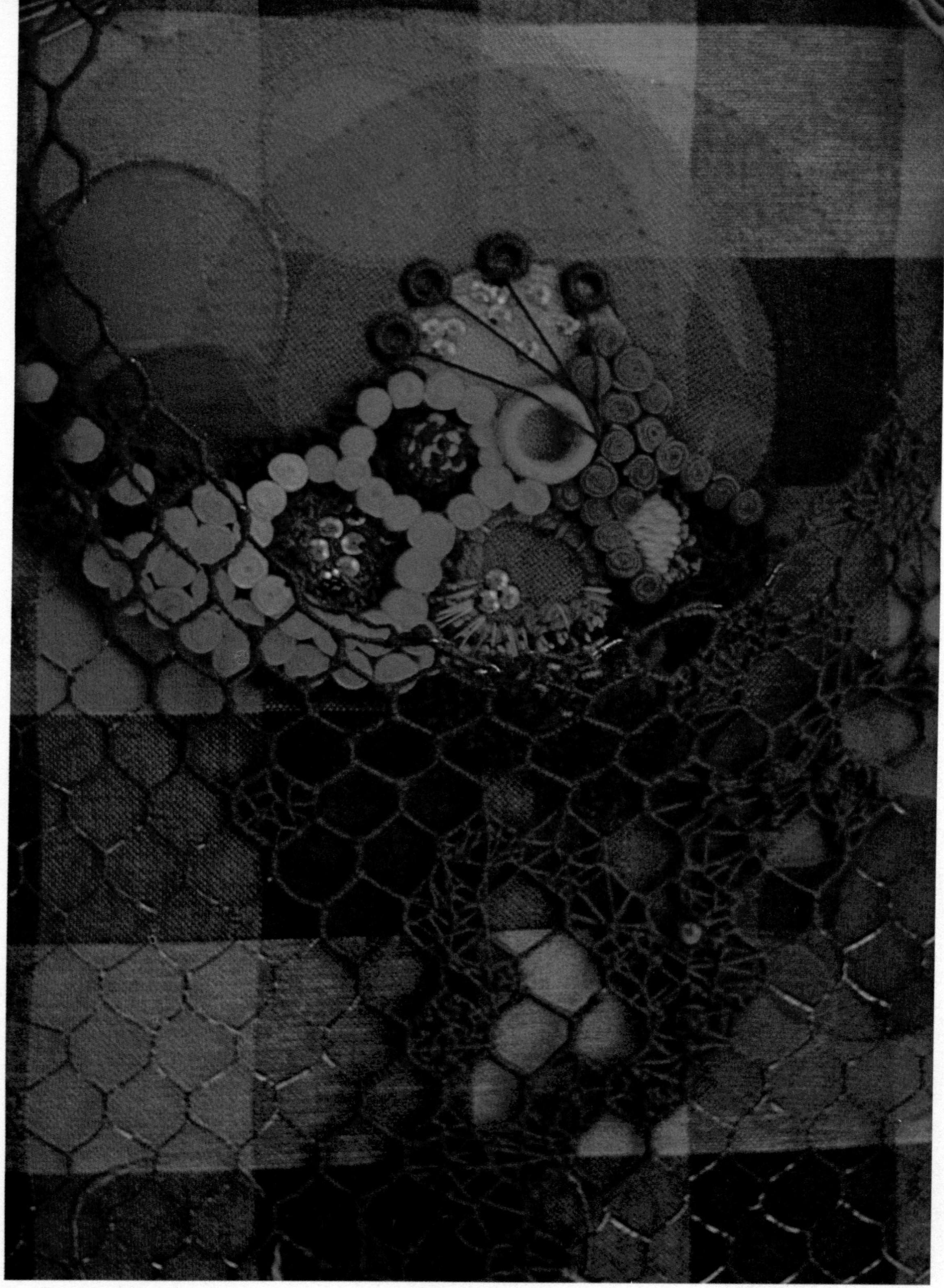

29 *Detail showing experimental use of chicken wire partly covered with wool and felt scrolls (Stephanie Groves)*

30 *Fabric and thread interpretation of plan of symmetrical town, Fig. 138*

31 *An individual interpretation of pregnancy (Elaine Davies)*

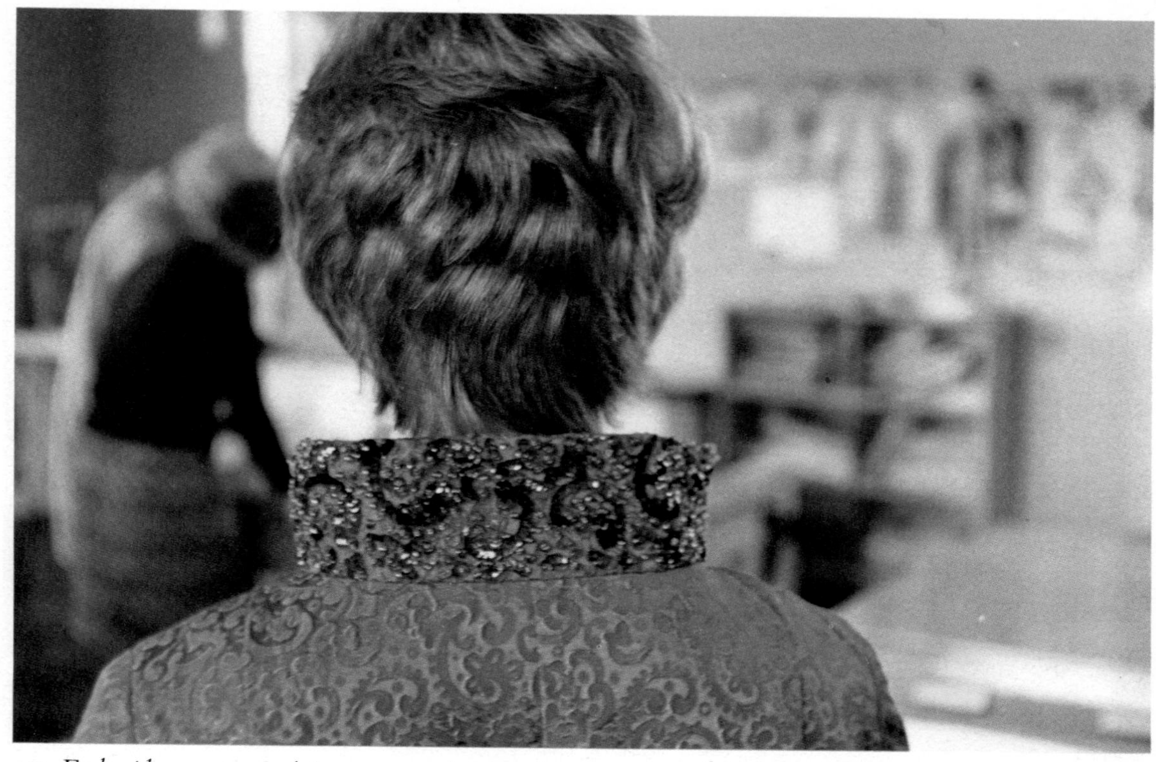

32 *Embroidery may exploit a patterned fabric by following the pattern*

33 *Softer fabrics with good draping qualities may have the folds enriched with smocking*

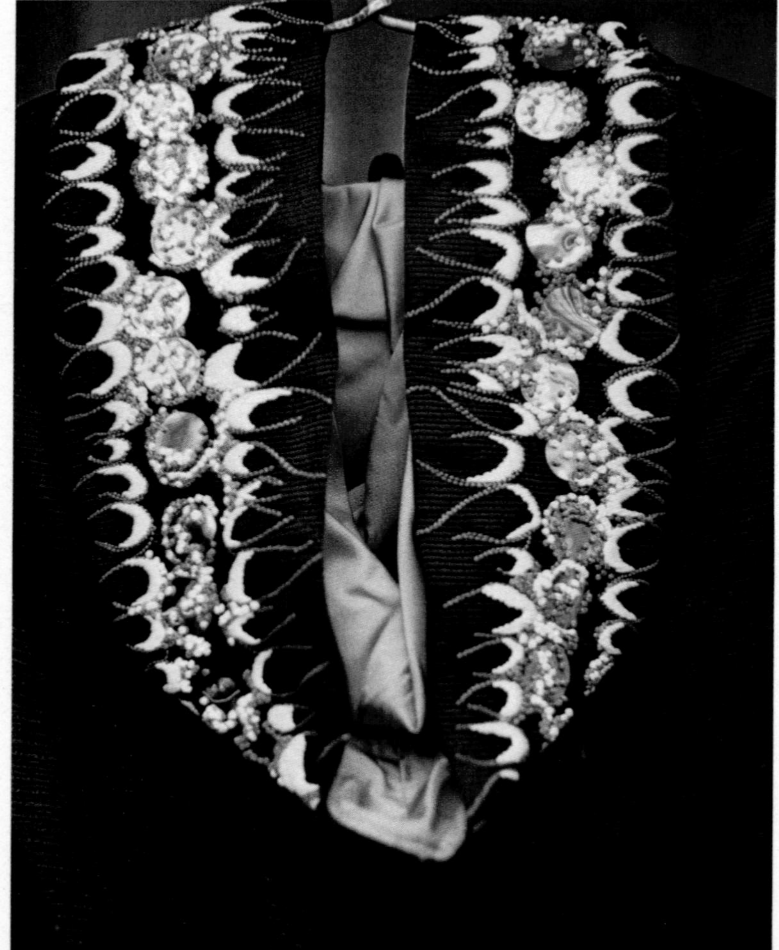

34 *(above) Section of bodice textured with applied padded shapes, beadwork and French knots*

35 *(left) Hood with border design in machine cable stitch, further embellished with satin stitch and French knots*

Fig. 2b

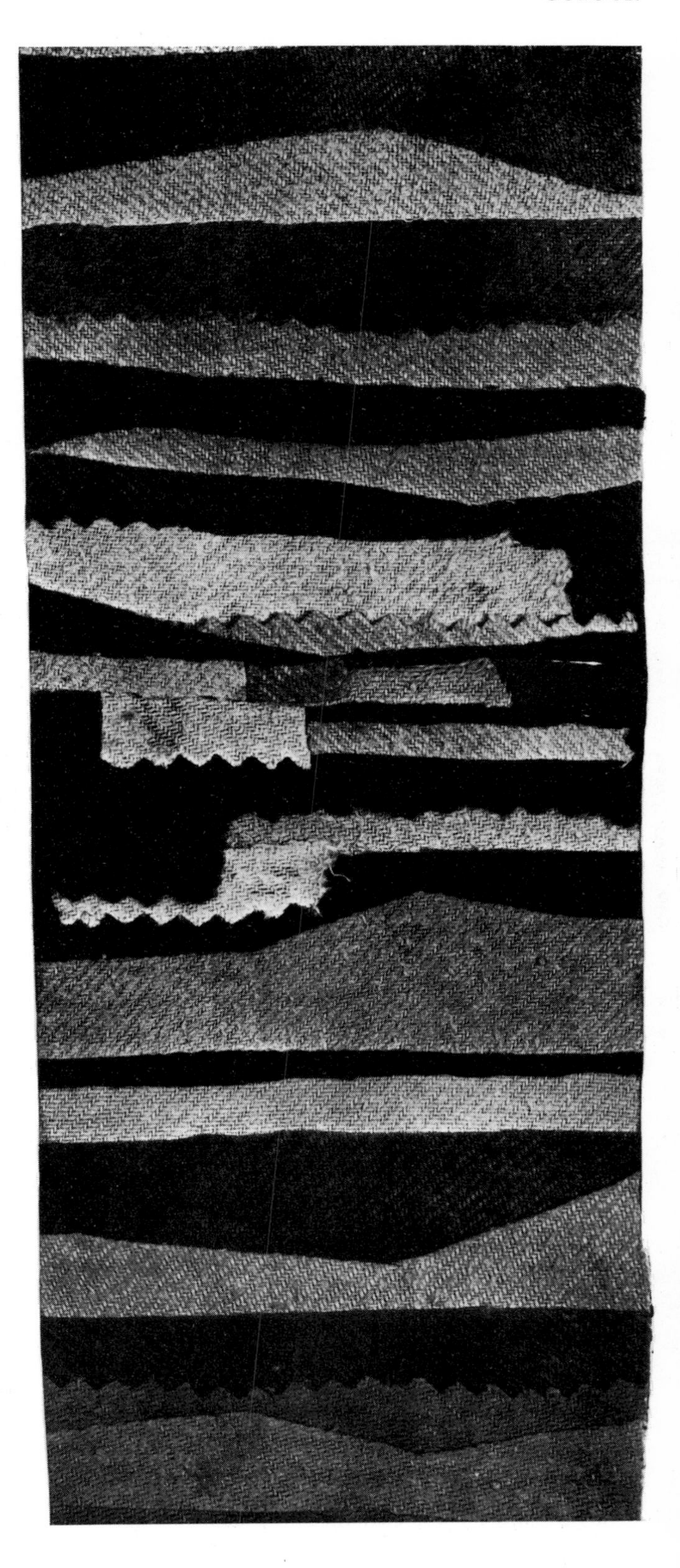

this should be exploited to attract the eye to an important part of the design. Strong contrast of this sort should be avoided on the edges of the work where, if black or white appear, they should be supported by greys that are not too far removed from them tonally, so that the eye is not drawn from the central part of the work (Fig. 3).

Fig. 3

We have given this example of tone using black and white because it is easily imagined, but tone could be applied to any colour because all it means is the amount of light and dark in it. Tone has the power to create space. Let us look at an example of this. We see things that are near more clearly than those that are at a distance. So a white wall with a dark shadow on one side would appear to have its strongest contrast of tone–the strongest light and the strongest dark–in the foreground. As the wall travels into the distance, the atmosphere dims the view, with the result that the white becomes a light grey and the black becomes a dark grey. This continues to happen until the light and the dark are indistinguishable (Fig. 4).

Fig. 4

This is what happens to tone in nature. In a two-dimensional design, black supported by white can therefore be made to come forward and attract attention, whereas the greys could take their place behind, in a supporting role.

INTENSITY

Colour plate 3 shows the family tree of colour. In the row on the left, working from bottom to top, the three primary colours, red, blue and yellow, are the parents of the three secondary colours, violet, green and orange, in the next row. These in their turn beget the tertiary colours on the far right, olive, citron and russet. The primary colours are pure and cannot be mixed; you have to buy them. But given these colours, all other colours can be made. Notice how the purity, the brightness, becomes dimmed by mixing, and the colours lose their intensity. The primary colours are the most intense–gay, fresh, garish, cheerful, brash–and the tertiary are the most sombre, subtle, dull, muddy, subdued, refined (the adjectives chosen depend on which sort of colour is admired). Both kinds are needed in colour schemes.

A very subtle colour scheme made up of well mixed colours like the tertiaries might be chosen but it would probably be enhanced by a contrast, either of tone or intensity, as there would be little of either in such a scheme. At the other extreme, success would be difficult in designing anything with the three primary colours, unless it be a flag to be seen instantly in the heat of battle or on the horizon at sea!

TEMPERATURE

Colour plate 3 shows a circle of colour and it is easy to divide it into two parts–the one warm or hot and the other cool or cold. The warm area is the larger and this is easily explained because two of the three primary colours are warm, namely red and yellow, whereas blue alone is responsible for the cool area. As soon as blue loses its influence, the colour becomes warm.

Warm colours have the property of coming forward and attracting attention, whereas cool colours tend to recede. Danger signs, fire extinguishers, and other similar objects that we must not fail to see, are painted red. In a less obvious way, warm colours are found in the foreground in a landscape and cool ones in the distance. Foliage that is near will appear to be a warm green, that is a green with plenty of yellow in it, but as the veils of atmosphere fall gradually with distance, blue takes over, the foliage becomes at first a bluer green, then more and more blue, and finally, on a far mountain, appears to be blue. So temperature like tone of colour can be used to create a spatial effect. Shapes in design, flat shapes, may be made to stand out or to recede according to their temperature.

A contrast of colour temperature can be very effective, as can be icecream with hot chocolate sauce! However, do not use equal amounts of warm and cool colours. Let one be dominant and use the other sparingly.

You can now re-read the paragraph on abstracting colour from nature with more understanding of how you may exploit the possibilities in the particular choice you make. Natural colour schemes are limitless and very satisfying. Remember that the proportion of colour in the specimen is very important. If this balance is altered it is quite possible to dislike a colour scheme that was originally admired.

It would be useful to have a notebook, and to keep both written notes and colour analyses together in it. In order to analyse and abstract colour from nature, the designer must select, narrow the field, simplify and make a personal comment.

THE COLOUR CIRCLE

We have already looked at the colour circle in colour plate 3 when considering the temperature of colour. Let us look at it again. This wheel of colour is inspired by nature. Here all the colours of the rainbow, the spectrum, are arranged as an aid for discussing the theory of colour, in a never-ceasing flow of colour. In the rainbow, nature shows her purest colour, her most intense colour, as clear as light shining through stained glass. The three primary colours are arranged at intervals of a third around the circumference of the circle.

PRIMARY COLOURS

These are mid-red, mid-blue, mid-yellow. This is important. The red must not have any tendency towards either an orange-red (vermilion) or a violet-red (crimson). The reason for care in getting the exact mid-colour is because this red has to mix in turn with yellow and blue to make the secondary colours, and vermilion could never produce a violet because of the yellow content in it. It would make a brown.

SECONDARY COLOURS

These secondary colours are also mid-colours. Mid-violet, mid-green, mid-orange are colours with a personality of their own and they do not favour either of the parent primary colours, i.e. a green that is not a blue or yellow green.
On each side of the secondary colours are the mixtures that they form with the primary on each side. On the yellow side, next to the green one finds yellow-green, and similarly blue-green on the blue side. This is a simple version of the colour circle, which could be made more complex by the addition of a limitless number of more subtle changes such as yellow-yellow-green and yellow-yellow-yellow-green.

We have already discussed the tonal range in colour when black and white have been added to lighten or to darken it. Here, the tonal range within the colour circle owes nothing to black and white. These colours, called hues, are pure. A good method of judging tone is to look with half-closed eyes. Yellow will be seen to be the lightest tone and the tones get progressively darker, step by step, until violet, which is the darkest in the circle, then the hues become progressively lighter until yellow is reached again. This tonal range in the spectrum is the *natural order*, i.e. the order of tone in colour found in the rainbow and generally in nature as a whole. There are exceptions, but we will talk about them later. Think how many flowers have dark violet petals, light yellow centres and mid-toned green leaves. Colour in nature is generally harmonious, and should be used in the tonal natural order if the desire is to create 'easy-to-live-with' colour schemes. Consider, for example, the common fuchsia–crimson, blue, violet.

MONOCHROME

On the colour wheel there are twelve hues, and, as has been said, there is a possibility of creating a great many more, which would take their place in between these twelve. Each of these hues could be taken separately and used in a mono-chrome (one colour) colour scheme.
In the section on tone, we said that white and black could be added to any hue to produce a tonal range from, say, dark blue, to pure colour, to light blue. These tones produced by the adding of black and white to the hue are called respectively, shades and tints.
Monochrome is a 'safe' colour scheme which never fails and can be used with great effect. Colour plates 4 and 5 show a design/study from a natural object using monochrome.

ANALOGOUS COLOURS

These, as the name suggests, are colours that are close neighbours on the colour circle and therefore chromatically related.

A one-colour scheme using analogous colours can be more lively than monochrome and easier to implement in needlecraft. One colour, such as red, is used to the exclusion of any other. This allows the use of reds that are almost orange and reds that are near violet, but do not actually go outside the range of red. This can be a very rich colour scheme.

A more adventurous use of analogous colours will embrace a wider range of colour. Take a wedge of colour from the circle, including one primary (if you wish) but not reaching the next. This will produce a harmonious colour scheme, easy to live with, which is excellent for interior decoration, e.g. orange, red, red-orange, red-violet, arranged in the tonal order of the colour circle. Colour plate 6 shows an example of the use of analogous colour.

DISCORD

The colour schemes above are easy to use, 'safe' ones, sometimes at the risk of being a little unadventurous. They could be greatly enlivened by careful use of discord. Discord is a very precious commodity in design and should be treated sparingly. To add discord to an analogous colour scheme is rather like adding spice to a cake mixture. Put too much and the real flavour of the cake will be lost. It gives a sensational effect, both pleasing and disquieting at the same time–a kind of bitter-sweet taste. What is discord that it is so effective in a disturbing way?

In studying the colour circle we have noted its natural tonal order. If that order is upset there is a feeling of uneasiness and this is precisely what discord does. It alters the tonal order of the colour circle. It may be that a light-toned colour such as yellow is darkened, so that in the design it appears darker than a colour that is normally darker than yellow in the natural order. Rarely is this found in nature, for example one finds, in autumn, Michaelmas daisies with pale violet petals and a dark yellow centre, and the effect is rather surprising. The more usual arrangement of colour in nature would be dark violet petals and light yellow centres. The former is a complete reversal of the tonal order. In addition, to add to the excitement, these are complementaries–complementary colours. To sum up, discord occurs when a colour is tonally out of step with the colours surrounding it, i.e. it does not follow the rule of the natural order. The effect is always scintillating.

For the analogous colour scheme the example considered was: orange, red-orange, red, red-violet, and violet. Add to these a shocking pink. This is a popular use of discord. Shocking pink is a tint of red and makes red appear lighter than orange and therefore discordant with it. This same principle could of course be carried out with other selections of analogous colours.

COMPLEMENTARY COLOURS

These are found opposite each other on the colour circle, on the diameter, and are difficult to use successfully. An example is mid-red and mid-green. When these two colours are used together a sense of visual vibration is set up. They complement each other in such a way that red is more intensely red if that particular green is present and green is more green in the company of the complementary red. In order to experience this visual vibration we suggest that you paint two sheets of paper of about 3″ × 6″ (7·5cm × 15cm), each with one of two complementary colours.

Then cut one of the sheets into strips and stick them onto the other.

A study of nature will guide us in the use of these complementary colours and it will be seen that where they appear together they are never of equal proportion. Red in a bed of geraniums appears brighter and harder than most reds. This is because that particular red is complemented by that particular green, a slightly blue-green.

However, it is worth noting that generally there is more green than red. With holly, red and green appear together, again less red than green, and the green is subdued to a shade, making it easier on the eye, in fact very pleasant. Here the intensity of colour has been varied.

Because two complementaries used together are visually hard to bear, they would not, in their pure state, be at all restful for interior decoration. The examples so far considered have been a primary and secondary colour, but they could just as well have been any hues that are found diametrically opposite each other on the colour circle, say yellow-green and red-violet. However, there is a way of using these disturbing, powerful colours that renders them as harmonious as analogous colours – and much more interesting. Try this little experiment.

1. Choose two complementaries, say orange and blue.
2. Prepare seven sheets of paper, say 3″ × 6″ (7·5cm × 15cm).
3. Paint one of these sheets orange. Keep the mixed orange paint in a separate place.
4. Mix some blue, and paint a second sheet of paper. Again keep the supply of paint apart.
5. Take five parts of orange and one of blue, mix them, and paint a third sheet of paper.
6. Take four parts of orange and two of blue and do likewise.
7. Take three parts orange and three of blue and continue as above.
8. Now two parts of orange and four of blue.
9. One part of orange and five of blue.
10. Arrange these sheets in a fan shape, like a hand of cards. Remove orange and look at the colour scheme. The colours remaining are blue and mixtures of orange and blue. All the mixtures contain some blue, however little, and so the scheme is unified by blue.
11. Try the same exercise but removing the blue. Orange unifies the colour scheme.
12. Make a small collage design using all the sheets except orange. Take a design like a knot-hole in wood and place irregular curved shapes one within the other. Use the colours in the order that seems most effective. It will be necessary to try all alternatives before deciding. Place the intense pure blue at the part to which the eye is to be attracted.
13. Make another collage using all the sheets except blue.
14. Make another collage using all the sheets.

Exercises 12 and 13 will have made unusual, subtle, harmonious colour schemes. In each, one colour dominates. Experiment 14 will be more successful if more of *either* orange or blue is used. If they are placed together, it must be at the centre of interest.

UNITY OF COLOUR

You will now have realised that in all these ideas of colour you are searching for some form of unity. With one-colour schemes the unity is built in. Similarly, if the range is narrow in analogous colours there is no difficulty. Designers can give unity to a colour scheme by adding a little of one colour to all. Interesting colour schemes can be created by dyeing a multi-coloured collection of fabric from the scrap bag in one unifying dye. This is in fact what you have done to give unity to complementary colours in exercises 10 and 11 above.

NEUTRAL COLOURS

Neutral colours are black, white, greys, and subtle colours that contain so much mixed pigment that they become subdued like the tertiaries. The tertiaries in fact are dark and too positive to be greys, but for example if white were added to lighten them and some red were added to olive to neutralise it, interesting neutrals would be made. Similarly, violet and green would be added to citron and russet respectively to neutralise these. It will be noticed that these tertiaries have a tendency towards green, yellow and red, and that the way to neutralise them and produce grey is to add the complementary.

We have seen the value of a mixed low-intensity colour being used as a buffer between two conflicting complementaries (the buffer colour being formed from the two complementaries) and making it possible for them to exist peaceably together. This use of 'neutrals' or 'grey' is invaluable in holding a colour scheme together by varying the intensity of colour in the design and in this case creating a related colour scheme.

Black is a most useful colour as a strong tonal contrast and as a barrier between very bright colours. It could be used in the way that lead in a stained-glass window is used to separate brilliant colour.

White is invaluable in giving life to the whole design. It provides a place of rest and refreshment for the eye, which has been taking in all the colour. White should be used sparingly, however, as it expands and so looks larger than it is. This must always be taken into consideration while designing. In contrast, black shrinks and allowance must be made for this. Designs could be made using different degrees of whiteness – bleached and unbleached, different materials, strings etc.

Black, white, grey and one bright colour is a safe colour scheme. The neutrals are a splendid foil for the bright colour and there is a good tonal range and variety of intensity (see colour plate 24).

ANALOGOUS WITH COMPLEMENTARY

We used discord as a means of enlivening a scheme of analogous colours. Another method would be to use a complementary. If this were a shade of the complementary it would not be at all disquieting and would add interest. A useful hint here is that the purer the colour, the less it should be used.

STARTING POINTS

How does a colour scheme start? Some of you will have no doubts about the colour that you wish to use and can now look into the theory to see how to use it to advantage. Sometimes a design suggests a colour. A design composed of restless shape might call for a complementary colour scheme to carry the theme further, or an analogous one to stabilise it. One could think in the same way for a design which was easy-going and harmonious. Either push it further into harmony with analogous colour, or give it life with complementaries.

A limitation in the form of a lovely piece of fabric may present the starting point, or some thread or beads. This is a good way to start because already the materials would be taking over and this is what should happen. A limitation such as this, contrary to what might be expected, is in fact an inspiration. The designer knows in which direction to go. When all the choice in the world is available it is difficult to know where to start.

Colour can also create mood. Blue can be melancholic or romantic and dreamy. Orange has the cheerfulness and warmth of the sun and is thought to give a sense of well-being. Colour can also be used symbolically. Green gives an idea of growth, of youth and freshness. White is the symbol of purity, while violet and gold suggest royalty.

CHECKING POINTS

No matter what colour scheme is chosen there are certain guidelines which it would be wise to check.

1 Have variety of intensity of colour, i.e. not more than one primary colour.
2 Have variety of tone–with care, however, that this does not make for unplanned discord. Discord used well is invaluable, but used badly it is disastrous.
3 Have variety of the amount of colour used, remembering that the brighter the colour, the less it should be used.
4 Have unity of colour. Let one colour dominate the scheme.

We would further urge you to examine colour wherever you encounter it. Go into our contemporary-style stores and look at the furnishing fabrics. It will be an exhilarating experience. Make notes of the colour combinations seen. Analyse, thinking of the colour theory, what it is that the contemporary designers have done in using colour and use the same ideas, perhaps with a different range of colour. Cut out and arrange in a grey-paged scrapbook examples of colour schemes that are pleasing and try to work out into which category they fit. Sometimes an illustration in a magazine will supply several ideas. Cut down the pictures, destroying the pictorial content, until the only concern is colour, and not the drama. Mount the chosen sections and draw a black felt-pen line around them to show that they are independent of one another. It will help when examining them to have some loose sheets of grey paper to cover up the other examples on the page. A bright cutting could draw all the colour out of a subtle, delicate one.

In the last chapter we said that design was, among other things, a sense of order. There is a very real sense of order and unity in the colour in nature, as has been seen. Human beings sometimes make chaos out of it by using it badly. The designer may want to be more adventurous than nature while taking a lead from it. Whatever is attempted with colour, the designer should aim to present a planned order of related colour, which should give unity.

3

SHAPE & SPATIAL RELATIONSHIPS

Shape is more important than colour in design. Colour gives an immediate attraction, and effective schemes can be achieved by following certain guiding rules and exercising personal judgement as to the proportions used, but it is necessary to experiment with cut paper to understand shape. No amount of theory could make up for practical experience of this kind.

Shape is the very foundation of design, the skeleton that holds the whole design together. The design can fail if the shapes are weak; it can succeed on its basis of good related shapes. No amount of 'prettying up' with sequins and bits and bobs will put right a needlecraft design that is weak in its foundations, just as no amount of trimming can redeem a badly cut garment where basic line and shape are poor. In all design, whatever the subject matter, whatever purpose it may fulfil, shape is fundamental and the designer has to solve the same problems.

SIMPLE SHAPE DESIGNING

There is a shape to be decorated. This may be a rectangular panel for a wall-hanging, or a curved yoke of a dress to be embroidered. This shape must be accepted with its size and limits marked before starting. It is the negative shape and it must be considered as the background material on which to work. Fig. 5 shows a rectangular panel.

Fig. 5

The designer then selects a positive shape and places it within the negative space (Fig. 6).

Fig. 6

Immediately, a relationship is set up between the two areas. The negative shape around the positive can be changed by the positive being moved about, the negative being in a passive state and the positive being active (Fig. 7).

Fig. 7

People who are not used to designing frequently make the mistake of considering only the positive shape, whereas to ensure success positive and negative shape must work together to make a good design. The negative shape requires more consideration once the positive ones have been selected.

Fig. 8

The designer adds a second positive shape (Fig. 8). This one has to relate not only to the first positive shape but also to the negative one, and so it goes on, becoming more and more complex, just as human relationships become more difficult when more people are involved (Figs. 8, 9, 10).

Fig. 9

Fig. 10

The selected shapes for a design should be related. Those used in Figs. 6–10 are related, being formed from the same square and cut out with a unified system of curved lines. All circles are related whatever their size, so are all squares.

Similarly, certain shapes in nature, such as the seeds in a pomegranate, are related. They are each unique but they bear a family resemblance, being fashioned within the same spherical shape and fitted together wonderfully in order to accommodate each other, building up to make a sphere. Water-lily leaves fill a pond surface with related shapes in a variety of sizes.

In the simple exercise shown, the shapes chosen are all different, yet related. The designer may, however, choose to restrict himself to the use of one shape and try by experiment to discover what different results can be achieved with this self-imposed discipline. The shape becomes a module in a design made up of many identical shapes (Figs. 11, 12, 13).

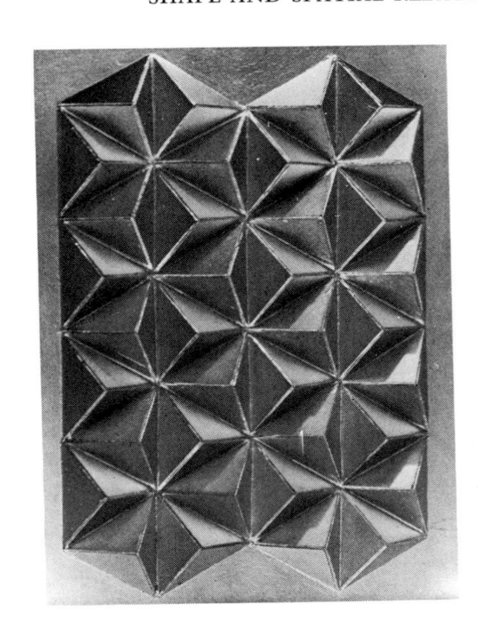

Fig. 13

Fig. 11

Fig. 12

The designer has selected one shape in each of the above examples and has used it:

1 (a long rectangle) to achieve a static arrangement, giving interest by the spaces created between the uniform shapes (Fig. 11).

2 (a long rectangle, the same shape) to give movement, in this case a spiral. As the rectangles turn in this three-dimensional work, the short ends of the rectangle appear as smaller forms. This is how interest is added and monotony avoided in this limited choice of form (Fig. 12).
3 (a triangle) to build up a larger pattern relief of cellular shape (Fig. 13). This kind of effect has been carried out with patchwork in two dimensions using triangles, honeycomb shapes or rectangles. Often the tone of the pieces chosen gives an appearance of three dimensions.

These identical shapes can be arranged without overlapping but making good use of the negative shape, or they may be overlapped. If transparent materials are used, the overlap forms new, yet related, shape, which gives the same variety that we have seen in Figs. 11, 12 and 13 where the spaces and shorter ends of rectangles give a different scale to the work (Fig. 14).

Be highly selective and deal with one idea at a time. The designer who decides to use circles, squares, diamonds and triangles all at once is giving herself a much more difficult problem to solve than the designer who settles for one of these shapes at a time. If you decide on triangles, you would be advised to choose one particular kind, e.g. right-angle triangles, and to experiment in many ways with this limitation.

A circle remains unchanged, however it spins around its axis of symmetry, the diameter, and has been a favourite motif for design from ancient times to the present day. The rectangle or square presents more difficulties because it is angular and becomes restless on being turned.

Consider for a moment the circle and its possibilities. If a circle of paper is cut from a square and placed on a sheet of differing toned paper, a positive circle is surrounded by negative shape (Fig. 15).

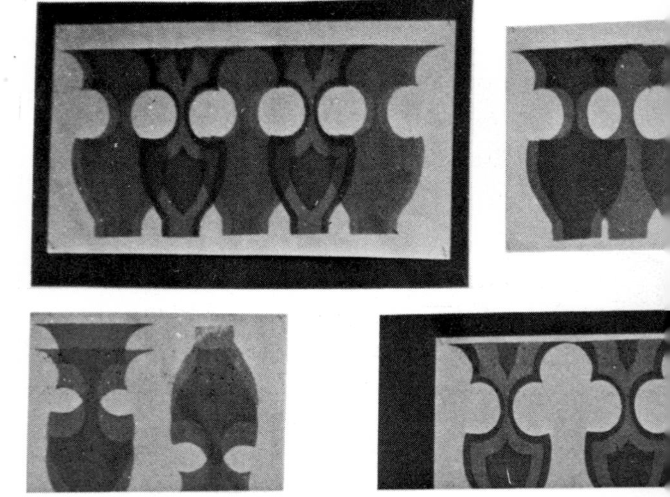

Fig. 14

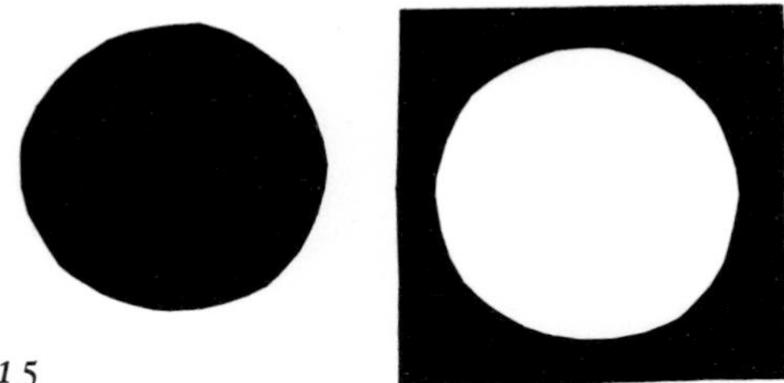

Fig. 15

Place alongside it the original square of paper with the circle removed and the reverse is seen, like the negative of a photograph, namely a negative circle and positive surrounding shape. Figs. 16–19 have resulted from accepting this limitation and playing around with it. This will produce a counterchange style design with all the shapes related because they originated from the square and the circle cut from it.

Fig. 16

Fig. 17

Fig. 18

Fig. 19

Try the same limitation of shapes but using a differing scale. It might be best to choose squares, the sides of which are fractions of the original square, say a half or a third, so that the new shapes are related in size as well as in form (Figs. 20, 21).

Fig. 20

Fig. 21

Circles may be arranged in a seemingly haphazard way, as confetti appears on the pavement after a wedding, but however seemingly casual the arrangement, it really must be most subtly careful. No design is ever haphazard. The designer chooses a positive shape and plays it off against the negative shape. Fig. 21 shows a free use of the theme, whereas Fig. 20 is a more classical style with the shapes arranged in a more orderly way, the sides of the squares being aligned with the sides of the ground shape. This will make for a serene and restful design. Whatever system is employed, there must be a sense of purpose and understanding.

Colour plate 24 shows a collage by Shân Humphrey Thomas where the shapes are limited to circles and the negative shape around them. It also illustrates how good black and white can look with one bright colour.

Let us try another experiment with the circle in cut paper. In the examples shown in Fig. 22 the circle has been cut into shapes, exploded and the negative shapes carefully considered. A limitless variety of designs can be done in this way. Note that each design has a unity of cutting, either straight, curved, wavy or jagged.

Use the following process:
1 Take a circle and cut away approximately a third of it. Decide on your method of cutting and maintain it throughout the exercise. The proportion

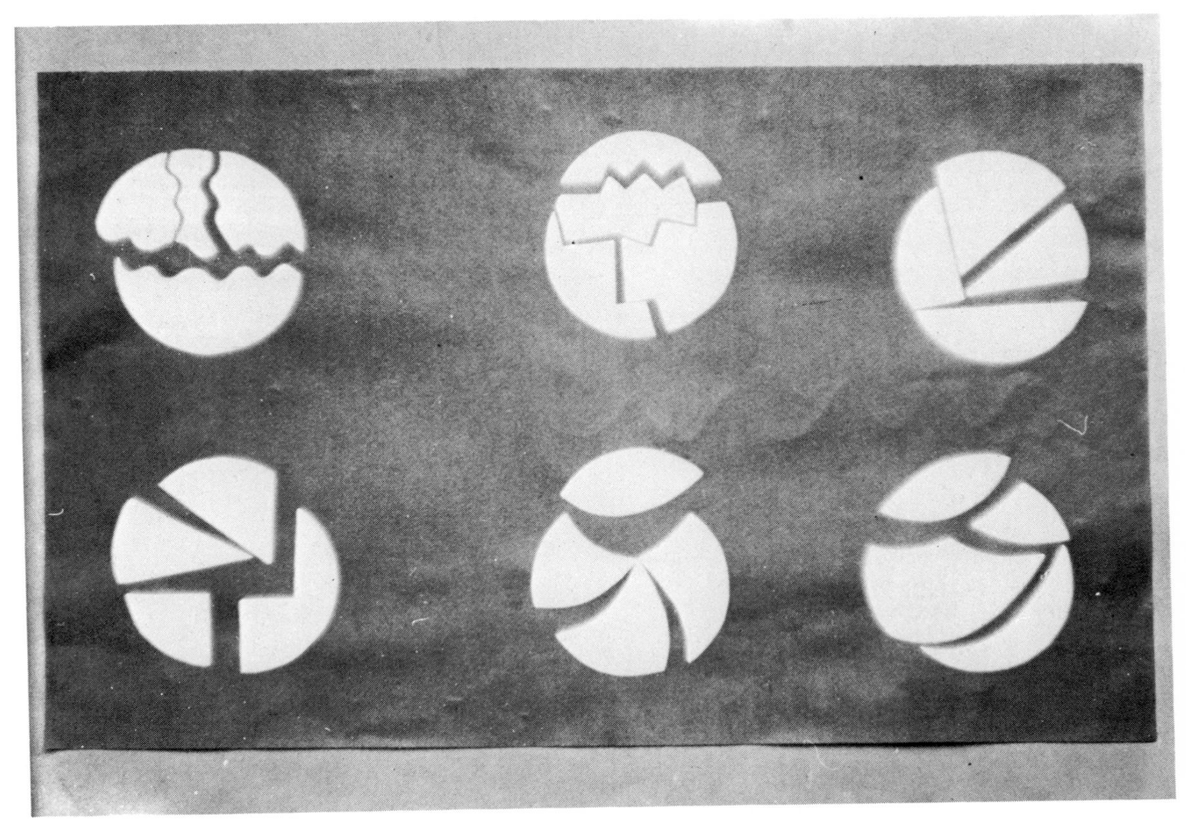

Fig. 22

of a third is chosen because of the Greek division of a line at the Golden Mean, which comes roughly on the third. This proportion, used by the Greeks in their architecture, has been appreciated and used throughout the history of art.

2 Place the two pieces on a sheet of contrasting toned paper. Part them, move them up and down and note the ever-changing negative shapes between.

3 Take the larger piece and cut a third of that away, maintaining the unity in cutting. Place the shapes down and make up the jig-saw puzzle to form the original circle. Now move the pieces apart.

4 Repeat exactly the same process until there are four pieces. Now move these about on the background as before watching the negative spaces formed.

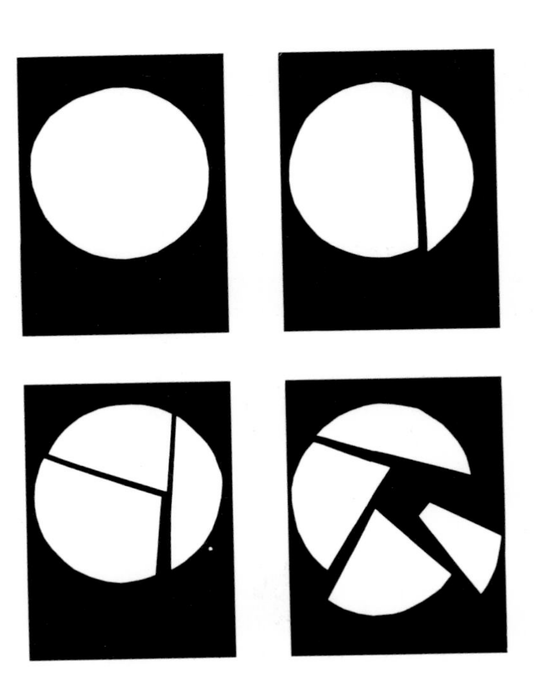

Fig. 23

Finally settle for an arrangement where there is a grouping of three and one (Fig. 23). In the final grouping try to have as much variety in the size of negative shape as there is in the positive.

There are several good design points to be learnt from this simple exercise:

1 All of these shapes are related shapes: (a) because they came from the same circle; (b) because they were cut in a unified way. In consequence all the shapes contain a part that bears the outline of the circumference of the circle and a part that has been cut in a chosen manner.

2 The division in design at the third. This is off-centre and divides into unequal parts, which are more satisfying than equal ones, and infinitely easier to use in design.

3 Uneven numbers are better than even ones in design. One, three and five look better than two and four. After five you no longer count at a glance and so it does not matter so much. Hence the grouping in Fig. 22 and the final ones in Fig. 23.

4 Variety of size of shape adds interest to the design, and this applies as much to negative as positive shape.

5 The negative shape becomes every bit as important as the positive shape, perhaps more so.

Other regular shapes may be treated in exactly the same way. However, when polygonal figures, which have a more complicated symmetry, are used, i.e. squares, diamonds, hexagons etc., the designer faces fresh problems. Squares cannot be swivelled around without creating movement and possibly chaos. Design must have a sense of order, so the designer might be advised to arrange the vertical and horizontal sides of shapes in order to respect the rectangle of the ground shape. It is all a question of being sensitive to what already exists in the design when adding to it, and this includes the shape of the background. An arrangement that has vertical and horizontal lines will give a sense of security, an architectural feeling of buildings solid on their foundations. Oblique shapes give a sense of insecurity such as one experiences viewing the Leaning Tower of Pisa.

We would suggest yet another way of creating related shape with cut paper shapes, while emphasising that there are many, many more possibilities. Our purpose is not to give you a recipe of how to design as we would design, but to give you a sense of being creative so that you will go on, unafraid, to discover for yourself.

Fig. 24

The last example (Fig. 24) shows that a shape has been selected, an ellipse, and parts of it have been cut off and used. The designer has contrasted the curved elliptical shape with a long rectangle, which she has related to the ellipses by cutting out elliptical shapes in one of them to form a counterchange effect of an ellipse. This again could give a limitless source for design using other shapes, the circle for example.

DESIGNING WITH A BALL LETTERING PEN

Designs already suggested in cut paper seem suitable for appliqué or collage work, but the needlecraft designer needs to appreciate shape for other purposes. The successful placing of beading depends also upon an understanding of positive and negative shape. For the following experiments we suggest that you obtain an ordinary writing or drawing pen and some ball lettering pens. These are available in a variety of sizes. If the pen nib is placed on the paper so that the round nib lies flatly it will draw a round spot.

1 Choose a small piece of white paper, say $2\frac{1}{2}'' \times 3\frac{1}{2}''$ (6·5cm × 9cm), and work with black ink, thus getting the maximum contrast of tone. Make a cluster of spots that do not overlap. Think of them as being water-lily leaves on a rectangular pond. Concentrate the spots off-centre and let them thin out as they reach the borders of the rectangle (Fig. 25).

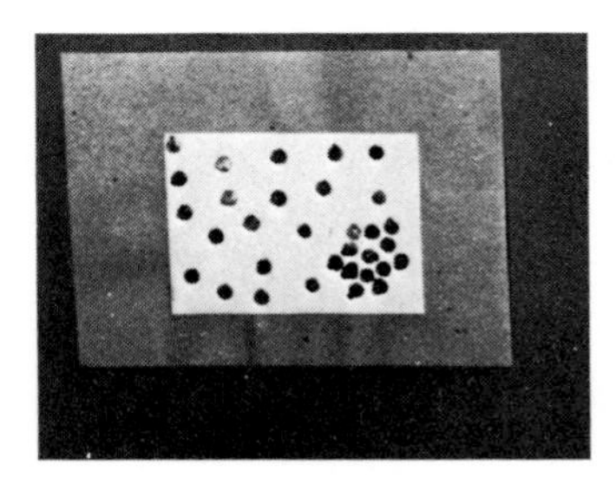

Fig. 25

2 Take a bird's eye view of a football ground at the finish of the game. The crowd, which thickly surrounded the ground, is invading the pitch. Try to concentrate the spots this time around the edges of the rectangle and let them thin out towards the inside, leaving a white negative space, off-centre. This is the exact opposite of the last exercise (Fig. 26).

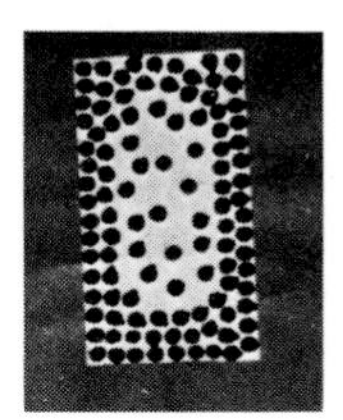

Fig. 26

This looks like child's play and any child could do it, but with varying success. The more this sort of experimental designing is practised, the greater is the understanding of the value of positive and negative space working together to form a whole, and their ability to play the principal or supporting role and change and change about. For example, Fig. 25 shows a positive cluster of spots that dominates the composition, but in Fig. 26 it is the negative white space, which is consciously left, that claims the attention. Both of these exercises have complete unity of shape, being composed of circles.

Unity of design can be carried a step further by using a unity of movement with shape.

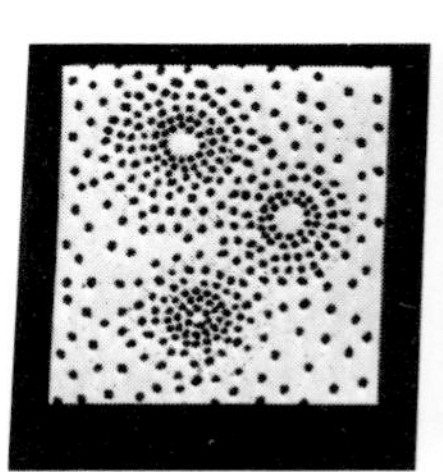

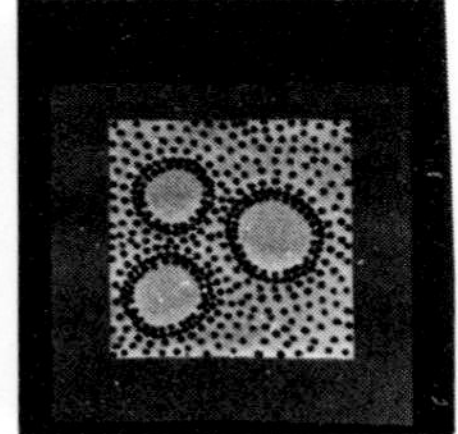

Fig. 27

1 Form three circles with spots, placing them within a rectangle (these spots should be placed close together). Then fill in around each circle with more rings

of spots, letting them thin out as they reach the border of the rectangle. These circles will stand out as negative shapes in a background of varying intensity of circular shapes (Fig. 27).

2 Form a circle composed of varying sized spots off-centre, and from there develop a circular movement suggested by soapsuds swirling around a square or rectangular sink and disappearing down a plug-hole (Fig. 28).

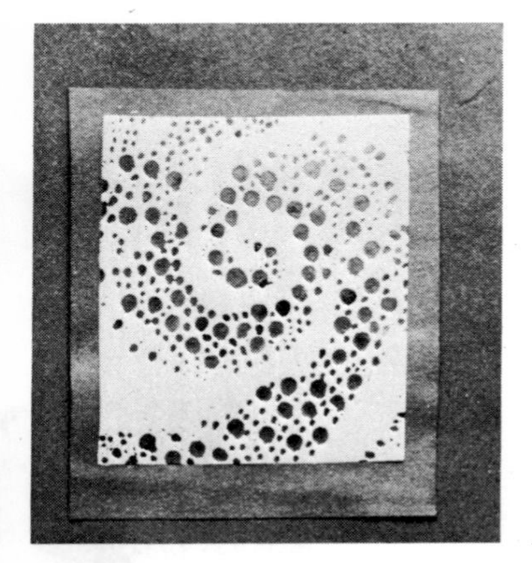

Fig. 28

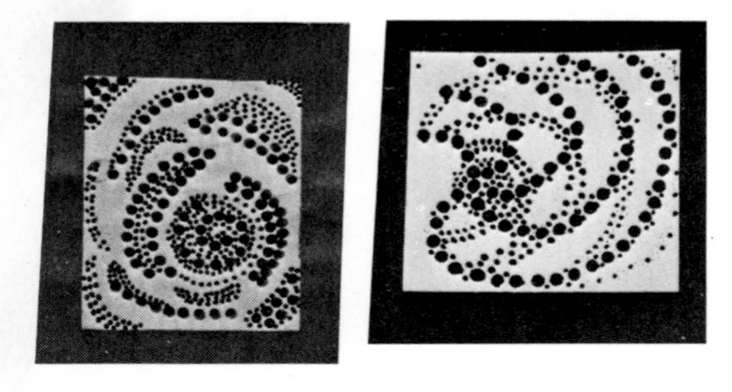

Other designs, suggested by rock-pools, seaweeds or islands in the sea, have been worked out using these pens (Fig. 29). They started with the placing of the dominant areas in the design; then they were developed by the linking up of the shapes, forming surrounding space in sympathy with existing ones. The important word is 'sympathy'. The designer must be sensitive in adding to the design – sensitive to all that already exists in the design.

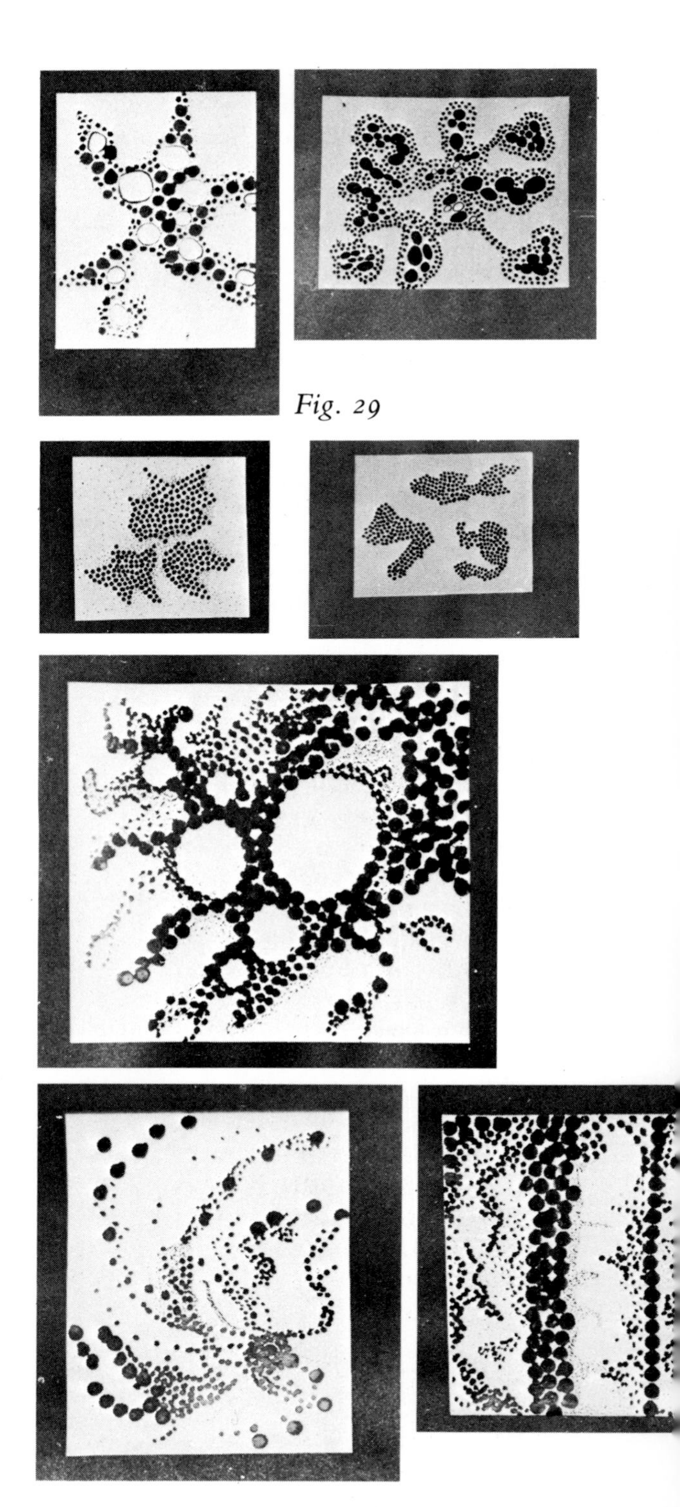

Fig. 29

To summarise, shapes should be related, should have unity, should be arranged in such a way that they give a sense of planned order. Space need not be always filled; indeed, space is valuable, a rest for the eye, and the amount that is acceptable will vary with fashion, but there should never be any unconsidered space. Negative shape is as important as positive shape, and the two should work together as parts fit in smooth-running machinery.

Unity of shape or related shape can be achieved:

1 By repetition with the same scale.
2 By repetition with varying scale.
3 By repetition with overlaps forming other related shapes.
4 By using shapes derived from the same parent-shape.
5 By using related shapes found in nature.

Experiments with these simple ways of designing should start to develop an appreciation, an awareness, of shape, and alert you to see shape wherever you look. The purpose of giving these exercises with simple shapes is to teach the principles so that you will apply them to more complicated shape as it attracts you in your environment. A later chapter will deal with subject-matter for design. We all differ in our interests and each designer must form her own collection of design materials.

By collecting cuttings of shape, which either pleases or in some way arrests attention, the eye will be trained in observation and selection. These may be natural forms such as trees against a skyline, or man-made objects such as a beautifully shaped piece of pottery or factory chimneys in an industrial scene.

Make a scrapbook of these shapes for future reference. Try also to make pages on which all the shapes are related to each other. Cut out and arrange them so that you have pleasing negative space between them.

If the source of material comes from women's magazines, lots of cosmetic advertisements and pictures of food will be found. There will be eyes, mouths, fingers, legs, eggs, fruits, cakes and perhaps bunches of carrots. Eyes and mouths are elliptical shapes and in this respect are related. A fried egg might also be considered related to an eye shape. Legs and fingers, however, are more closely related in shape to tree trunks and carrots, although in subject-matter and associations of ideas they are more closely related to eyes and mouths, being members of the human body. Remember that the ideas are to be related *visually* and not mentally.

Collect all circular shapes, and observe the different ways in which the basic shape is sub-divided. Consider half an orange, wheels, a dart-board, a snail-shell, a fir-cone, a daisy. Similarly, collect oblong shapes. Time spent on this sort of observation is never wasted; all the time powers of selection and arrangement are being used. Try to get so absorbed, so interested in the subject, shape, that when by chance you come upon an electric pylon or a giant crane in the peace of the countryside, you will admire the beauty of the engineered shape instead of regarding it as a blot on the idyllic landscape. The engineer often produces structures that function well because of their symmetry, which is also why these structures can appeal to the eye.

The public in general believes that there are those who are creative and those who are not. The truth is that there are those who look and see, and those who only look. A designer has to train herself to look and see and then to experiment as we have suggested in this chapter. There is no royal road to learning of any kind, you must be patient, practise, experiment and become involved.

4
LINE & TEXTURE

Shape is the foundation of design, giving stability by its mass. Line is a foil to this mass and adds lightness and movement. So far, we have encountered line related to shape (all shapes are formed by an outline) and we also considered cutting lines through shapes and maintaining a unity in the manner of doing this (see Figs. 6–10, 22, 23).

In other crafts mass and line are used effectively together. In ceramics, mass is often enlivened by the use of trailed slip, or a sgraffito line scratched into the soft clay. Similarly, pen and ink line is often added to mass washes of watercolour to enrich the textural effect. In needlecraft, the mass is the shape, perhaps cloth appliqué and the line is stitchery. Thread suggests line and can be used in limitless ways for linear design by machine *or* hand.

MOVEMENT

Line will give movement and direction to the design. Vertical and horizontal lines give stability, an architectural, classical feeling, a restful quality.

Oblique lines give a sense of insecurity and of falling, which can be uncomfortable. However, the two ideas can be skilfully used as a foil for each other. A regular grid of verticals and horizontals broken by an oblique can add interest. Too much variety of this sort could, however, destroy the unity of the design. A row of verticals broken by an oblique has the surprise effect of seeing a soldier fainting in the line. This could be exploited in order to draw the eye to a centre of interest that is out of step with the general pattern of the design.

CHARACTER

A line may be straight, curved, angular, flowing, curling, scribbling, whatever is wished, but whatever it decides to do, it must not be half-hearted about doing it. It should be vigorous and purposeful. It should have the strength of natural growth or functional equipment. A plant stretching up to the light grows boldly, however fragile it may be. Films have been made in which the growth of plants is speeded up, and show the amazing strength and confidence in this movement.

Try to design boldly when using line, never rub out, correct with a stronger line or a different medium. Never mind if it goes wrong. It is much better to have several attempts and in so doing to practise and gain confidence. It would help to try out the line in the air above the paper, like a dance movement, and then to draw boldly, using the whole arm. Line drawing needs to have this natural confidence.

We have already stated that the design need only be a mere germ of an idea on paper before you work directly with the tools and materials. The true character of needlecraft line can be discovered only by working with thread and needle by hand or machine. If thread is couched, you should try to let the yarn fall in a way that comes naturally to it while taking the direction you have planned. It may be that the original plan was not really suited to the craft and then it will be necessary to compromise and adapt to the needs of the material. Good line in machine embroidery can be achieved only when you have arrived at fluency through understanding and practising with your machine. Design should come easily from a sympathetic use of the materials and tools.

Let us imagine that we are uncoiling a coil of wire straight from the iron-mongers. What a vigorous spiral it forms! It is a living line. The wire is not very pliable and an attempt with fingers to make a spiral that is smaller is a difficult task (second attempts and corrections all show, and cannot be smoothed out). It is a very different line from the lively spiral that sprang from the original coil. It is nervous, tentative and weak, and has just the kind of character that should be avoided in line.

RHYTHM

Line surrounds us in everyday life. Let us consider the pattern of a row of park railings (Figs. 30 and 31).

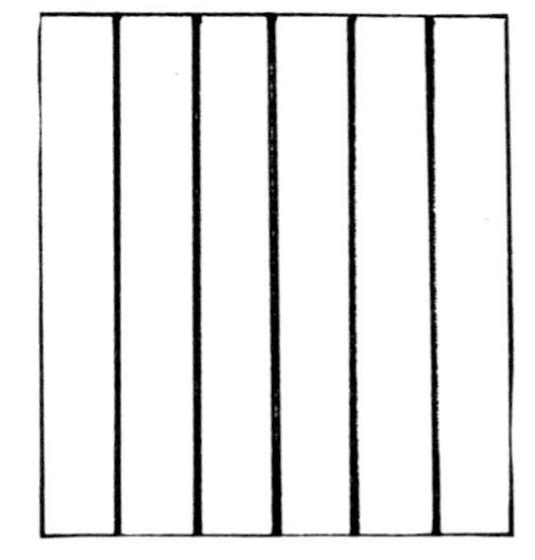

Fig. 30

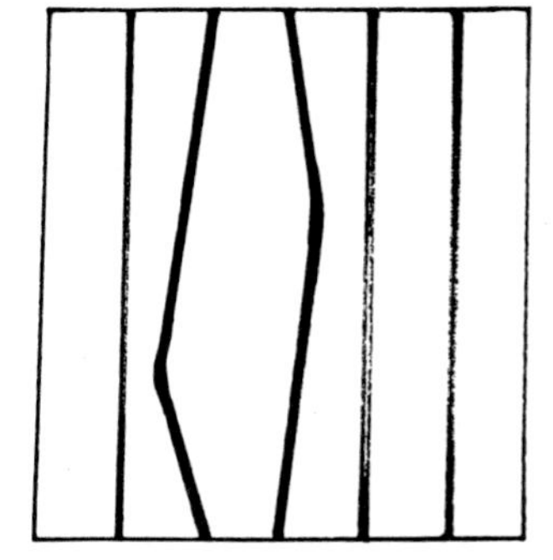

Fig. 31

They form a vertical stripe pattern of lines of equal width with equal spaces between them – a monotonous rhythm, a beat without variety. But some small boys have made their way through the railings, forcing them apart in their passage, bending the iron (Fig. 31). Already there is life in the pattern, due to the variety of the line and the interval shape. We are back to positive and negative shape, and all that has been said before applies here.

There must be variety. Either the positive must have changing thicknesses of line or the negative must have variety of interval between equal thickness of line. It does not matter which. Fig. 32a shows the same thickness of line used with good variety of interval. This variety of width of negative or positive shapes will give life to the design.

Fig. 32 *a* *b*

In Fig. 31 it will be noticed that we chose to bend the line so that the angles did not come directly opposite each other. This is stronger than a symmetrical arrangement. In nature a hollow on one side of a form is often compensated by a bulge on the other side. This makes for a stronger construction, and is found in human limbs. Man-made objects on the other hand may be completely symmetrical. Table legs turned on a lathe curve in or out on both sides identically.

TONE, TENSION AND RELAXATION

Fig. 33

With half-closed eyes consider the tone in Fig. 33. There are white negative areas, nearly black positive ones where the lines get close together, and varying effects of grey according to whether the lines are packed close or spread out. This packing and spreading gives rise to a feeling of tension and relaxation respectively, and this can be exploited to give excitement or peace to the design as required.

We have already discussed the effect and spatial power of contrasting black and white. The designer can arrange to have an area in which black and white come very close together and create a centre of interest. White, remember, expands, while black contracts, so be inclined to use more black than white and do not leave any unconsidered negative shape that is white. Grey it down with line, spaced to give the required tone. It would be best to grey down all white spaces near the edge of the design in order not to lead the eye away from the centre (see Fig. 33).

We are talking as though the designer were working with black on white because the pen illustrations in this book are so coloured, but she could equally well work on black fabric with white thread, when the problem would be reversed. In actual fact she would probably use colour. All colour has tonal value and it will be necessary to weigh this up whatever colour is used.

It would be a useful exercise for you to try out striped pen patterns using straight, waving, zig-zag lines etc., experimenting with one size of nib at first, and then with a variety of sizes. Consider the tonal values each time and the tension and relaxation. Keep a unity in the designs by limiting the use of one kind of line to each piece of work (see Fig. 34).

Fig. 34

LINE DESIGN

In general we would say that line in design plays a supporting role to shape, but there are times when it stands alone as design in its own right, as in some machine embroidery. It seems to us, however, that you would be wise to use the discipline of some construction with shape to guide the line. This would only be a construction that would not be seen in the final result.

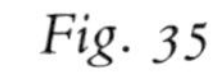

Fig. 35

For example, make a design within a shape, say a circle (see Fig. 35). The actual circle does not appear in the design, but its disciplining influence is felt, because all the line employed is in sympathy with the shape and remains within it. The negative of this could be used too (Fig. 36).

Fig. 36

Similarly, in preparing a border pattern or an all-over one, the placing of obstacles that the line must negotiate is helpful and will help in creating a sense of order (Fig. 37).

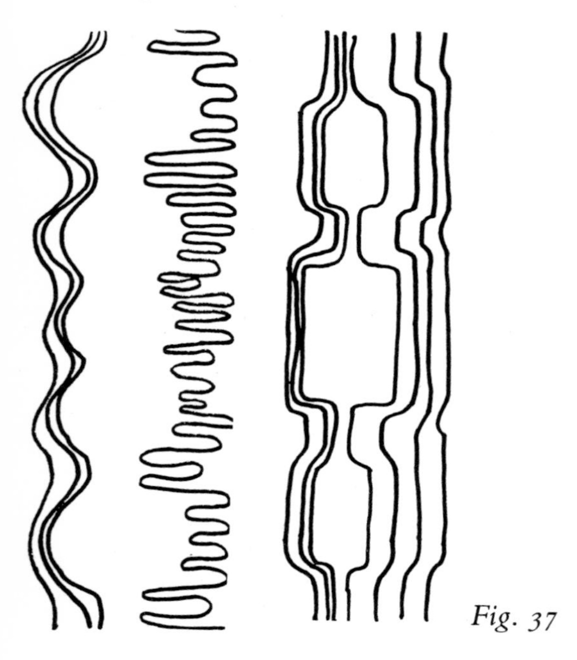

Fig. 37

We find also that a structure of shape in the form of bands of different widths can discipline the line, which wanders freely within the area allotted to it (Fig. 38).

Fig. 38

LINE SUPPORTING SHAPE

It seems that line and shape are rarely separated. In the last paragraph we saw that shape can support line, but more often it is line that supports shape.

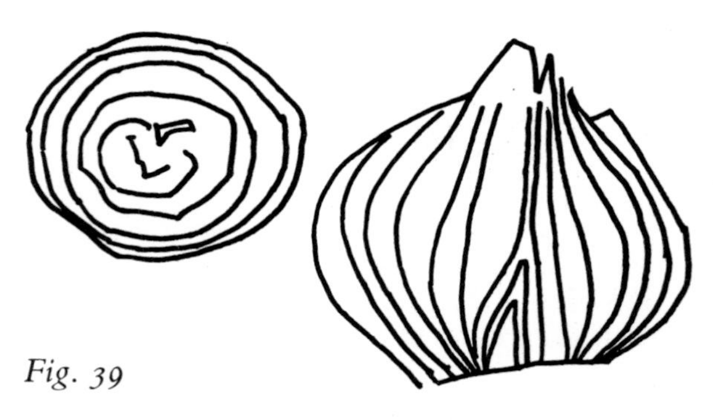

Fig. 39

A study of nature will help to show how line can support shape. Consider a section through an onion. See how the lines become more and more bulbous on either side of a line of symmetry until they form the outline. Or the designer may find an onion that is not perfect and may find it more interesting to make an asymmetric design (Fig. 39). This is an example of line pattern filling a shape and doing so in such a way as to be sympathetic with the shape.

Another example from natural form will illustrate the last point in a slightly different way. In wood grain the lines tend to run parallel to each other at various distances apart until they meet an obstacle in the form of a knot, then, just like water in a stream flowing around a boulder or several stepping stones, the line must accommodate the knot shape before continuing on its route (Figs. 40, 41).

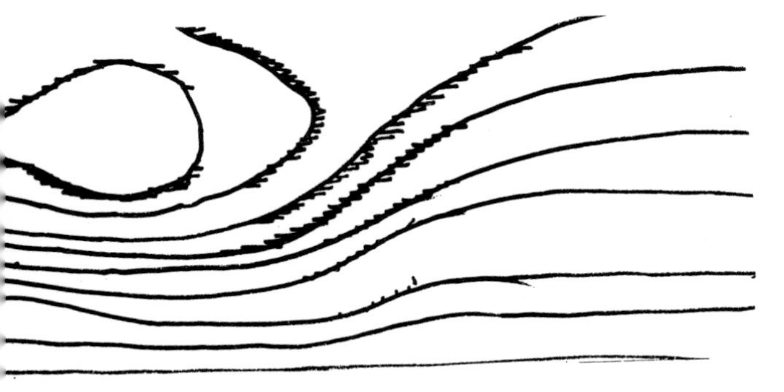

Fig. 40

Fig. 41

Similarly, the shapes used in design might be rectangles. To preserve the unity, line in the background might consist of verticals and/or horizontals. These would echo the shapes in the design and the edges of the ground (Fig. 42).

Fig. 42

It has not been easy to separate the elements of design from one another because they are interdependent, but it seemed less confusing to concentrate on one at a time. It is, however, quite impossible to separate texture from line, because apart from line's function of outlining shape, line is also texture. Here line will appear as thread – texture – in the final work although it is only a pen line in the design.

TEXTURE

Texture, in general use, refers to the structure and surface effect of textiles. A surface has tactile qualities that make the beholder want to touch what she sees. One of the great pleasures of contemporary embroidery collage is the lovely contrasts of surface textures. Obviously you can appreciate that surface textures are harsh, silky, lumpy, hairy and so forth, by handling them. But you can also tell, just by looking at the fabrics, how they would feel to touch. Hessian and velvet are obvious examples of contrasting tactile qualities.

We have seen that for the designer texture could mean a series of pen lines, a semblance of what will be true texture in the final work. A painter in his painting may use a medium that is lumpy (palette knife with oil paint) to create true texture that could be felt with the fingers. With a smooth medium he can create tactile qualities that are only illusory, but give us the same sense of wanting to touch. We would cite the sixteenth-century Venetian painters who gloried in rendering lifelike silks, brocades and furs. This is obtained by placing different touches of colour side by side, and so producing a broken surface – a pattern seen, not felt. These areas of broken surface give life to the work of a painter. The same possibility is open to you. You can enliven your embroidery collage by true texture surface or broken surfaces of colour.

BROKEN SURFACES

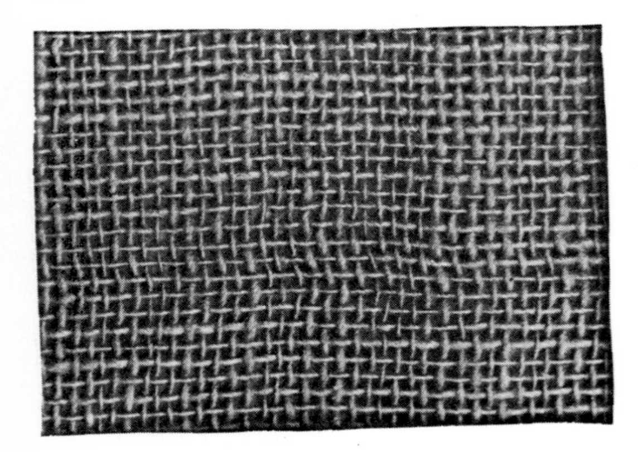

Fig. 43

Surface textures of textiles, both seen and felt (Fig. 43). You could make a collection of different textures of this sort, and make a textured collage, limiting the colour to white and making the design depend on the variety of texture in the materials. Unity would be preserved by the colour, and there would be the opportunity to be adventurous with contrasting textures.

Fig. 44

Patterned fabrics (printed and woven): a broken surface seen but not felt (Fig. 44). No one needs reminding that caution is needed in mixing these in a design. A little of this kind of pattern goes a long way and should be separated by areas of plain fabrics. A repetition of the same pattern, be it in a different scale, is better than too much variety. Unity is always the aim. The pattern should be related to the design as a whole. Choice of checks and stripes would work well with a design based on horizontals and verticals. Another collage might be tried on this theme. Broken areas give life to the design; conversely, plain areas provide restfulness and stability. It is necessary to find a balance of these two surfaces.

The line filling the onion shape in Fig. 39 is also texture, and so is the wood grain line in Fig. 40. Both these examples are showing line used as texture – supporting shape. We have said that shape is fundamental and that line is added to lighten, to enrich, shape. It is usually added after shape has been established, and it is important that it does not go counter to what already exists in the design. It must never seem to cross out, but to reinforce. It must be sensitive to what is already placed, just as the water in the stream accommodated the rocks in its path.

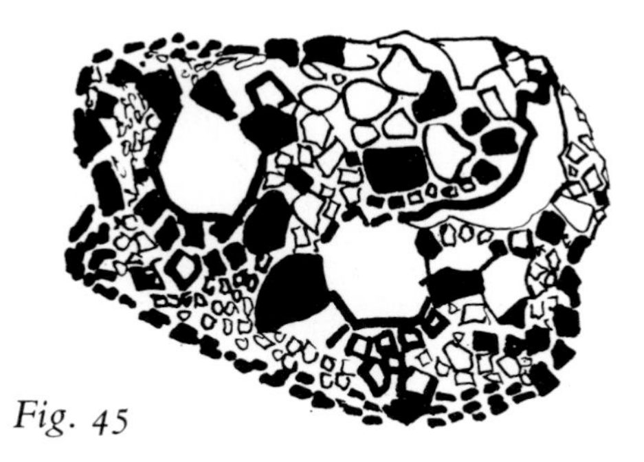

Fig. 45

Texture may be spot pattern, French knots, beads, sequins etc. Ideas for beautiful grouping or spot pattern can be observed all around us in nature: birds' plumage, eggs, snakeskins, insects, flowers, animals, or a chance discovery of small stones encased in concrete, as Fig. 45 shows. The same object inspired very different treatment in Fig. 160 (see page 113).

In the chapter on shape we discussed the organisation of spot pattern and everything said there holds good here. The spots need grouping and scattering to an organised plan (Fig. 45). The difference here is that they will not exist in their own right. This texture will very probably be added last of all, in the form of beads, sequins, French knots or other stitchery, and they must be used sensitively to fit in and enhance what is already established, be it machine embroidery or mass appliqué shape. They may fill a shape, follow a contour. They may provide a great deal of excitement in the design, giving richness and life, but being part of the total whole, they must fit in.

Related line and spot texture can unify shapes that may be dissimilar and give harmony to the design. They can also give variety of surface treatment to relieve monotony in a design, where a shape has been used as a repeated unit, and be its source of life. This point is dealt with further in Chapter 8, page 91.

A common fault in contemporary embroidery collages is that the texture is too varied. Here again the aim must be for unity in the design. Try to use similar shaped beads, ovals or circles and vary the scale rather than the shape. Repeat and carry an idea through. If a start has been made using needleweaving or other drawn thread work for the textural effect, be content with this and do not add beads as well, unless the beads are incorporated in the needleweaving. It is useful to try out ideas on separate pieces of cloth and to keep them handy as samplers, to select what is needed for a particular piece of work.

We suggest that you practise pen drawings of line and spot patterns and draw such textures from natural objects. The scrapbook cuttings should also grow alongside these. A collection of textures would be invaluable material for designing.

It seems that in this chapter we have emphasised the subsidiary role that texture and line play in the design process. But how important a part this is will be shown in the next chapter.

5
COMPOSITION

Because colour, shape, line and texture are interdependent elements of design, they rarely make sense on their own. Composition is concerned with this interdependence – the putting together of the vocabulary to communicate visually, to make sense.

In composition the craft designer becomes involved with an idea, which she interprets into the basic elements of design, disciplined by the characteristics and limitations of her craft. She channels her desire to be creative, on a chosen theme, through this discipline. This would be a very complicated process to explain if we had not attempted to consider each element separately in preceding chapters.

Although a great deal of composition is done by flair and instinct without apparent intellectual effort, a great deal can also be achieved by thinking and working out your problems of composition. Generally speaking, we feel that you should aim for a variety of size of mass, i.e. shape, lightened and enriched by line and texture.

You are likely to face three problems of composition in your craft. Design for:

1 A single unit – a decorative panel, wall-hanging, mobile etc. – within a shape. This could be a rectangular or circular panel to hang flat on a wall or to hang in space as a mobile and to be viewed on both sides.

2 Filling a shape that is irregular – part of a garment: a yoke, bodice, sash, half-belt, buttons, pocket.

3 A repeating pattern: a bodice, hem, evening bag.

In all three cases, scale needs to be considered. There is a fitness of scale, which works within a given shape. Designs that are too big will appear overpowering, whereas those that are too small will seem lost and insignificant. Practice in designing and a constant assessing of negative and positive shape should give you this sixth sense for scale. It is difficult to give specific instructions for acquiring it. Trial and error at the designing stage should show what is acceptable.

It should be seen that no part of the design has unconsidered space. This does not mean that you should avoid space. On the contrary, a well-planned space can be very valuable and necessary, so long as it registers as a shape and not as emptiness. It will always be helpful, while composing, to look at the design in a mirror. The eye can become tired and so accustomed to the work as to become uncritical. Seen in reverse the problem is viewed afresh, and often what has seemed to be balanced can be seen in fact to be awkward. We would advise using the mirror often during the designing process, in order to discover weakness before it is too late to put things right.

THE SINGLE UNIT

A design, already in the mind, may dictate the size and proportion of the panel to be composed. A piece of cloth suitable for the ground may present itself, or there may be a certain space on the wall to be filled. In any case the ground is the first consideration, its measurements, proportion, colour and tone. A mid-toned, low-intensity colour is very suitable and should present the minimum of difficulties, because it allows both light and dark colours to show up well on it and will be a good foil for high-intensity colours (Fig. 46).

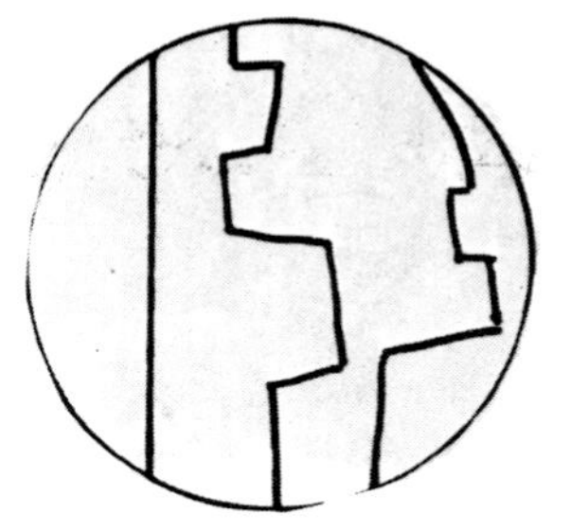
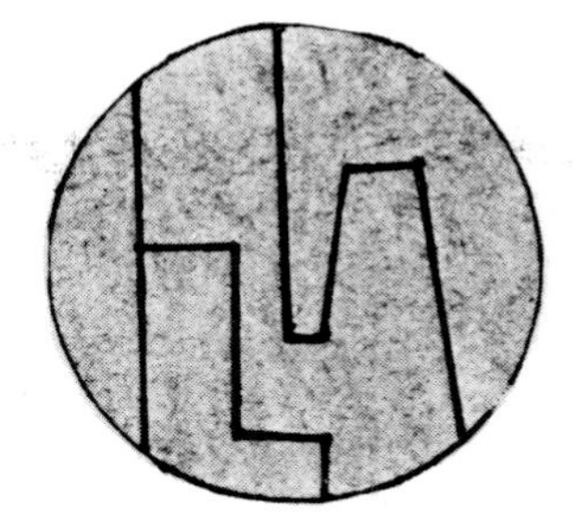

Fig. 47

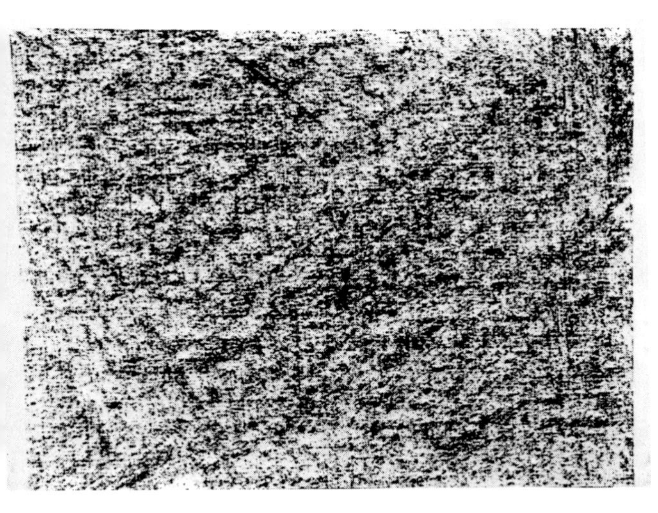

Fig. 46

Fig. 48

If you were using an exploded circle, as already discussed in Chapter 3, Fig. 22, you would already have a unity of related shape by the method of cutting from a parent shape and the overlap of transparent material. In this example transparent shape echoes the opaque one. You could also experiment by cutting another circle of transparent material, in a similar manner, e.g. angular cuts as shown in Figs. 47 and 48, thus maintaining a unity of shape but more variety. The use of transparent material in this way unifies the colour scheme too.

The panel should have a feeling of completeness. To produce this effect it is essential to have a focal point, to which the eye is continually drawn. The eye should wander with interest within the panel but never want to look outside its boundaries, and should return to the special interest, the focal point. There may be a secondary interest or interests, which play supporting rôles and these may echo the chief interest in colour, tone and shape; but the echo should be faint, supporting and never competing. Theatrically speaking, the focal point is the star of the production with many spotlights centred on it, the secondary interest has one spotlight and the rest of the stage depends on footlights and overhead lighting so that at times the stage may be lost in darkness and half-light. There must be no clash of personalities. The secondary interest plays a minor rôle – but a very essential one.

This explanation is on purpose dramatic to give you a picture in your mind's eye of the kind of organisation that takes place in composing. If it were followed out too slavishly, the result could be overdramatic and crude, but it would also be possible to work very subtly, bearing in mind the principle of this order of importance and attention.

PLACING OF THE FOCAL POINT

We have already encountered that aesthetically pleasing division of line at the Golden Mean. This device has been used by artists, by instinct or design, through the ages. For our purpose the approximate division at a third will suffice. Place the focal point so that it lies a third of the way in from either side of the panel and a third of the way up or down (Fig. 49).

PLACING OF THE SECONDARY INTEREST

The positioning depends on that of the focal point. It should come in the area on the diagonal from the focal point, not to emphasise the diagonal but to ensure that the balance of interest is maintained and that no big area is devoid of interest (Fig. 50).

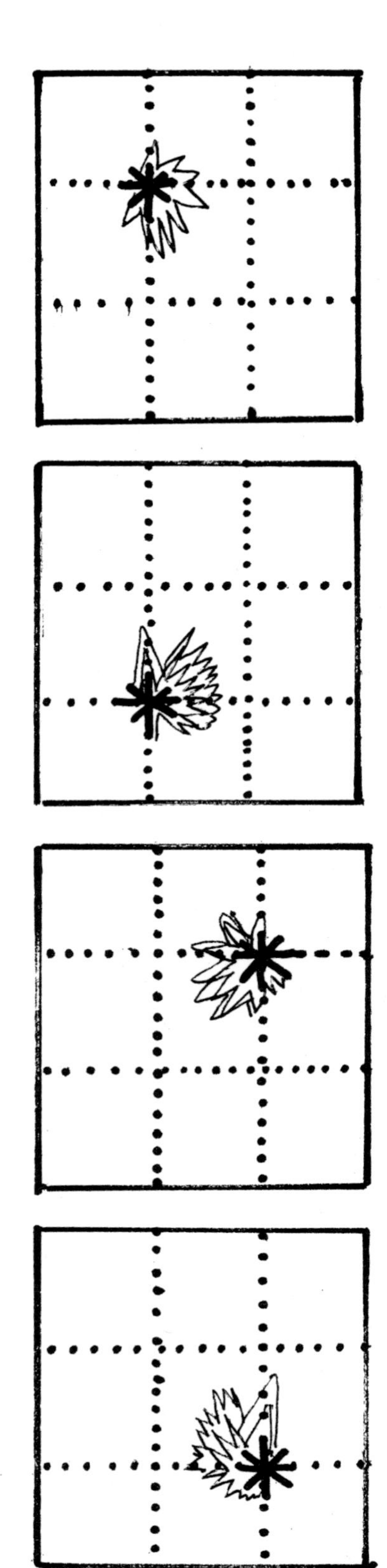

Fig. 49

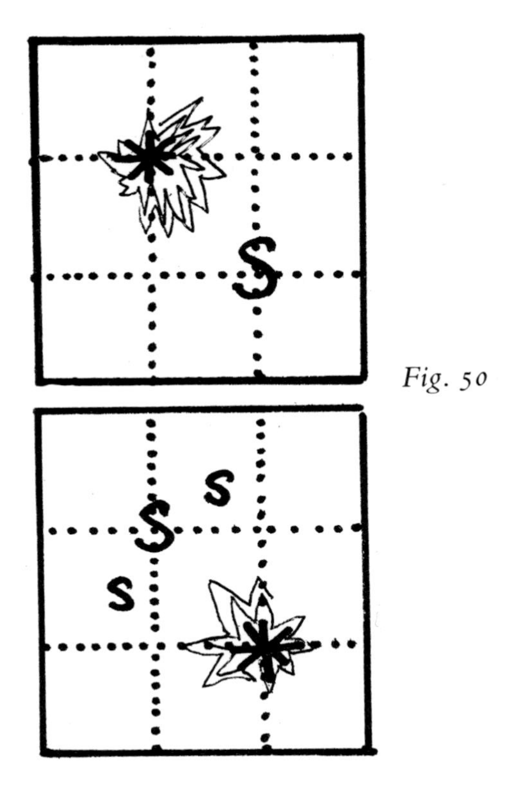

Fig. 50

HOW TO ACHIEVE THE FOCAL POINT

There are many ways of attracting attention visually in design. The reader will recognise methods from other chapters summarised below.

1 A change of scale in shape: e.g. small, fussy shapes at the focal point and larger, steadier ones surrounding it.
2 Colour:
(a) Intense colour surrounded by more subtle ones.
(b) Strong contrast of tone surrounded by a mid-toned range.
(c) Discord in the midst of harmony.
(d) Complementary colours.
3 Texture: the tension, be it in dot or line, would be intensified at this point, like a honey guide on a flower.
4 Movement: a change of movement, such as an oblique line among verticals and horizontals. A swirl of action leading up to the focal point.

Any one or a combination of these devices would attract the eye to the centre of interest. The whole design then revolves around and plays up to this point. If, for example, two complementary colours were used at the focal point, *one* of them might be repeated at the secondary interest. Similarly, if discord is used, it might be repeated at the secondary interest, but used there with a surrounding colour that is less disturbing. For example, shocking pink could be used next to orange at the focal point (thus reversing the natural order of tone) but next to red-violet at the secondary interest. (Shocking pink is a tint of red and red is lighter than red-violet in the natural order, so the tonal order would not be reversed at the secondary interest as it would be at the focal point.)

In order to give the impression of completeness, the panel must exist as a unit in its own right and never appear to be a fragment cut from a larger design. It can be likened to a television camera zooming down on a chosen subject, placing it well within the screen. Certain shapes in the foreground and background might be out of focus, blurred. One accepts this in photography.

While absorbed in looking at the main interest, one is barely aware of the surroundings, yet these surroundings are a very important part of the composition. Nothing must appear cut off at the edges, although it is possible that shapes will be incomplete. The colour and tone must work in order to 'frame' the design and let the edges fade out. An explanation of how to achieve this has been given in Chapter 2. The edges of the panel should be quiet areas without contrast of tone or colour or intense colour. While the edges of the panel retire, the focal point should claim the limelight, supported by its secondary interest. The mid-toned ground is helpful in making quiet areas at the edges. If a light-toned ground is used it may be necessary to subdue the edges by applying net or 'greying down' with line or texture as was explained in Chapter 4.

Line has been used just as a corrective for ground that claims unwanted attention, but these lines would play a dual part, for they would also be taking a direction in sympathy with the shapes already established in the composition. The whole act of composing is a 'fitting in', a team effort if you like, towards the common goal of unity and completeness. These lines will react like water negotiating stones, flowing around and onwards, echoing and reinforcing the shapes by their movement and setting up their own system of relaxation and tension areas. There may also be shapes that will be enriched *within* by line and spot texture.

When placing the mass shapes at the outset, provision should be made for the addition of line and texture in between the shapes. This textural effect of beading or stitchery could also lead towards the focal point and enrich it. This is the important part that texture has to play. It is the final embellishment and it should not be applied until the underlying foundations are ready to take it.

When composing for a single unit panel, the designer aims for unity of shape, colour, line and texture and a completeness of the whole. As a general rule she could work towards this end using a logical sequence of action. Heulwen Parry Jones, a student, has developed an exercise (shown in Chapter 3, Fig. 23) using opaque and transparent fabrics, thread and beads. We show below a way of working, while showing a specific example which proves that each design presents its own set of problems to which there are not any cut-and-dried solutions.

Fig. 51

1 Choose the ground; lower range tone (see Fig. 51).
2 Cut the mass shapes in paper and arrange them on the ground, bearing in mind:
(a) Positive and negative shape.
(b) The placing of the focal point.
(c) The secondary interest or interests.
(d) Spaces between the shapes, which may at the outset seem bigger than is aesthetically pleasing, to allow for line and texture.

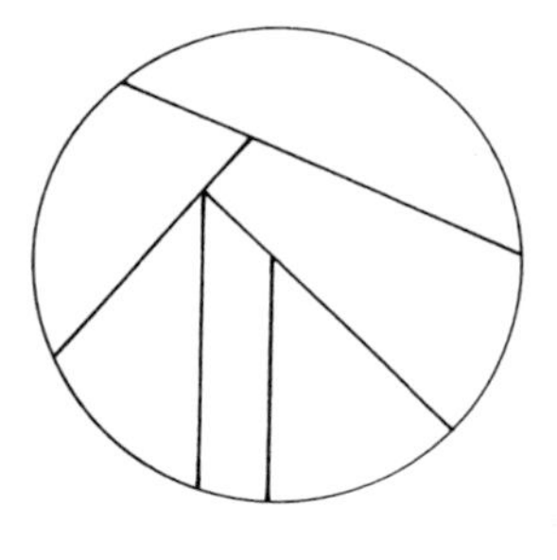

The example shown above follows most of the advice given: (a) Is the negative space varied enough? Further development will show if this is satisfactory; (b) The focal point will be placed in the space on which all shapes converge; (c) There will be no secondary interest.

3 Choose a colour scheme, related to the ground already selected, planning for:

(a) Focal point.
(b) Secondary interest.
(c) Surroundings and edges.
(d) Replace the cut paper with cloth, bearing in mind variety of tone against the ground and texture (Fig. 52).

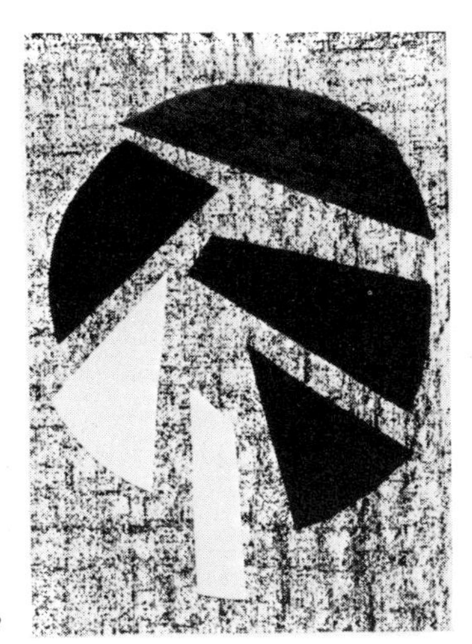

Fig. 52

This time our example follows 3(d). The ground chosen, dyed sacking, will take care of 3(c). The colour scheme is a monochrome and so our main concern is tone, and that is why we can show this in black and white illustration. What we cannot show is the extreme intensity of colour represented by the white shapes (see colour plate 7).

Fig. 53

At this stage, before attaching anything, look and ponder, often and long. Put it aside and come back to it with a fresh eye. Use a mirror. Does it seem too hard and naked? Try breaking the edges and changing the colour and tone by using transparent material. This gives a softer effect with more variety of related shapes (Fig. 53).

4 Link the shapes with line. Lighten the mass with line and texture, giving variety, movement, reinforcing shape, a lead to the focal point or a build-up of the focal point by means of applied texture.
5 Continue adding line and texture, building up tension and relaxation areas.

Fig. 54

Most of this advice has been followed in Fig. 54. It will be seen that the line giving life and change of scale is sometimes on the cloth shapes and sometimes on the ground, linking the design together and echoing both the angular and curved quality of the shapes. The focal point is a tension area of texture, texture that is circular in sympathy with and so related to the original parent shape.

This example shows the thought process and order of working that may be followed. We have chosen to experiment with a simple exercise – an exploded circle. Had we chosen to work from a natural object, as may be seen in Chapter 9, colour plate 26, the problems posed would have been similar, but less clearcut, and more easily faced after undertaking an exercise such as this.

DESIGN FOR EMBROIDERY ON PART OF A GARMENT

The principal difference between design for embroidery on clothes and that which we have just discussed is that in the former case the decoration will not lie flat but will be viewed on the individual wearer in three-dimensional form. It would obviously be wise to place a paper pattern of the area to be embroidered onto the figure before starting to design, and to realise how the three-dimensional form is being highlighted. Decisions on which part of the garment should be embroidered will be discussed fully in Chapter 10.

Once this all-important decision, which makes for success or failure, has been made, the design problem is similar. Shape, colour, line and texture are to be arranged within a given shape, but this time it may be an irregular shape. The same order of working may be observed.

1 Consider the ground, from the point of view of colour, tone, and, above all, *shape*. No preconceived plan for design can take preference over the ground shape to be filled. Whatever design is used it must be related to the shape. For example, if a yoke is to be embroidered, the design must accommodate the outline of the armholes, neck, and the line that joins it to the garment. A half-belt with two buttons needs to have a design that considers the rectangular shape of the belt and the round shape of the buttons, which will interrupt the flow of the design. A border design to go around a cuff must be so arranged that it will make a perfect join without interrupting the flow of the pattern (see Fig. 55).

Thus it is necessary to consider first the shape of the ground and then any other feature the design must accommodate.

2 Place the shapes on the ground, being as aware of negative as positive shape.

3 Form a focal point. This may well be an area in which line machine embroidery produces an area of tension by the placing of the line closer together at a chosen part, or an area of relaxation where the lighter ground becomes the special interest. The focal point as described for designing a panel may well be too dramatic and showy, but a variety in the interest will enhance the design.

4 Choose a colour scheme related to the ground.

5 Add line and texture.

REPEAT PATTERNS

It may well be that a repeat pattern might be used for embroidering the bodice of a garment, and there would be certain design problems to be solved to make it fit the shape of the bodice, but here we

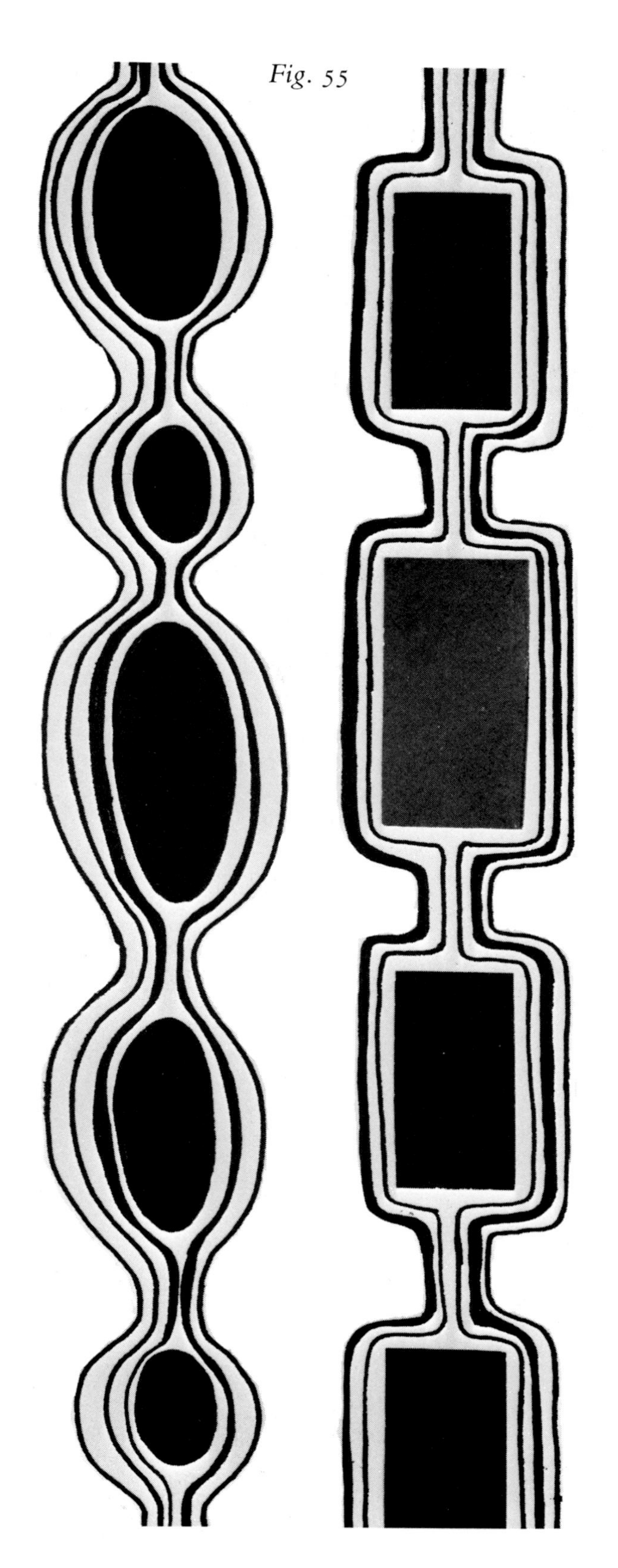

Fig. 55

want to consider repeat patterns without their being applied to any specific purpose. This is an easier design problem to solve than either that of the single unit or a feature on a garment, because any motif repeated makes a rhythm and looks better in repeat than as a single unit. Even a sheet of stamps seen in the post office makes an all-over pattern, which nevertheless is composed of single unit designs. Units that are designed for repeat patterns take into consideration the negative shapes between the positive motifs.

A design may grow from any beginning, however simple. You must accept a motif and then experiment with various arrangements of it.

Fig. 56

The drawing in Fig. 56 was done by a fourteen-year-old schoolboy. It is part of a hydrangea flower, two of the many units that make up the whole bloom. He drew this with careful consideration of the shape and of the varying scale of petals and achieved the blocklike form of the flowers. It is a drawing very suitable for design because the concern is for shape and line even though he was drawing a flower. It is harder to design using a motif that is representational, much more difficult to be detached and analytical when drawing something beautiful like a flower. We thought we would use a representational motif for this part of the chapter, because so far we have concentrated on geometric shape with cut paper. Let us then accept this simple drawing as the basis for a repeat pattern.

1 First take some tracing paper and trace from the drawing, reducing it to simpler terms, using a felt pen. Draw a rectangle around the tracing and cut it out. This will be the unit for repeat. Consider the negative shapes in the unit. If they are too big, cut the rectangle smaller (Fig. 57).

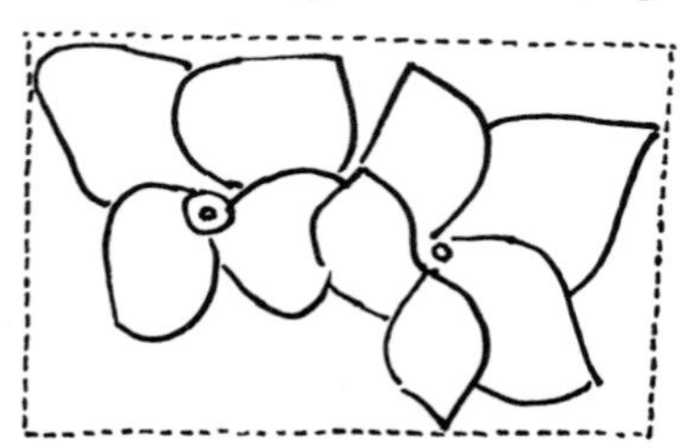

Fig. 57

2 Take a larger piece of tracing paper and try a straightforward repeat pattern, tracing the unit by placing it under the paper and moving it on. Fig. 58 shows the plan for the units and the resulting pattern. The way in which the unit is used will be indicated by the symbol in the rectangles. In this case, Fig. 58b, all are lying in the same direction.

Fig. 58a

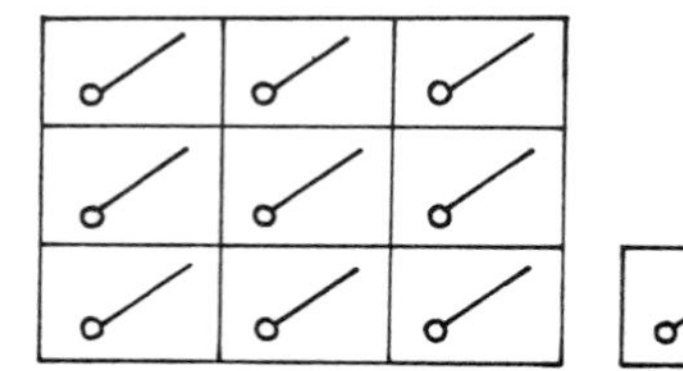

Fig. 58b

The important point to consider now is the negative shape. This registers as a shape, but there may be more satisfying negative shapes to be found by different arrangements. Would it be better to overlap the rectangles of the unit of repeat and so pack the positive shapes more closely?

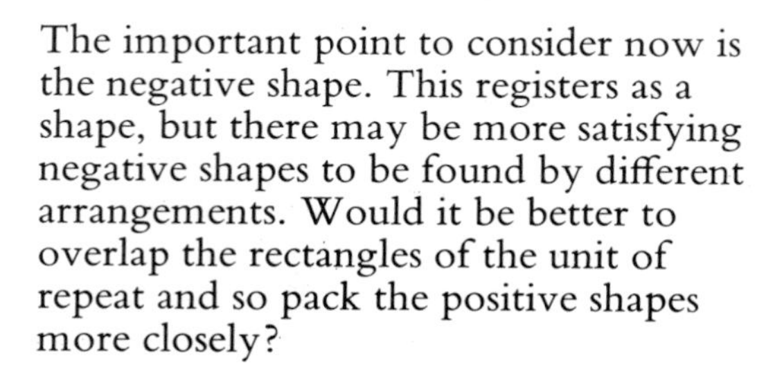

3 Try overlapping the unit and at the same time turning it around on alternate rows. The plan, Fig. 59b, shows how the units are arranged and the working out of the pattern can be seen in Fig. 59a. Notice the variety in the negative shape now shaded to give it prominence. Between the rows of units now appear a narrow shape and a wider shape. Is it better than the last example? The decision is left to you. Are they still too far spaced? It depends for what purpose the design is required.

Fig. 59a

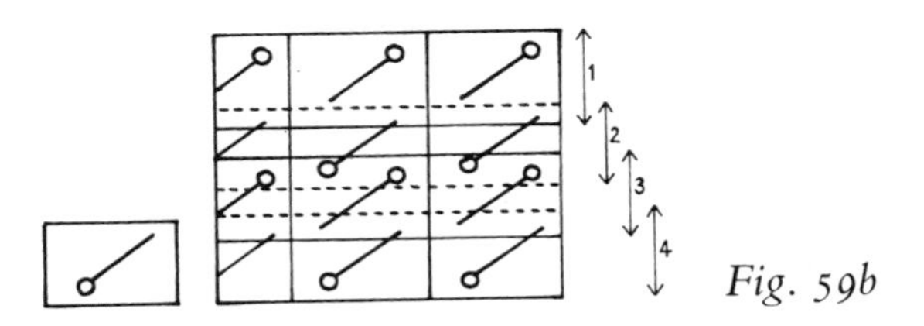

Fig. 59b

4 Let us try to get the flower motif really closely packed. The plan on the next figure, Fig. 60b, shows how the unit has not only been overlapped from top and bottom but has edged sideways sufficiently to allow the motifs to interlock. Alternate rows again as for the last design. Look at the negative shape. It is still varied and there is less of it.

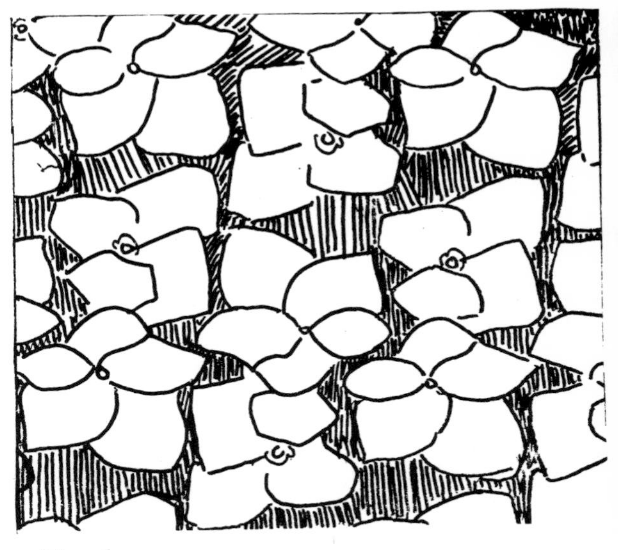

Fig. 60a

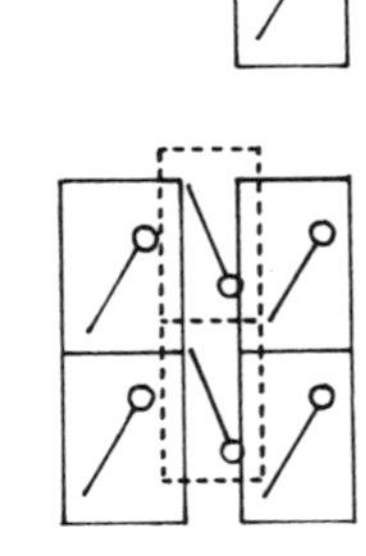

Fig. 60b

5 In the last pattern the unit was moved sideways as far as the pattern demanded. There is a traditional movement, called 'half drop', when the blocks are moved to exactly halfway along the adjacent unit. Fig. 61b shows how this has been done here.

The negative shape seemed to work out well, but needed some help to fill it. In all arrangements a second motif may be used instead of reducing the negative space, which is what has been done in Fig. 61a.

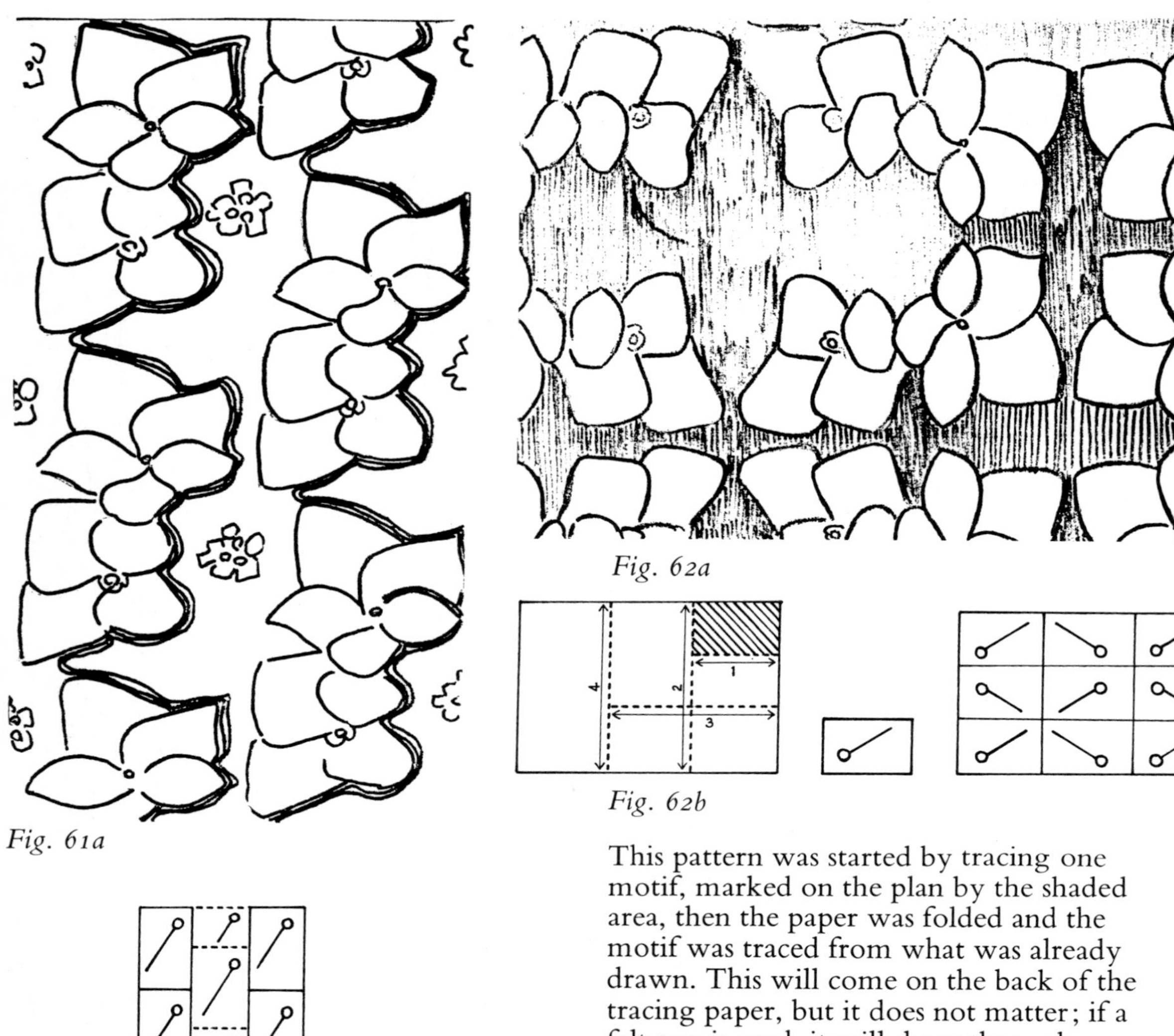

Fig. 61a

Fig. 62a

Fig. 62b

Fig. 61b

Line has been added to link the repeats and to emphasise that it is a stripe pattern. Try to make the second motif seem related to the first.

6 It will be realised that there are limitless ways in which to use a design motif. Once the choice of a unit is made, it is fascinating to try it out in this way. One more try is shown in Fig. 62.

This pattern was started by tracing one motif, marked on the plan by the shaded area, then the paper was folded and the motif was traced from what was already drawn. This will come on the back of the tracing paper, but it does not matter; if a felt pen is used, it will show through. This system continues as the plan indicates. Folding and tracing – the little unit of repeat is no longer used. The result is a larger symmetrical unit made of four motifs with fascinating negative shapes. This is a much larger repeat and many repeats of the larger unit would be required to see the real effect. It may prove interesting as an experiment but not necessarily suitable for the purpose.

From the very beginning we have emphasised the importance of negative shape. Nowhere is it more important than in a repeating pattern. Although, possibly, all the work will go into the positive shape, it is often the negative that registers more strongly at a distance, especially if the ground is lighter than the embroidery or more intense in colour.

7 When the arrangement of the units is decided upon, each motif requires a focal point (the centres of flowers provide a first and second interest in this case). This little accent of colour or tone or texture will add interest and avoid monotony. The design is a starting point for designing with materials. Fig. 63 shows the motif used as a repeat pattern for appliqué.

The blocklike form could be used in more repeats as above, and form a deep decorative area on a jacket or waistcoat. Felt has been used in the example, but other non-fraying fabrics would have been equally suitable, e.g. suede. The method employed is described in Chapter 6. Some areas have been cut away, so that only the outlines of the petals remain, giving a line which is a foil to the mass. The centres of the flowers have been given an accent of colour and texture with wooden beads, felt and textured threads.

Flower designs are very suitable for machine embroidery, but this would need to be adapted to a continuous flowing line, which would keep the machine moving. In order to achieve this flow it would be necessary to loop the line. Fig. 64 shows a paper collage made from the hydrangea motif and a rubbing of the collage. This shows the possibility of using the motif with a continuous line. It might well be that modifications would be needed to adapt the design to the flow of the machine. This will soon be realised once machining starts. It is essential that the machine works freely and creates its own design.

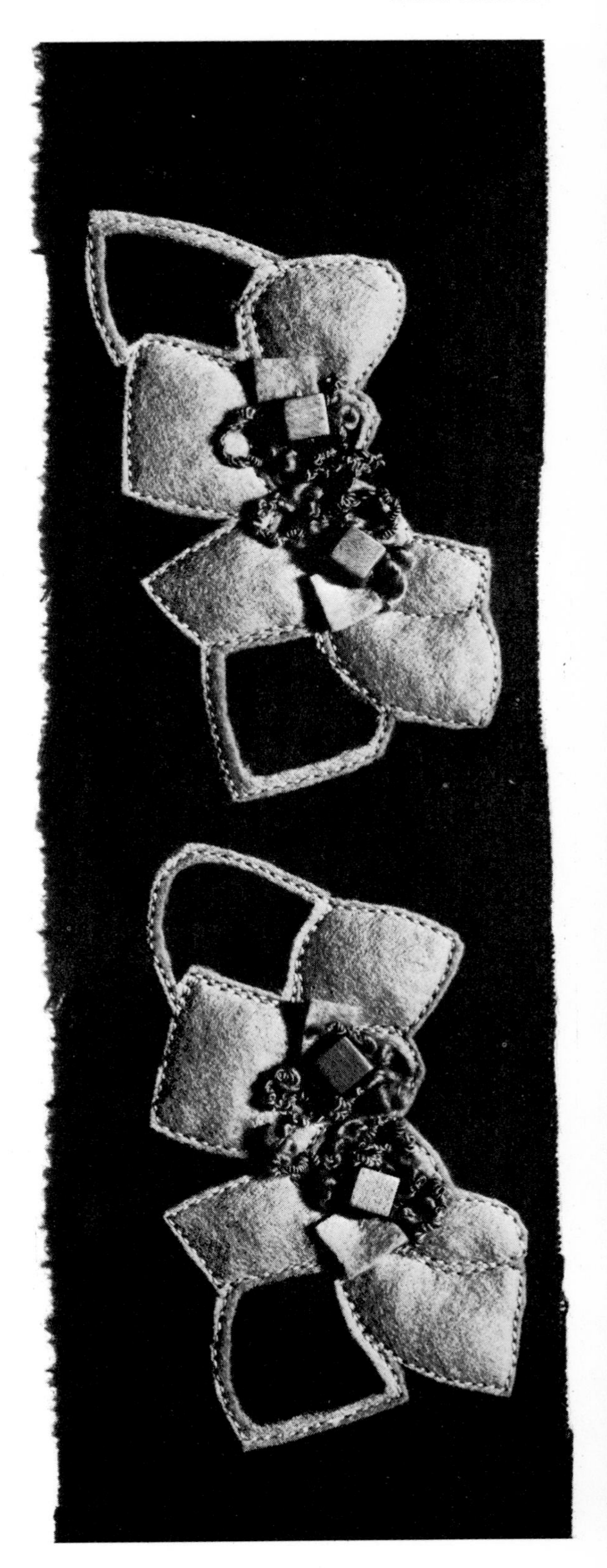

Fig. 63

Fig. 64

The motif could then be used en masse in an all-over pattern. An example of how this could look is shown in Chapter 10, Fig. 184. Note how the centres of these shapes have accents of texture to give interest.

Always work designs to a reasonable size and try to work accurately. It is easier to work on a big scale and a successful large design will reduce well. Assessment of the merits is possible only if the repeats of positive and negative shapes are accurate. If the scale of the drawing is not right, it is an easy enough task to reduce or enlarge it, as can be seen in Chapter 8.

These instructions should be sufficient to start you experimenting. You may like to go further into the problem and use some of the networks shown in Figs. 65a–e. Further study of a book that deals entirely with pattern would give a fund of ideas.

Fig. 65a Diamond

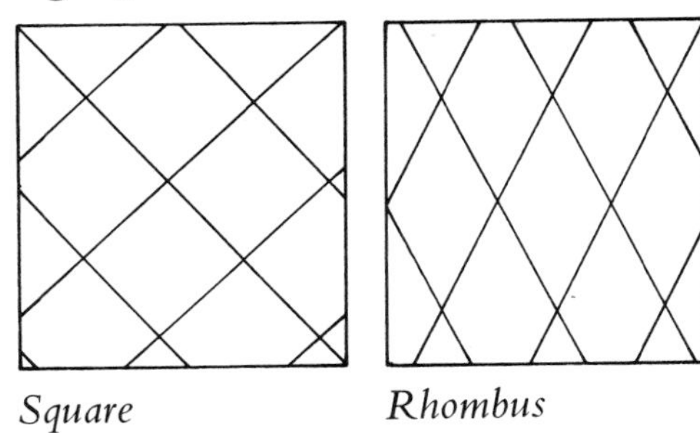

Square *Rhombus*

Fig. 65b Triangle

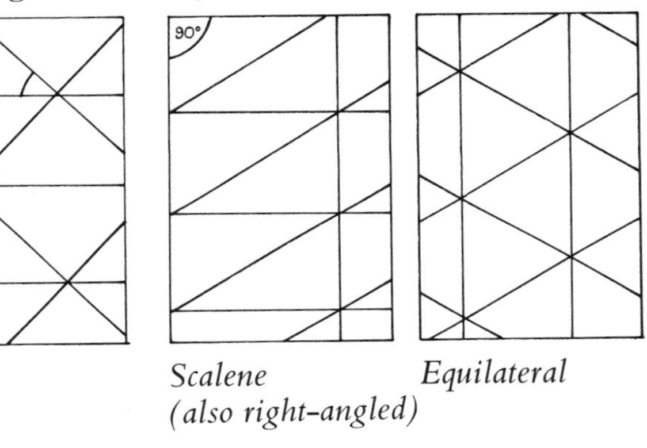

sceles *Scalene (also right-angled)* *Equilateral*

Fig. 65c Ogee

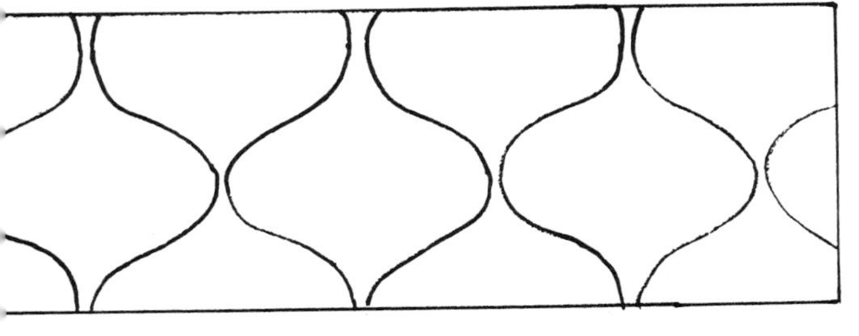

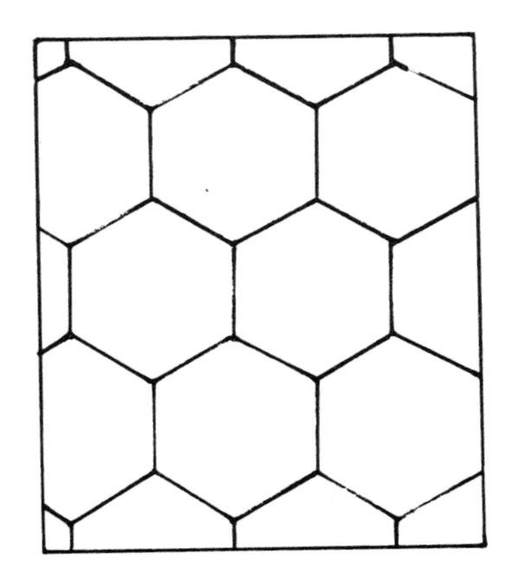

Fig. 65d Hexagon

Fig. 65e Circle

INTRODUCING PATTERN, ITS DEVELOPMENT AND APPLICATION

It cannot be emphasised enough that trial and error are essential in composing for embroidery. Time must be allowed for experiment. There must be no rush. Mature thought is needed while looking, changing, adding and taking away. Half the secret is knowing when to stop and what is superfluous. Experiment, there is nothing to lose at this stage! Find excitement in it.

As designer for needlework you are both composer and performer. You must take time and thought that your composition is worthy of performance. You have an infinite variety of effects upon which to call. You can play with contrasts and harmonies, positive and negative shape, intense and subdued colour, restful and restless shape and line. Each of you will have a natural emphasis and will show preference for some aspect of design. One of you will be particularly interested in shape, another will be, above all, a colourist, another will have a marked linear quality in her work. A personal style as easily recognisable as your handwriting should develop naturally, without any conscious effort on your part.

6
MATERIALS

We have said that true design for a craft grows naturally from a sensitive use of materials and tools. In this chapter we shall be dealing mainly with the materials used for fabric collage, although many of the explorations are applicable to dress.

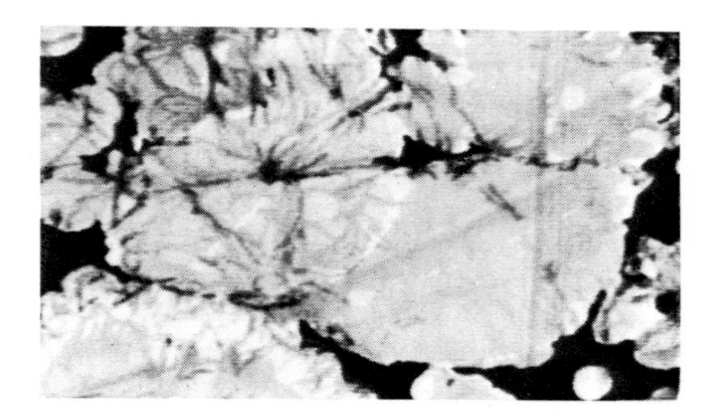

Materials of all kinds may be used. In fabrics the variety is vast. Threads, beads, sequins, plastic in all its forms, metal, wood, practically anything that can be stuck or sewn on. All have possibilities to be explored and exploited. Colour plate 11 gives an idea of the excitement such materials create.

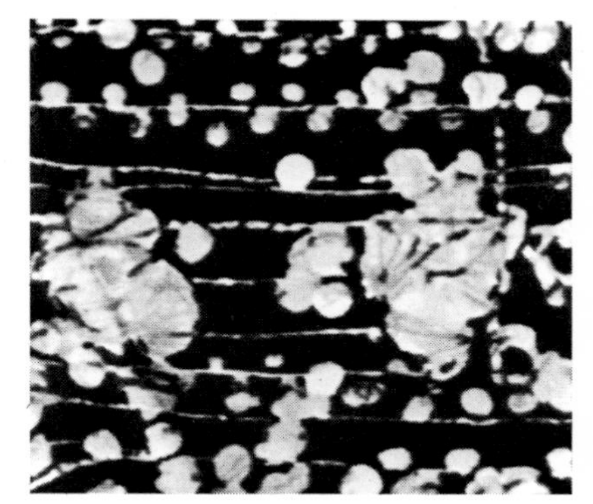

Fabric is the basic and most important material we are going to use, so you should (a) be aware of the wide range available; (b) be prepared to experiment with it.

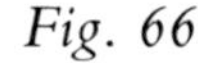

Fig. 66

We have already mentioned the need to make a personal comment in creative work. Personal choice is exercised in selecting the fabric to be used. You may choose a fabric for its colour, texture, weave, matt or shiny surface, pattern, handle, or because it is patterned by printing, weaving, or is embossed, and you will use these characteristics in your own way. You may be fascinated by the reaction of one colour to another, contrast in texture, scale of pattern or weave. The scope is limitless. (See Figs. 66 and 67.)

Fig. 67

Whatever the reason for the choice, ultimately the way the fabric behaves becomes important. So much frustration is avoided if you can combine an understanding of the properties of the fabric with its aesthetic quality. Two important elements affecting the behaviour of the fabric are the fibres used and the manner in which they are constructed. Most of us find it increasingly necessary to handle and experiment with new fabrics flooding the market in order to make the best possible choice for the task in hand.

Basically, fabrics can be woven or knitted (by hand or machine). Decorative fabrics are also constructed from threads, macramé, tatting, lace, crochet etc. Or they can be non-woven – felt or Vilene, for example. There are combinations of woven fabrics with a bonded knitted backing. You will really have to learn by handling and experimentation. (See Fig. 68.)

Fig. 68

Pulling in both warp and weft directions shows whether the fabric stretches a little, greatly, or not at all. Its recovery should be observed, that is its reaction to crushing, folding, pleating. Notice its effect one way up, or the other. These are superficial assessments of a fabric's properties, of course, but they help in making decisions whether to use it for one purpose or another. A fabric's reactions to heat and moisture are important, for very practical reasons – ironing and pressing.

Sometimes just seeing a fabric on display will suggest possibilities. Draped qualities suggest folds and gathers in dress, semi-transparency necessitates thinking of the shape to be made and the shape that will show through – applicable to dress and fabric collage. Handling will give information about the feel and weight, which are very important in dress because they affect the comfort and hang of the garment.

WOVEN FABRICS

The weave of a fabric can be used as a basis for design. For example, the open weave of the fabric chosen was the basis for the embroidery collage in Fig. 169 (page 120). The vertical and interwoven horizontal threads provide a framework. This can be accepted and exploited in a sensitive way. In a simple tabby weave (see Fig. 43 on page 38) the threads can be withdrawn easily – but carefully in order not to distort the rest of the fabric.

The possibilities of fringing could make it very exciting.

The range is extensive, from sacking to very expensive linens. Many curtain fabrics permit work on a scale of design otherwise impossible. Drawn thread work has been practised for many years, but not in a free creative way. Art is a freedom and a discipline. Discipline in the past has had the upper hand. The true discipline is that imposed by the material. We suggest that you start with sacking or hessian; it is cheap, easily available, and will accept a dye readily.

EXPERIMENTS USING THE WEAVE OF THE FABRIC TO ENCOURAGE CREATIVITY

1 Withdraw some threads and substitute other more interesting ones. (The exercises done in line pattern should be remembered here.) Consider variety of thickness and texture (Fig. 69). Note the reverse in texture (Fig. 70).

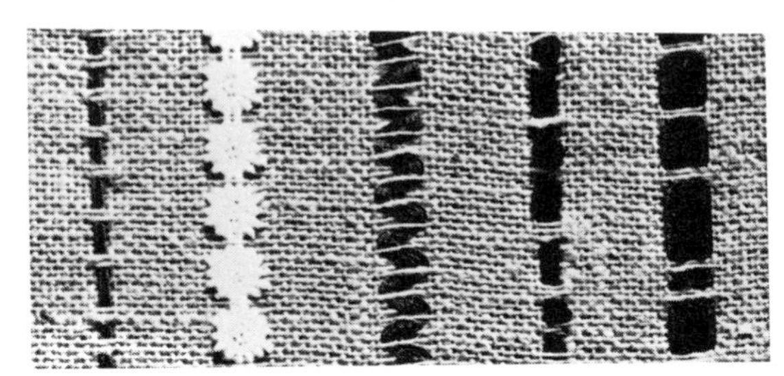

Fig. 69

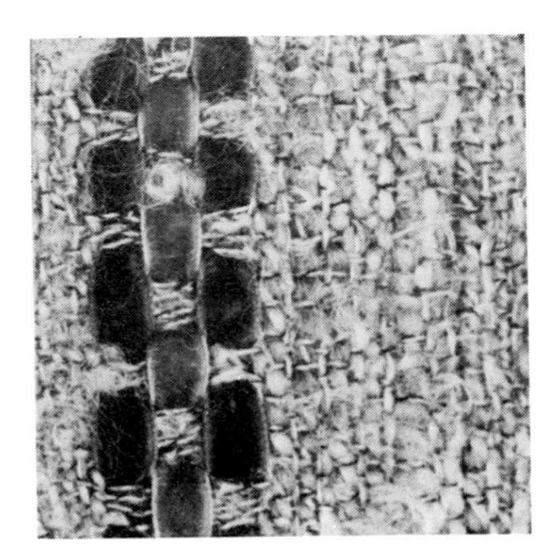

Fig. 70

2 Expose broad bands of warp and weft, find alternative ways of filling in or arranging threads (Fig. 71).

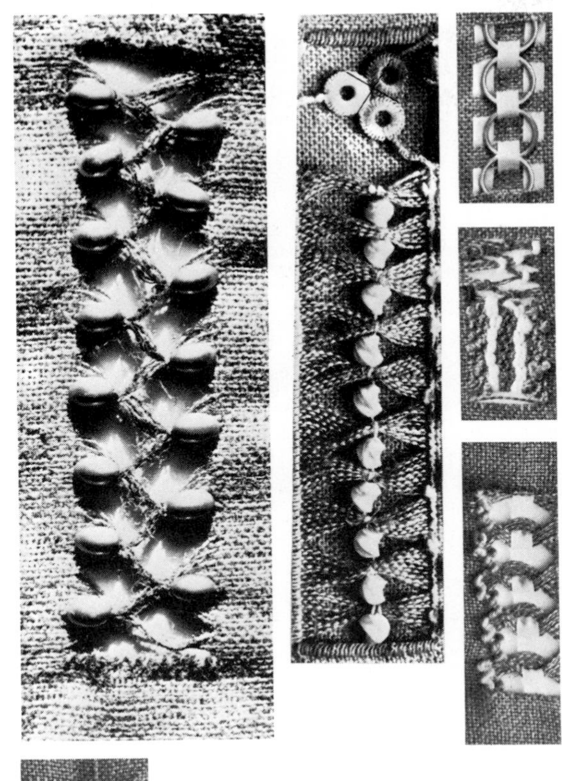

Fig. 71

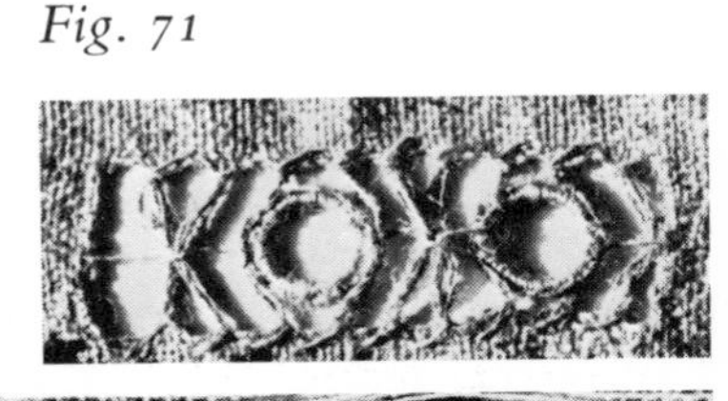

3 Note spaces left where warp and weft threads are removed. Try filling in these shapes, maybe with some kind of lacy infilling or peepholes to things of further interest beyond (Fig. 72).

Fig. 72

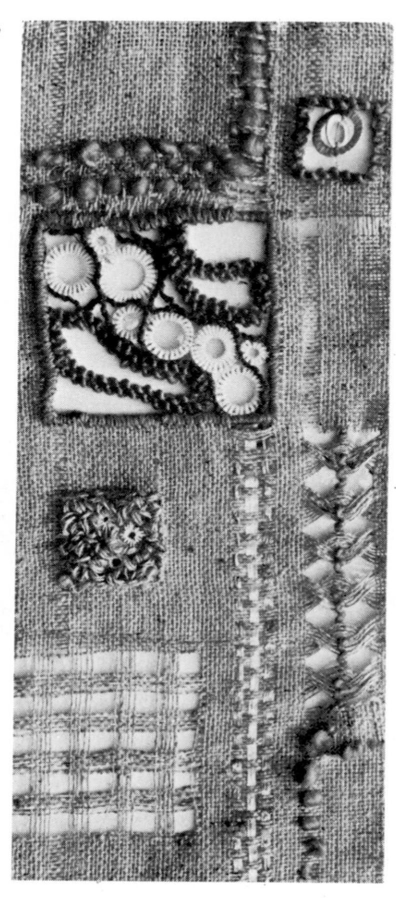

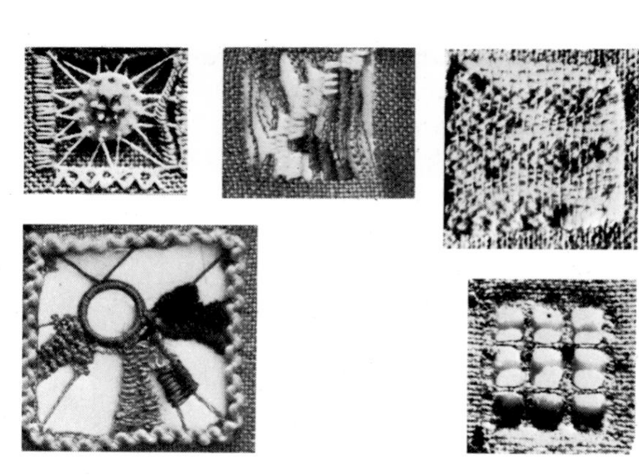

Fig. 73

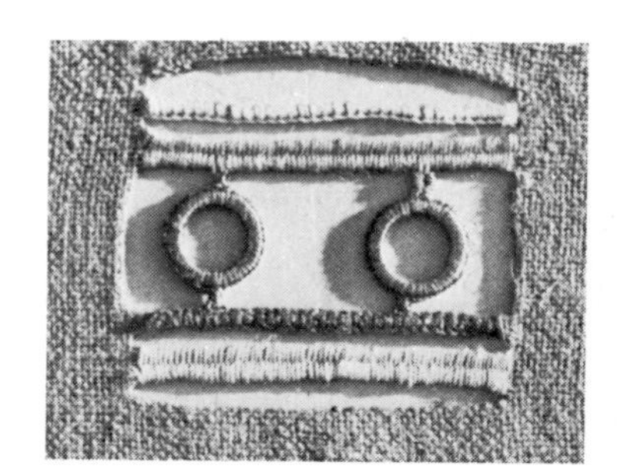

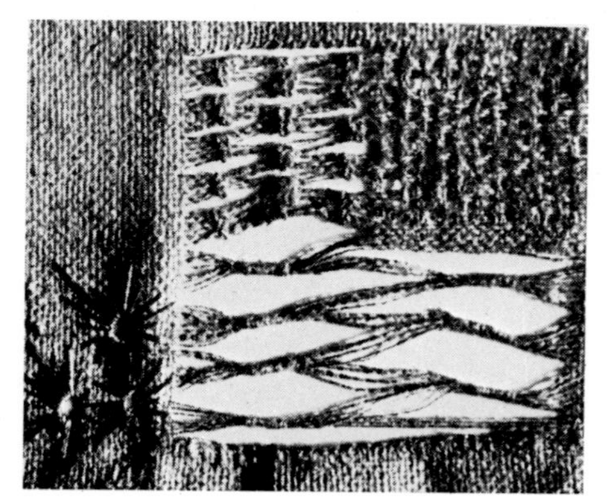

At first work only in small areas. There is no point in labouring long once a discovery has been made. Move on to further experiment. Try different ways of securing the ends of the withdrawn threads so that eventually you will have a choice of methods for different pieces of work. Sellotape the ends to the wrong side of the fabric as a temporary measure and get on with exploring the fabric.

4 Instead of withdrawing threads, pull them apart and keep them apart with stitches (Fig. 73).

5 Poke holes in the cloth with a thick knitting needle and keep these holes open. Experiment with stitches that will keep the threads where you wish them to be. It will be found that threads frayed from the edge or withdrawn will be useful for this. This self-coloured stitching will be unobtrusive and will not distract from the shape created. The shape is the part to be appreciated, not the stitching, whose function is just to hold it firm (Fig. 74).

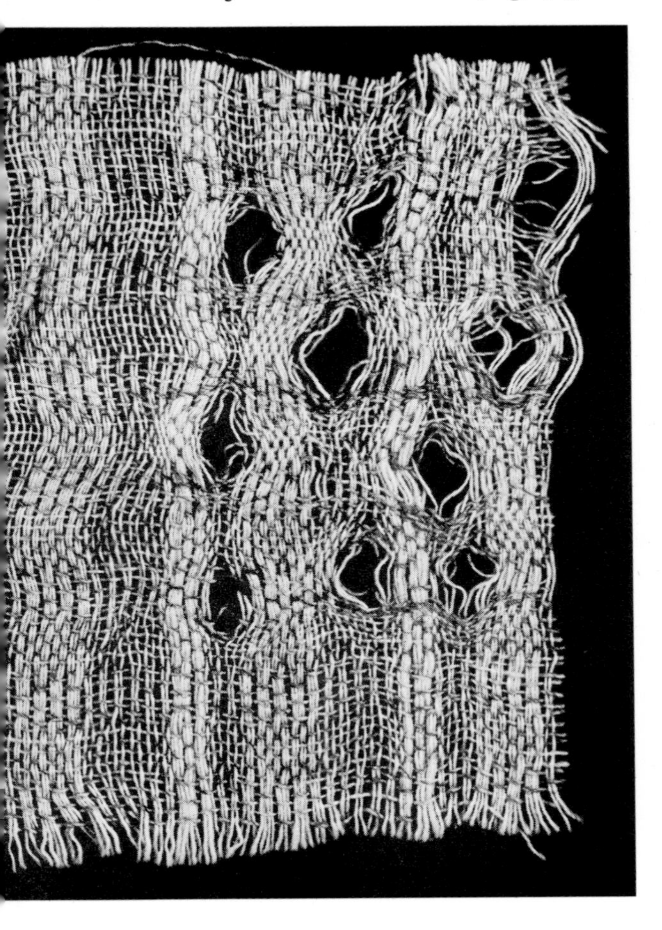

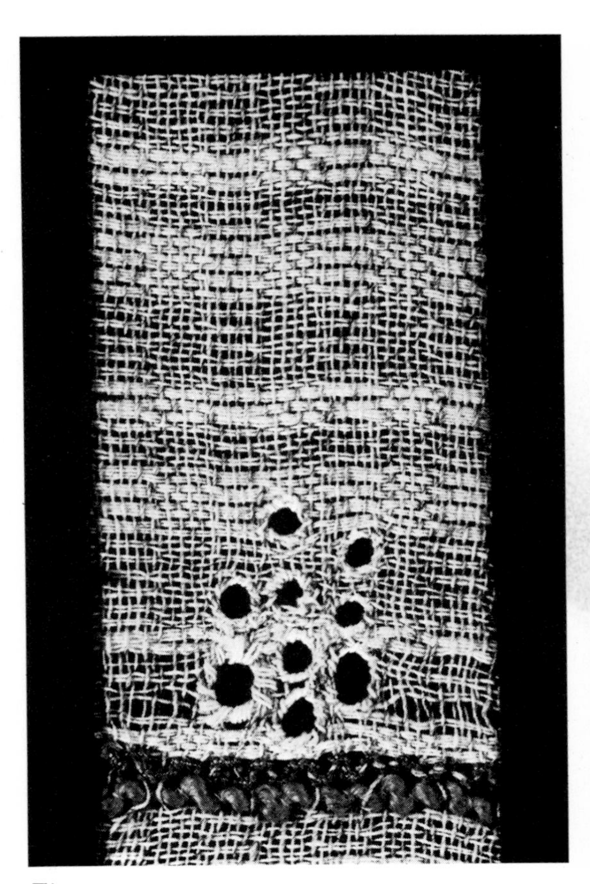

Fig. 74

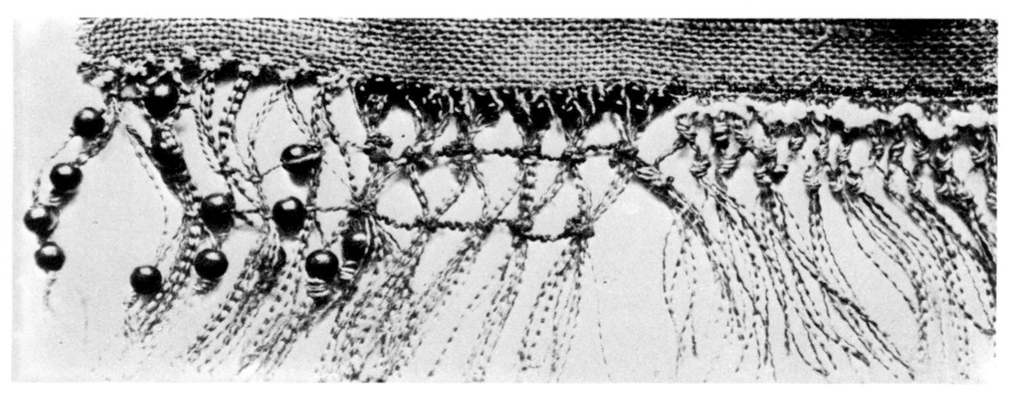

Fig. 75

6 Fray the edges and use the wispy, shaggy quality of the threads. Control them and make them decorative by knotting, plaiting, beading or a combination of all three (Fig. 75).

In the above we suggested designing freely and directly onto the material. They are exercises, not finished pieces of work, and should act as references for the future. If a finished piece of work were being carried out, confidence might be gained by quickly seeing the final effect after cutting and pinning on strips and rectangles of paper before withdrawing the threads (Fig. 76).

Fig. 76

The design should be your own creation and have contemporary expression. Only then will you feel the excitement of being creative. While admiring the skill of past craftsmanship, you should not hold it in such reverence that it inhibits you. What was an expression of a bygone era is not contemporary expression. We must live in *our* world and express it.

The use to which the work will finally be put will dictate the finish. Dress or household articles will require a more exacting finish than collage, which may be under glass or stretched over hardboard.

PATTERNED FABRICS

Patterned fabrics, either printed or woven, can form a basis for embroidery. Gingham checks, spotted or striped fabrics can be developed by the addition of embroidery stitches (Fig. 77).

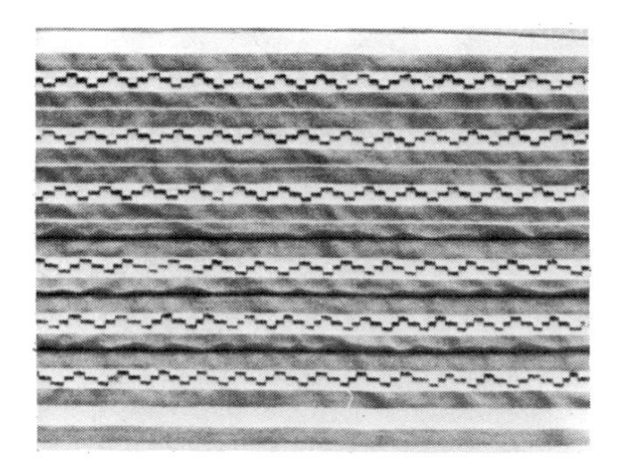

Fig. 77

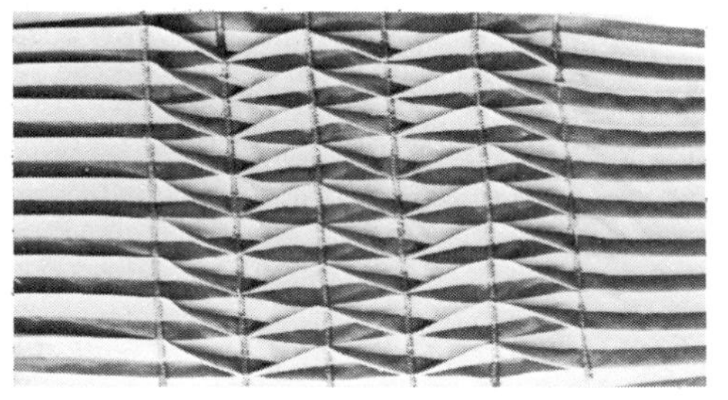

It has been done before, but the ways of tackling the problem are ever new with each piece of fabric, and the results are very satisfying. A fabric that has an interesting shape in its printed or embossed pattern might also be developed (colour plate 32). Painting the lily if you like! It could be terrible done badly, but with selection and restraint can be very effective.

This leads us to the possibility of developing prints that have been done by hand or tie-dyed patterns. If you are interested in this aspect you should study the books suggested in the bibliography on printing and tie-dyeing of fabrics, respectively.

SPECIAL EFFECTS WITH WOVEN FABRICS

Some fabrics have a pile or sheen. Velvet, corduroy and needlecord are among these, and can look light or dark depending upon the direction of the pile. This richness is used in dress, soft furnishing and decorative work, sometimes ensuring that the pile is running in the same direction, giving a consistently light or dark appearance, sometimes deliberately alternating the direction of the pile for effect (Fig. 78). Crushed velvet has its own areas of light and shade.

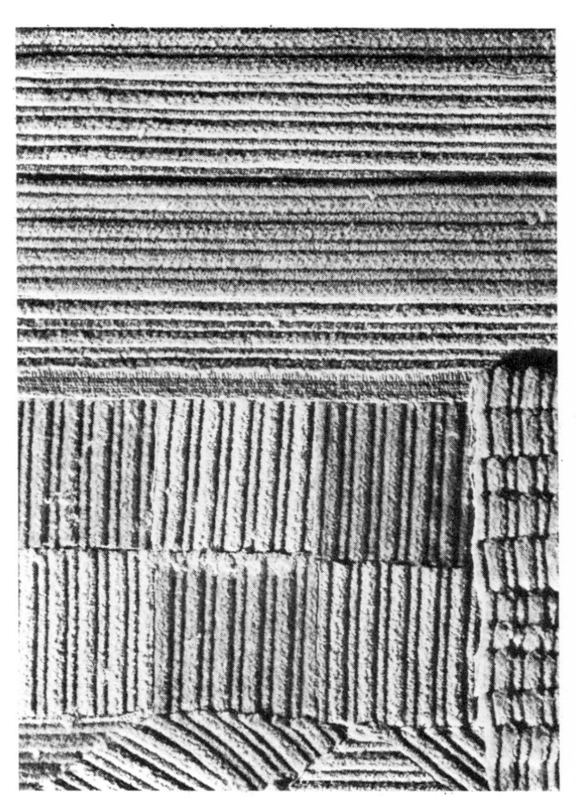

Fig. 78

Shot taffeta or chameleon taffeta is woven in contrasting colours of warp and weft in equal proportions. It appears one colour from one viewpoint and a different colour if turned around. This effect without the sheen can also be seen in some Welsh tapestry. Warp and weft of complementary colours, red and green, produce a subtle blend when woven. A bedspread seen from the head of the bed may seem to have a green bias, whereas from the foot it seems to be bronze. Obviously this effect might be worth exploiting in collage work.

The illustration of moiré taffeta shows a watery pattern, which has interesting shape and line used for its own watery effect or for inspiration (Fig. 79).

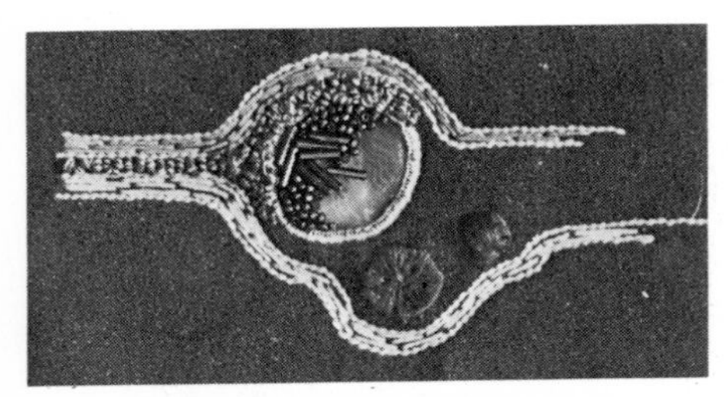

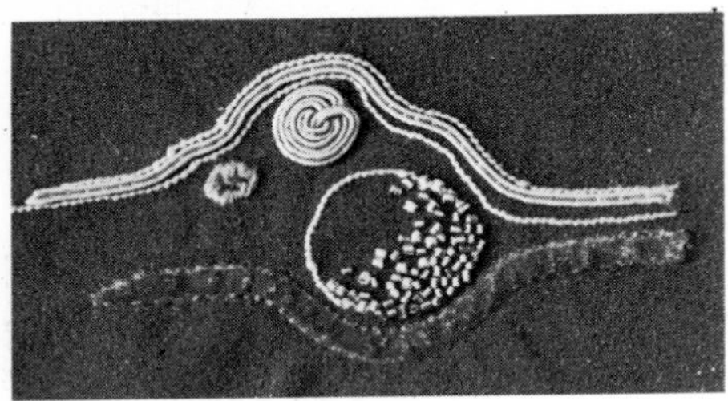

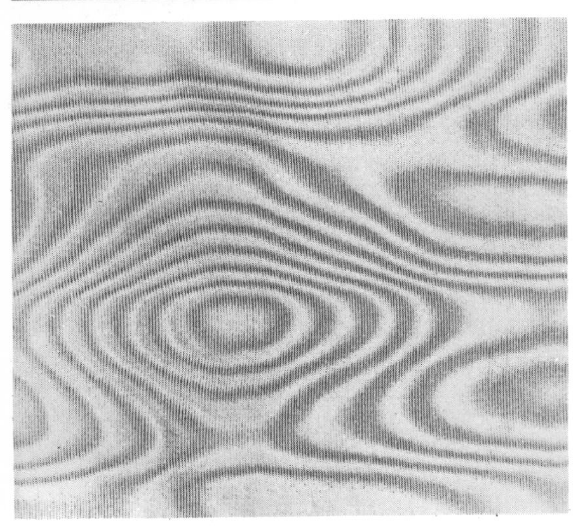

Fig. 79

KNITTED FABRICS

Knitted fabrics, whether made by hand or machine, have more elasticity and tend to be less stable to handle. Many have excellent recovery properties, and are ideal for garments. The finer, closer knits are much easier to handle and can be used for appliqué. Some exciting shapes can be hand-knitted, making holes and creating texture within the resultant fabric.

NON-WOVEN FABRICS

These bonded materials, such as felt and Vilene, have the advantage of having no grain line and so can be cut without fraying (Fig. 80). Because of this lack of grain line they can be cut and used as one would use paper. The designs with cut paper in the chapter on shape could all be carried out in felt. The shapes could be turned around, used at any angle, also pieces left in the background could be used without fear of a grain line. Felt is effective in layers, giving the appearance of rocky strata, each stepped back from the one below. It can also be rolled. Felt is made in a wide range of colours and although it is expensive there need be little waste.

Fig. 80

PVC (Poly Vinyl Chloride) is available in a variety of forms. Plain, embossed, printed with pattern, and either opaque or translucent. If it has a knitted cloth base it has quite good stretch properties and is easy to apply.

Gold or silver kid, used a great deal in ecclesiastical embroidery, is luxurious and expensive. There are synthetic alternatives which are cheaper.

All these non-fraying materials are excellent for providing clean-cut shapes and can be stuck down or sewn, as you think appropriate.

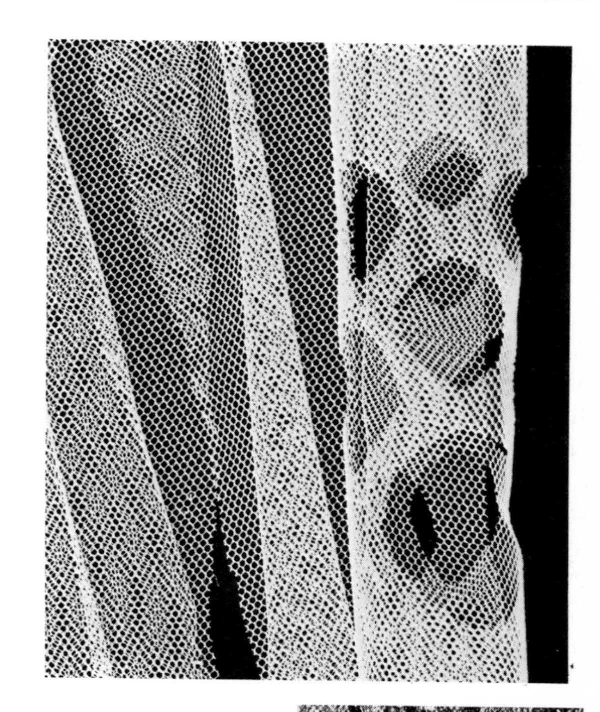

Fig. 81

TRANSPARENT FABRICS

Transparent fabrics allow the underlying fabric to show through (Fig. 81), sometimes reducing the colour of the underlying fabric yet exposing the texture. This power to reduce colour is useful. If the collage seems to lack unity of colour, nets can bring about a unity by giving the effect of looking at the embroidery through tinted glasses. Net is also useful to soften tones that are too contrasting and can be most effective, giving softness and mystery of shapes merged together. Nylon net has a functional use also. It is invaluable in strengthening large shapes cut in a top layer of a two- or three-layer collage.

It is not possible to deal with every kind of fabric you are likely to encounter. By the very nature of your interest you will collect a wide variety. We would say explore them for their design possibilities, test them for stretch properties and be aware how they will react to heat and moisture, in order to avoid a great deal of frustration and disappointment. This is particularly important when differing fabrics are to be used in the same design. This is the discipline materials impose on creativity.

METHODS OF ATTACHING FABRICS

The way one fabric is attached to another depends on the fabric, the effect desired and the purpose of the work. Anything that has to be laundered must be considered from the practical viewpoint, i.e. the fabrics used should react in a similar way when washed, and the method of application should withstand handling and wear. The relative weights of the background and applied pieces need to be considered to avoid any drag causing distortion.

The simplest method is to use an adhesive, and this is often appropriate. Experiment with the large variety now available. Adhesives are not suitable on transparent fabrics.

If a more secure method is required for practical purposes, then the grain of the pieces to be applied should be matched to the grain of the background fabric. This is important because it helps to prevent puckering and contributes to a good finish. Careful tacking is also important (Fig. 82).

Very thin opaque fabrics may need the support of iron-on Vilene (Fig. 83).

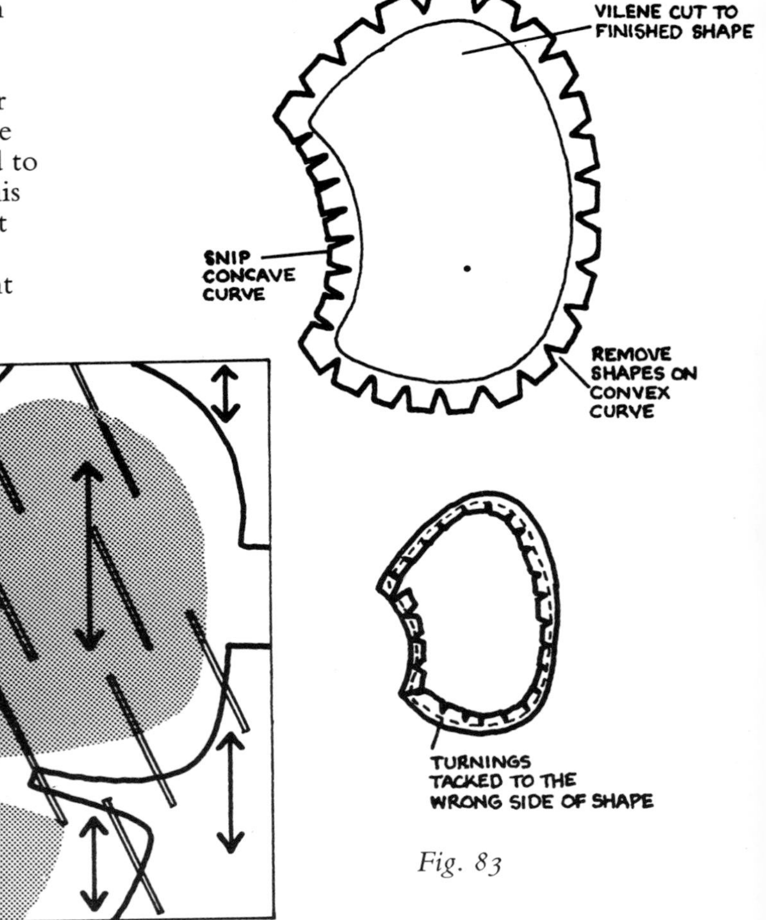

Fig. 83

Fig. 82

Sometimes the edges may remain raw, e.g. non-fraying fabrics, felt, suede, leather etc., and attached by hand or machine. Other fabrics, which are closely woven and fray only a little, need not be turned under, providing they are neatened adequately with a swing needle machine. Additional stitchery linking the appliqué and background adds strength as well as being decorative. Fraying fabrics of medium thickness can be turned in all around the edges, tacked carefully in position and hemmed or slip stitched.

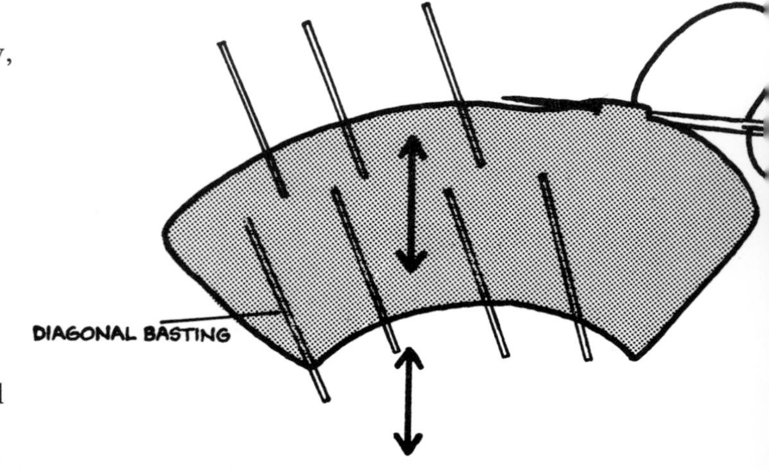

Shapes can be applied by using the method illustrated in Fig. 84a–d.

1 The design is transferred to the wrong side of the background itself, or onto a fine backing used to support the background, e.g. organdie (Fig. 84a).

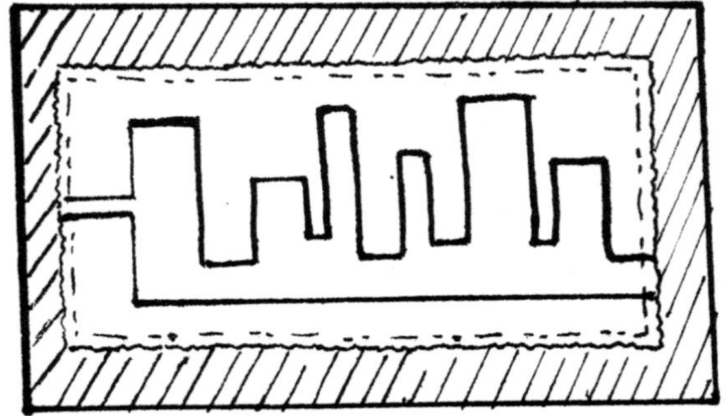

Fig. 84a

The fabric to be applied is very carefully tacked onto the right side of the background with the right side uppermost, with the grain lines of both running in the same direction. Ensure that the design area is covered (Fig. 84b).

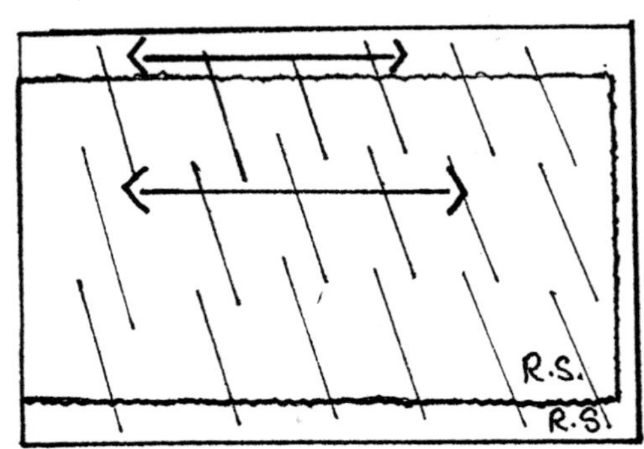

Fig. 84b

2 Stitch from the wrong side and carefully remove tacking and trim close to the stitched lines (Fig. 84c and d). Neaten and secure the raw edges with zig-zag stitch.

Nets, if used to give soft, shadowy effects, are better applied by hand because machine stitchery gives a hard outline.

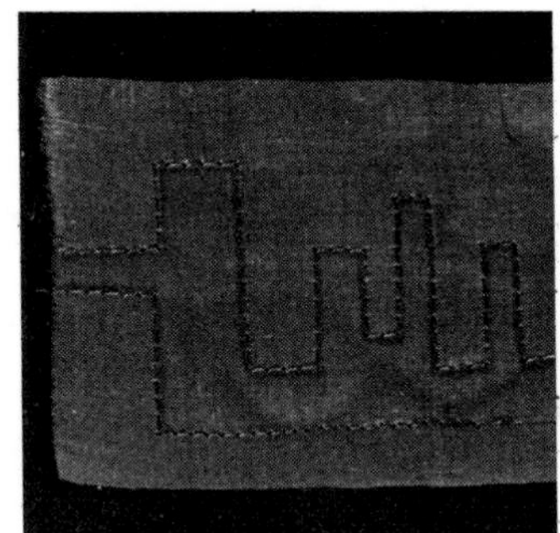

Fig. 84c

Fig. 84d

Catch the net down with a small stitch over the connecting net structure in the colour of thread of the background.

Applied shapes can be padded to give a raised effect by cutting successively smaller shapes than the shape to be applied in felt or fine wool, tacking and inverting the shapes so that the smallest is resting on the background fabric. Tack in position and cover with the shape to be applied. This gives a dome-like effect (Fig. 85).

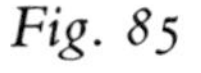

Fig. 85

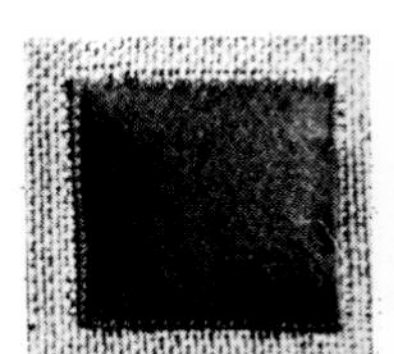

TRAPUNTO METHOD

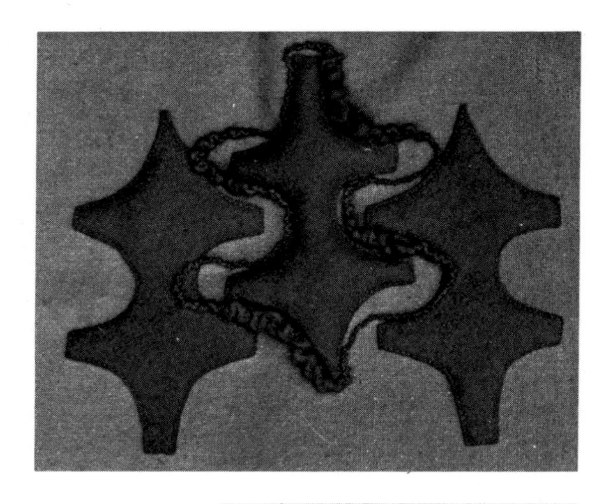

This can be done on areas or parts of areas that have been applied to a background, or on the background itself, providing there is another fabric on the wrong side, which will hold the padding – rather in the same way as Italian quilting has a muslin backing to hold the quilting wool.

1 Machine around the area to be raised. If this is an applied fabric, neaten edges if the fabric frays.

2 Turn the work on to the wrong side; the machine stitching will show the shape of the part to be raised. Cut a slit carefully on the straight grain of the fabric. Insert wool, reaching extremities with a knitting needle. Check to see the effect on the right side of the work. Do not overfill.

3 Draw the edges of the slit together with oversewing, secure threads. (See Fig. 86.)

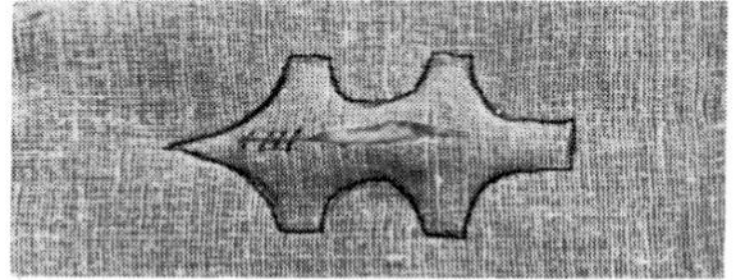

Fig. 86

You should visualise working from the ground both forwards and backwards. Working forwards involves applying fabrics onto the ground whereas working backwards entails cutting into the background and revealing a lower layer.

A different effect can be achieved by using a method practised by the Cuna Indians. Select up to five fabrics in different colours, put one on top of the other, baste together tightly. Cut a pattern in the top layer, and work your way down to the bottom. The pattern appears with all the colours stepped down in depth. Neaten edges.

Once you have tried various methods and observed the effects possible, you will find yourself combining techniques to achieve a desired result. Some people design directly with the fabric, others like the reassurance of a plan on paper and cut paper shapes. You should aim to evolve your own way of working; in this way you will achieve results that are individual and unique.

THREADS

One fabric may require to be sewn to another as invisibly as possible, or a thread may be needed to be decorative as line or texture. The modern embroiderer should make a collection of threads that are thin, thick, textured, shiny, matt, flat, rounded, hairy, smooth, and be eager and willing to find out how best they can be used.

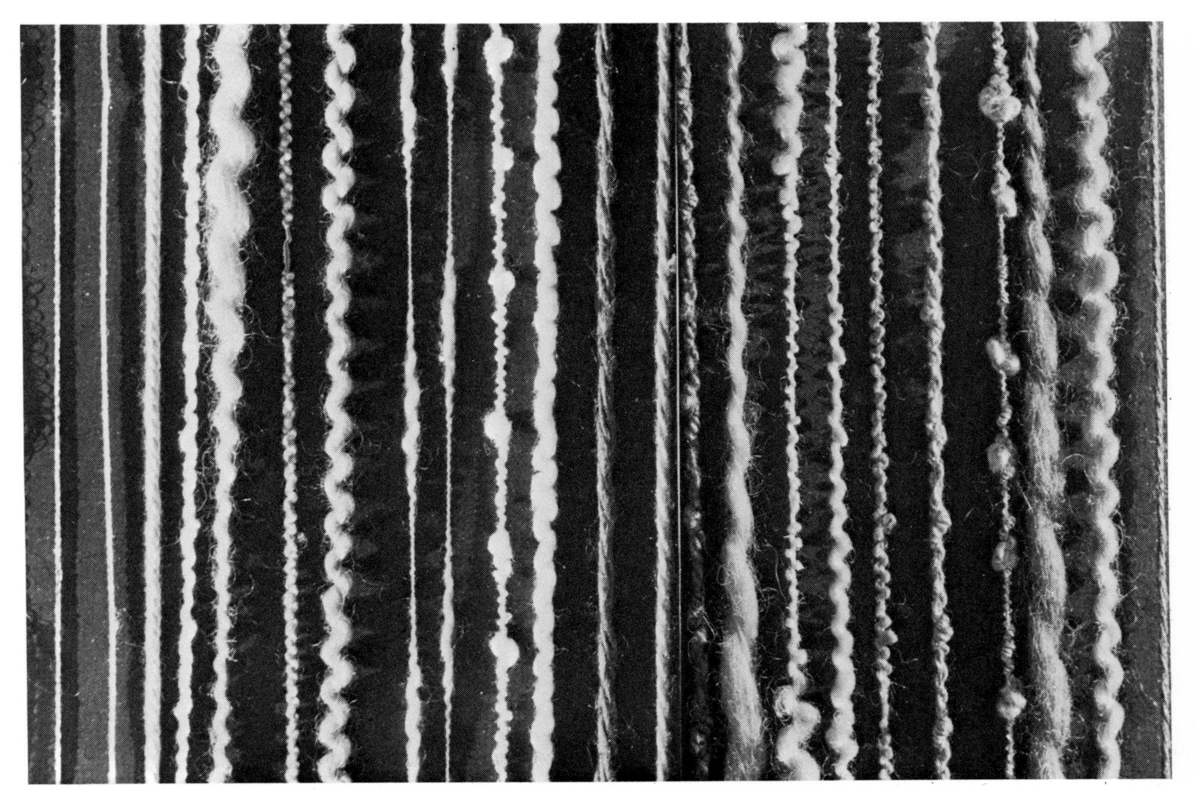

Fig. 87a

(See Fig. 87a.) The appropriate needle for hand or machine sewing will avoid unnecessary frustration. See equipment on page 70.

It will be observed that some of the thickly textured threads and strings are in fact weaving yarns and used here they are intended for weaving, couching and knotting. Combined with contrasting thinner threads they give very satisfying textured effects.

Collecting together sufficient material to give the inspiration to start working can be an expensive business. At the end of this chapter are some experiments with dyeing fabric, which you should find economical and at the same time creative in producing unity of colour.

It would be economical to buy a limited number of coloured threads and to dye these. If they are already of varied colours and are placed in a common dye, the dye will have a unifying effect and will produce something that is unique in colour schemes. Threads withdrawn from fabric, too, should be saved and perhaps dyed to suit a particular piece of work.

Woven cloth with warp and weft of contrasting colours, perhaps red or blue, giving a purple effect, can be embroidered with threads which are withdrawn, with the red or blue predominating.

BEADS, SEQUINS ETC.

These provide enrichment, giving textural interest and can be a dramatic addition to collage or dress (Fig. 87b). The range is great, both in shape and finish, but they are not cheap to buy. You should be on the lookout for old jewellery and

Fig. 87b

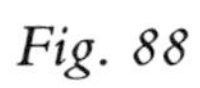

Fig. 88

second-hand beaded clothes. If the shape is right it is very easy to change the colour by spraying or painting. There are many ways of attaching beads. Try to vary methods. Combined with stitchery, beads can give unusual texture. Beads sewn on top of sequins or mingled with sequin waste are worth experimentation.

Many materials, such as coils of wire, metal and plastic curtain rings, chicken wire, plastic fruit bags etc., can be used (Fig. 88). It is impossible to name them all. Different things will spark off a reaction in different people and the time given to becoming involved and experimenting with whatever appeals will never be wasted. It all builds up to a visual and tactile vocabulary. An experiment tried one day may prove exactly what is needed for a finished work at a later date.

DYEING

Good colours are produced by subtle mixing of the pigment in the dyes. Cloth that requires a subtle mixing of colour can be expensive. (Colour mixing is dealt with fully in Chapter 2.) We have already advised a mid-toned, low-intensity coloured ground for collage. If there is a piece of cloth available, of suitable texture, that is too intense in colour or too light in tone, why not dye it? It needs to be a ground that is rich but will not drain the colour from the appliqué and embroidery placed on it.

An excellent texture for the ground is sacking. The natural fawn colour will have a subduing effect on almost any dye used. Always experiment with small pieces at first, and if the result does not please, either add another colour to the dye bath or dip the sample into another dye. Allow for shrinkage when the ground cloth is cut. It would be worthwhile measuring the small sample pieces before and after dyeing to estimate shrinkage.

If you want to do collage embroidery work we would urge you to experiment with dyes as suggested below. The results on fabrics and thread are stimulating, pleasantly surprising and inspire creativity.

COLOUR SCHEME EXPERIMENTS

Dye is pigment suspended in a medium such as water. In the process of dyeing, the dye becomes exhausted. The first experiment is based on this characteristic of dye.

1(a) Choose a strong colour hot-water dye and make up the dye solution with a pint of boiling water, adding 1 table-spoonful of salt. Put half of this solution into a dye bath and heat as suggested on instruction leaflet.
(b) Take 4oz of old cotton sheeting and cut into ten pieces of similar area. Wash the cloth.
(c) Place one of the wet pieces into the dye, keeping it covered by the liquid and constantly in motion until it is a rich colour.
(d) Remove it from the dye, squeeze back any surplus dye into the bath and rinse until the water is clear.
(e) Add another piece of cloth and treat in the same way. Continue with the rest, one by one, until the colouring in the dye has been so exhausted as to have little effect on the fabric.
N.B. Turn the heat low once the dye has boiled, otherwise it will evaporate before the experiment can be completed.
(f) Arrange the pieces to show the monochrome colour scheme produced (Fig. *2b*, page 13).

2(a) Take another dye and make up the solution as before, but this time place it all into the dye bath. It will be noticed that double the amount of dye is used for man-made fibres.

(b) Take 4oz of white fabric of as wide a variety of fibres as possible. Try to include such natural fibres as cotton, linen, wool, silk and rayon – man-made ones such as Tricel, polyester (Crimplene), polyester/viscose, viscose (triacetate), nylon (polyamide), acrylic.
(c) Add enough water to cover the material and place it wet into the dye bath.
(d) Bring the temperature slowly up to hot, under 100°C, and maintain this for 15 minutes, then rinse the fabrics.
(e) Compare the resulting colours. Natural fibres will have absorbed the colour well, whereas the absorption in the man-made fabrics is very varied. This does not produce a true monochrome as did the last experiment. When we used a red dye, the deep red colour of cotton, silk and wool seemed unrelated in colour to the polyester (Crimplene), which was a pale pink, or Tricel, which was almost orange and very satisfying in colour excitement among the rest, a discordant note in an analogous scheme. The bundle of cloth taken from the bath resembled petals from a half-opened rose.

3(a) Take the second half of the dye used in the first experiment.
(b) Take 4oz of different coloured fabric from your bit bag. Try to vary the colour, the tone, the texture and the fibres, both natural and man-made. Wash the cloth before dyeing. Colour plate 8 shows the materials before dyeing. They are completely unrelated, about twenty pieces of varying size were used.
(c) Cut a small 1″ (2·5cm) square of each piece before dyeing to keep as a control.
(d) Add enough water to cover the cloth and dye as for man-made fibres above. Rinse the cloth.
(e) Arrange the resulting colours and compare them with the originals.

The set of unrelated colour will be unified by the dye. We show two examples using Dylon red (9) and turquoise (33). Within this mixture there is also the variety of colour absorption, which we saw in the last experiment with natural and man-made fabrics. (See colour plates 9 and 10.)

If these experiments are tried it is difficult to imagine that anyone could fail to see the merits of using dye or to become an enthusiast for it. We could think of other experiments, such as selecting from a group of random colour pieces and dyeing by the first experiment method of exhaustion, or taking the white fabrics containing different fibres and allowing those that absorb less easily to enter the new dye first. We would then use judgement in selecting the order of dyeing and so gain experience in manoeuvring colour. These are only test pieces. If larger pieces are dyed for use in embroidery collage, do not forget to dye threads also.

EQUIPMENT

Sewing machine: Hand or preferably electrically operated. A zig-zag machine is more expensive but worthwhile. An extensive range is available; shop around and enquire about demonstration lessons and after-sale service.

Scissors: Large cutting out shears, medium weight. Small, sharp, pointed embroidery $3\frac{1}{4}$″ (8cm) blade for close cutting.
Paper scissors.

Needles: Machine needles range from fine No. 9 to heavy No. 18 and should be changed to relate to the weight of the fabric. Some hand sewing needles are illustrated in Fig. 89.
No. 1 'Betweens', for general use, are short and strong. Sizes 1-10.
No. 2 'Primary' needles for children; large eye for easy threading, small for ease in handling. Sizes 1, 3, 5.
No. 3 Embroidery, crewel needle, long eye for easy threading. Sizes 1-10.

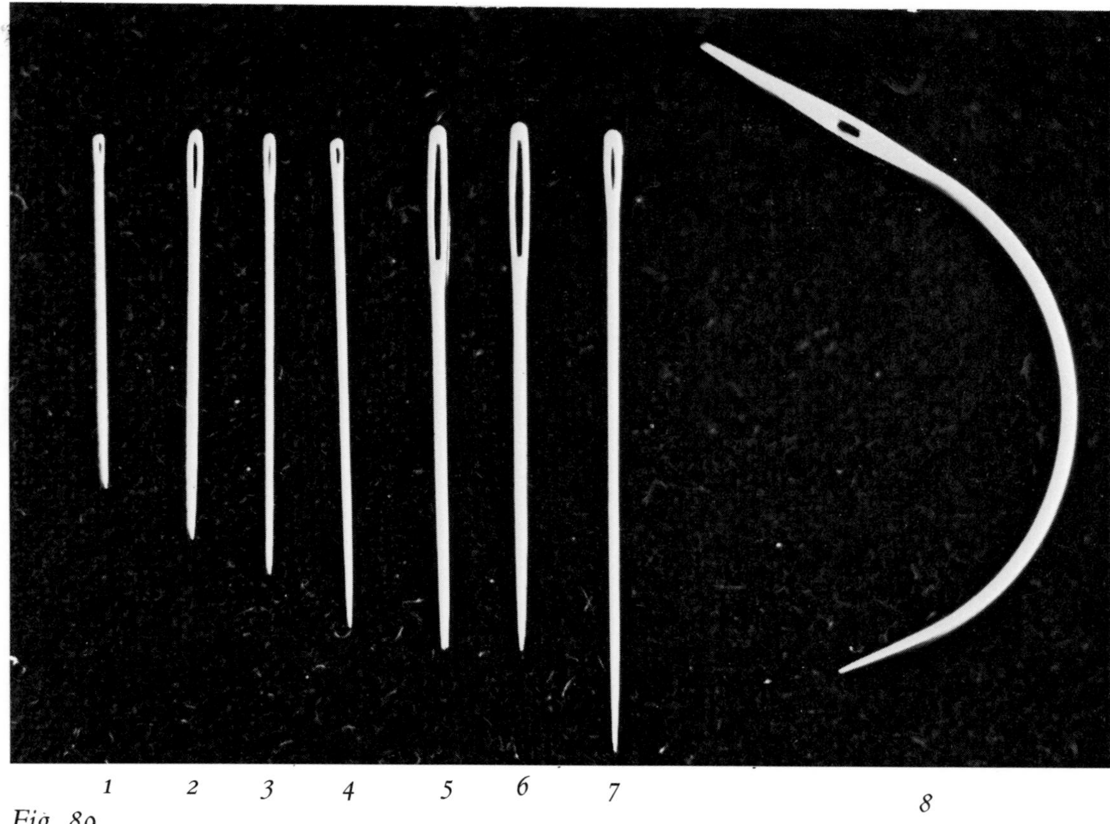

Fig. 89

No. 4 Sharps for general domestic use. Sizes 1–10.
No. 5 Tapestry – very long eye for wools and thick yarns; a blunt point for canvases. Sizes 17-24.
No. 6 Chenille – similar to tapestry, but with sharp points for closely woven materials. Sizes 17-24.
No. 7 Darners – long needle with a long eye for easy threading. Sizes 1-8.
No. 8 Upholstery, curved needle for sewing difficult areas where one is unable to draw the needle through.
Bead needle, not illustrated, very long and fine for bead work.

Tailor's chalk.
Tracing wheel, dressmaking carbon paper (yellow, red and blue).
Tape measure with metal end.
Thimble.
Pins – fine steel.

Stiletto – to make holes in fabric.
Tacking cotton.
Embroidery frame (Fig. 90).

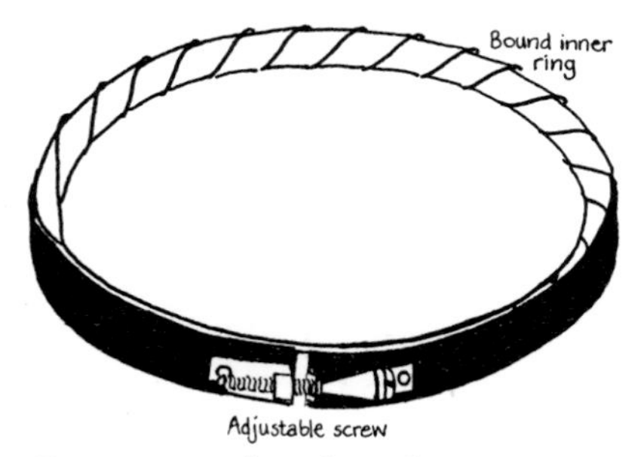

Fig. 90 Embroidery frame

Tissue paper (useful for placing under slippery or soft fabric before machining).
Tracing paper – for transference of designs.
Paper, pencils, brushes, paints for planning work.
Stretching board, drawing pins, blotting paper.

Millinery wire.
Thick towel – useful for pressing embroidery. The right side of the embroidery rests and sinks into the towel. The iron is pressed gently onto the wrong side.
Containers – preferably transparent – for holding beads, sequins etc.
Plastic bags and boxes for fabrics and other materials.

7

DESIGN WITH THREAD

Thread was used in the last chapter chiefly to aid the exploration of the structure of fabric. It is convenient to deal with fabric and thread in two separate chapters in order to study each, but of course one often depends on the other.

Fig. 87a shows what an inspiration thread can be for creativity. An open mind is needed when using particular threads, and experiment is necessary in order to discover which are best for specific purposes. This is the way to become inventive and selective.

Uses of thread to be considered are:
1 To construct decorative fabric.
2 To make decorative stitchery.
3 To join fabric.

CONSTRUCTION OF DECORATIVE FABRIC

We confine this to weaving, although knitting, crochet, tatting, lacemaking and macramé could all be used if the spirit of adventure continues. The bibliography will help readers who wish to find specialist books on these topics.

Fig. 91 shows a build-up of appliqué, crochet, weaving, couching, and beadwork and illustrates the richness that such additions bring to fabric collage.

Woven material was explored in the last chapter as a fabric ground for embroidery.

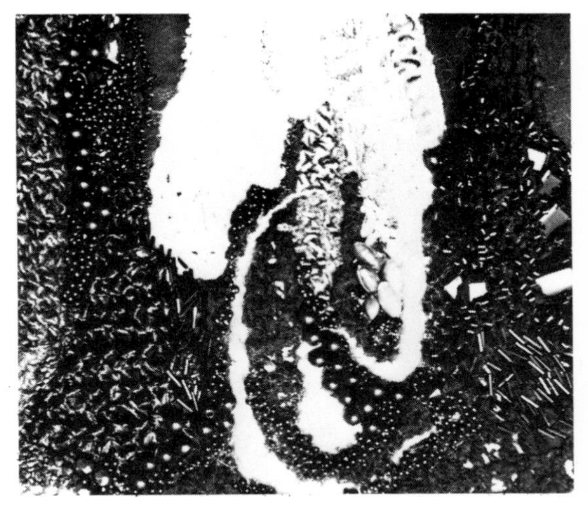

Fig. 91

We now want to consider interlacing threads as a decorative surface, be it for a wall hanging on a large scale or a fragile needleweaving for dress embroidery. We suggest that you become involved with the problems that experimental weaving presents.

EXPERIMENTAL WEAVING

In the past and today creative weaving has been carried out on a loom. We want to take a new look at weaving and take it out of the realm of the loom.

The spider swings his warp irregularly from post to gate, branch to branch.
If left in peace he will continue to weave his web with an interlacing circular weft.

Fig. 92

This is what we want you to try, to create a warp and weft that are your own. Like the spider you will need to look around to find a structure to hold the warp. It can be almost anything. Let us first think of it in two dimensions. Card may be cut to any shape or size. Polystyrene tiles, Perspex, hoops, picture frames, all these may be a starting point and have the advantage of looking pleasant after the work is finished (see Fig. 92 and colour plate 13), whereas with weaving card it is necessary to remove the weaving and remount it.

Whatever is chosen as the base must have the means of holding the warp threads in position. Each material will impose its own limitations and will dictate to some extent the method used. For example, card may need punched holes or a serrated edge, wood receives panel pins easily, Perspex can have drilled holes, whereas hoops and wire shapes will allow the threads to pass over them.

The weft is being visualised while the warp is being set up. Again the concern of the designer is for shape, both positive and negative; the positive being the thread, warp and weft, and the negative being the spaces between. Once the principle of weaving is established, it will be realised that it is the weft threads that make the shapes, which can be of a highly textured nature. A rich variety of threads, both in colour and texture, will stimulate the worker. The addition of other shapes, such as curtain rings, will make the shapes more complex, and beads and sequins will add richness. However, the stimulus of exciting shapes and spaces emerging is often enough, and some very spirited work can be achieved. (See colour plate 20.)

It may be that a sketch may spark off the idea. Fig. 93 below shows a detailed study of a rose hip. The drawing's linear quality suggested weaving to this student. A card loom with serrated edges was made to suit the design. On completion the weaving was removed from the card and transferred on to a background fabric. The spaces between the weaving were used for raised appliqué.

The obvious development from this creative two-dimensional weaving for embroidery is to create work independent of embroidery, on Perspex, wood etc. Further satisfaction can be derived by taking the experiment into the third dimension, where it would remain as a piece of experimental weaving in its own right. You will be familiar with the arrangement of two-dimensional shape. The problem is different when the work is in three dimensions. It is necessary to stand or hang the construction and to view it from all directions, looking at the lines created and the spaces between the warp thread and later assessing the shapes created and the spaces between them. Sometimes the frame itself is a good shape and the finished result has a sculptural quality. (See colour plate 14.)

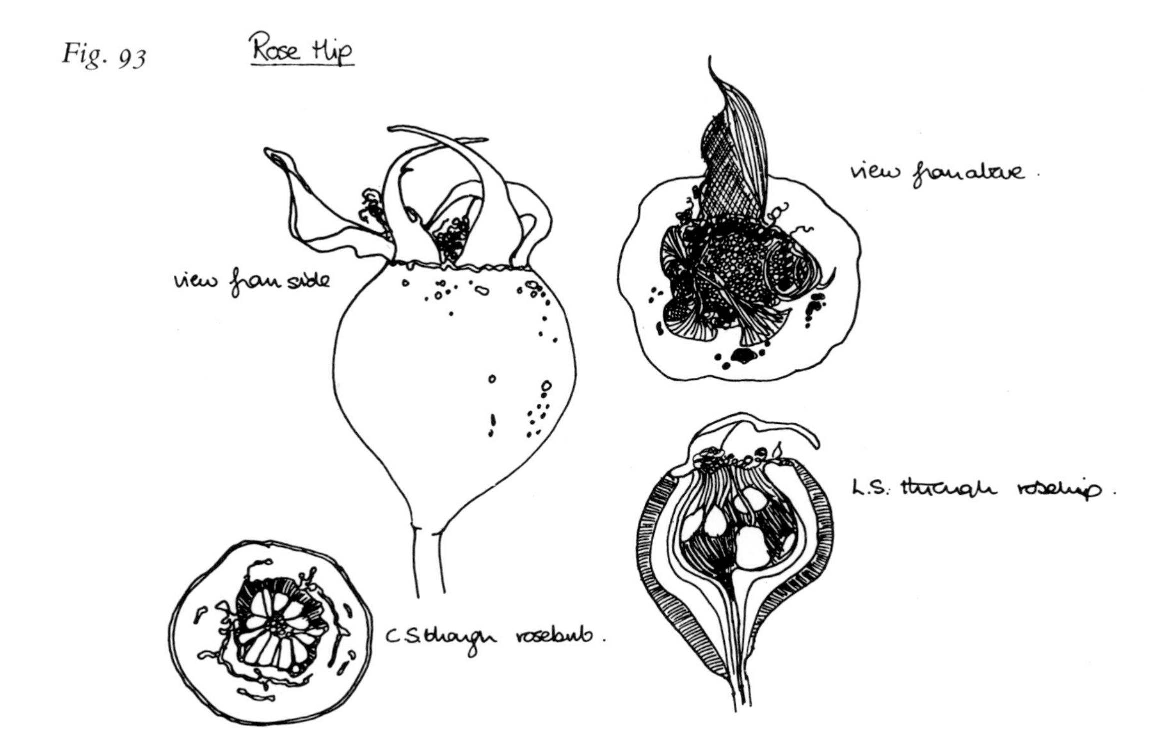

Fig. 93

These experiments may seem far removed from embroidery, the main theme of this book, but the embroidery will be enriched by a deeper understanding of textured threads and positive and negative shape which this experience will give. The next chapter will show these methods being used to interpret natural form, and the finished embroidery collages will show such weaving incorporated in the design. Two-layer collages are also shown and three-dimensional weaving and/or curve stitchery could start on one layer and lead down to the next. The age of purism in art is past, at least in our time. The sight of materials will spark off creative forces that can be expressed unfettered by tradition.

Embroidery on dress can be enhanced by the addition of weaving, which is not done into the fabric of the garment but added to the surface (Fig. 180).

DECORATIVE USE OF THREADS

Threads, rich in colour and texture, call forth a spontaneous wish to touch and to experiment. Just to see them on different fabrics is pleasurable, to contrast fine and thick, shiny and dull, to make doodles with them, to take them 'on journeys', to try out shapes with thread, all this handling and 'play' with a medium promotes an understanding of the characteristics and limitations of the craft. (Fig. 94).

Sometimes images so produced are pleasing and this leads to the desire to make them permanent, by sticking or catching the threads lightly to the background as surface decoration. The best way of doing this is by using couching stitch (Fig. 95). Couching can be purely functional, especially if done with a matching or invisible thread, or it may be made decorative (Fig. 96).

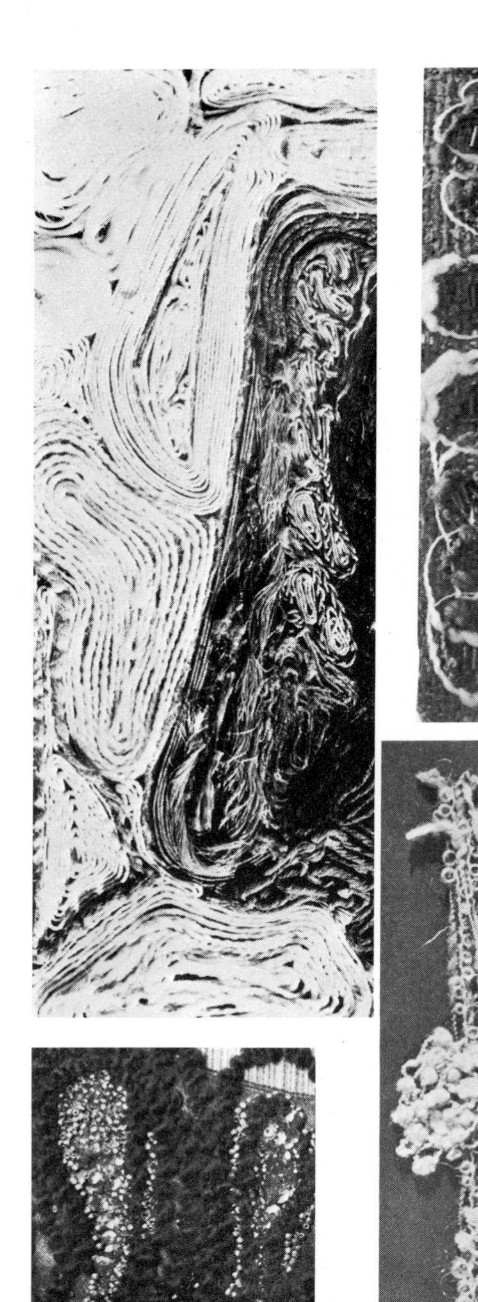

Fig. 94

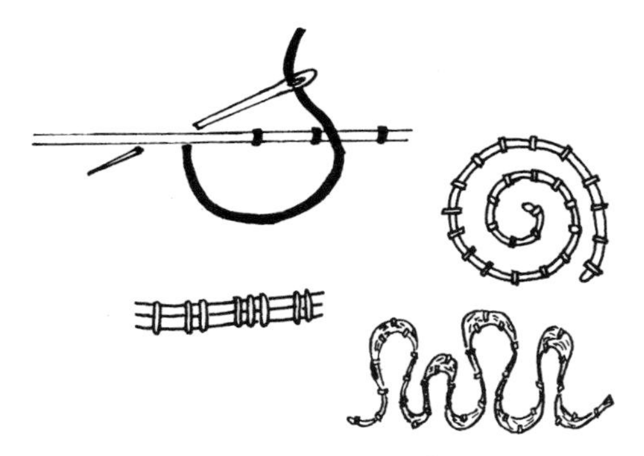

Fig. 95 Plain couching stitch

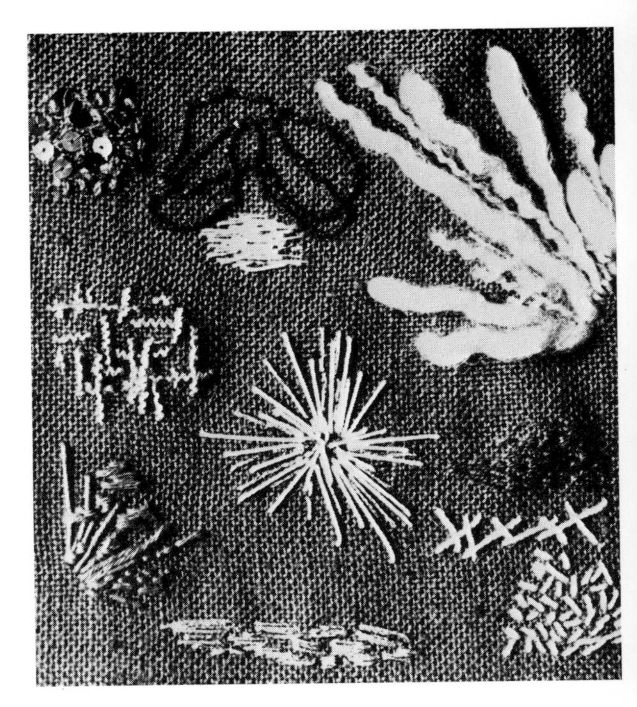

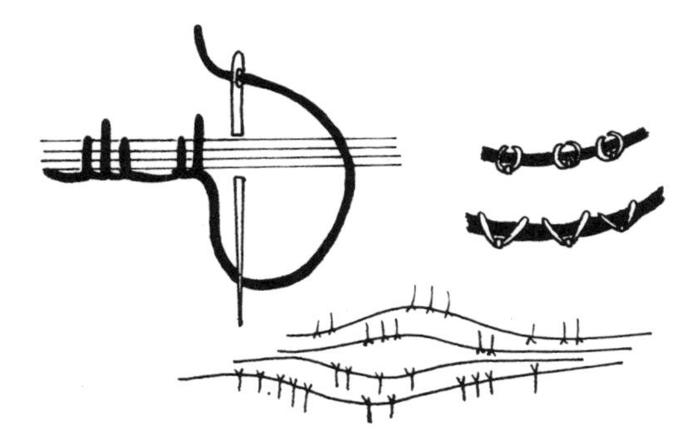

Fig. 96 Decorative couching stitch

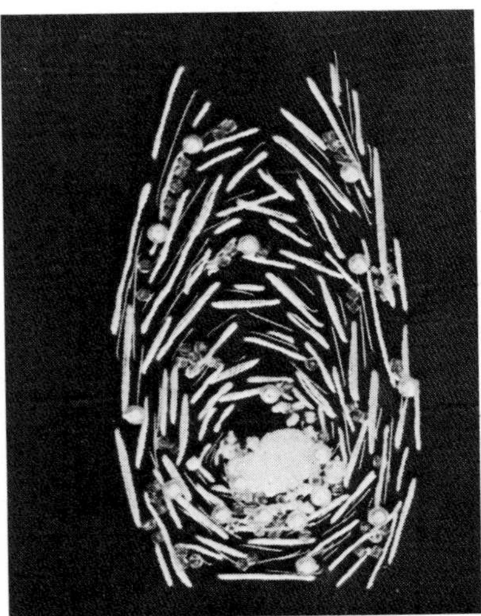

Fig. 97 Straight stitch

We offer some suggestions for a creative and free way of using thread to make decorative stitches. We hope that the principles of working will be absorbed and then that each of you will work in your own individual way. We all have a characteristic way of writing and if we use thread, which is linear, the result should be equally distinctive. While the ultimate effect of decorative stitchery is texture and pattern, it must be borne in mind that this must always suit the purpose. For example, large loose stitches are not suitable if they are liable to catch in anything in use.

Experiment, initially with simple stitches, e.g. straight stitch, chain stitch, fly stitch, couched thread (Figs. 97, 98, 99).

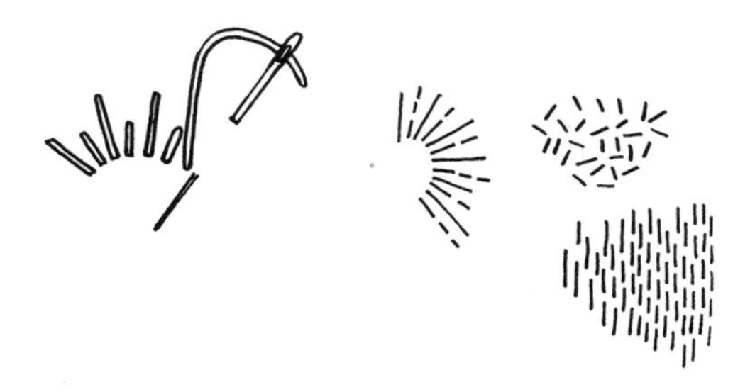

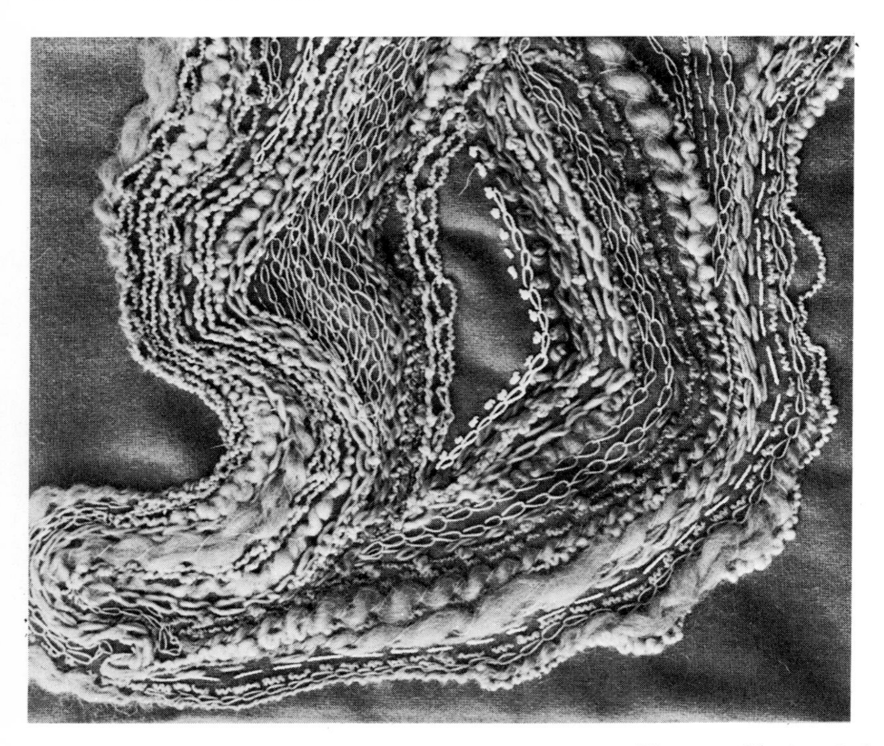

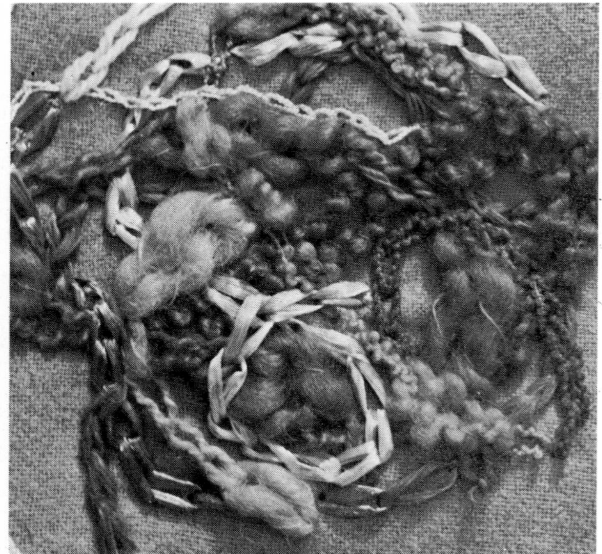

Fig. 98 Chain stitch

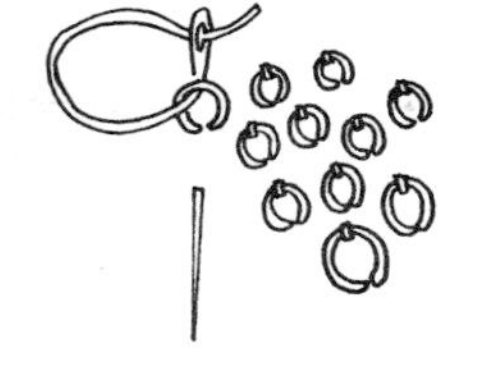

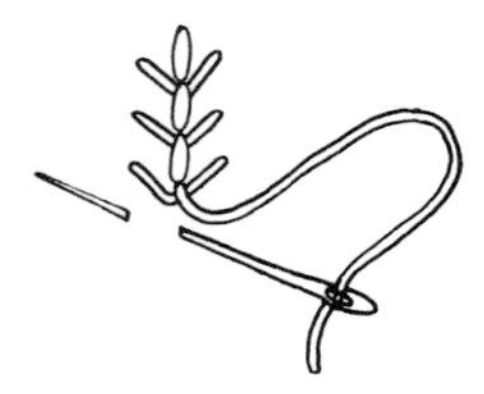

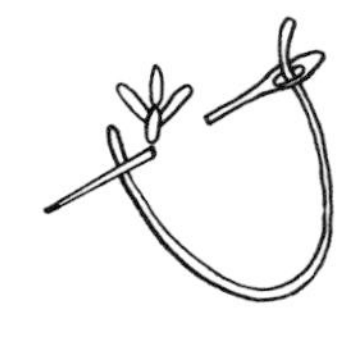

Fig. 99 Fly stitch

Start working on hessian (it is good-natured), then try other materials, adjusting the needle to the thread and fabric being used.

1 Use a variety of threads: thick, thin, textured, shiny and dull.

2 Widen, lengthen, shorten and change the direction of stitches.
3 Separate stitches.
4 Add variations to the stitchery.
5 Build up patterns.
The first attempts may be purely experimental, but will provide a background of knowledge for further development.

Every stitch has shape and when massed together they give an individual textured effect. Vary the use of colour, sometimes bold, sometimes delicate, vibrant colour as opposed to subdued colour. Build up technical skill so that the expression becomes fluent. Colour plate 15 shows how one student attempted this exercise.

Contrasts are always striking, and we have already seen the need to change the scale in line patterns, as well as the intervals between the lines. The combination of fine stitches with thick bolder threads adds variety to the work.

There will be a natural tendency for some of you to be drawn towards delicate stitches and fabric, whereas others will find their expression on a bold scale. Recognise your own tendency and do not be afraid of working in many different ways, which may at first seem strange for you. It is only when you have had this wide experience that you are able to take a long, cool look and objectively select which is best, and to reject the less good.

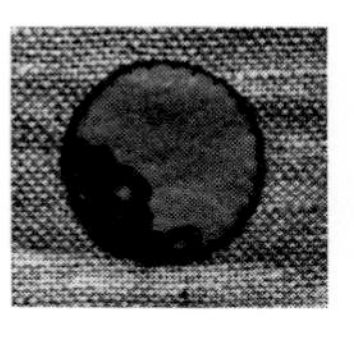

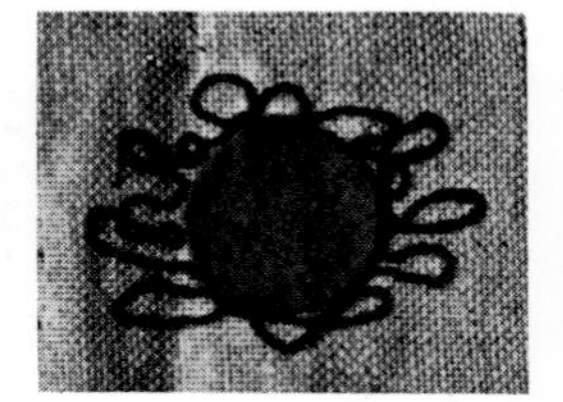

Fig. 100

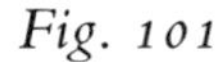

Fig. 101

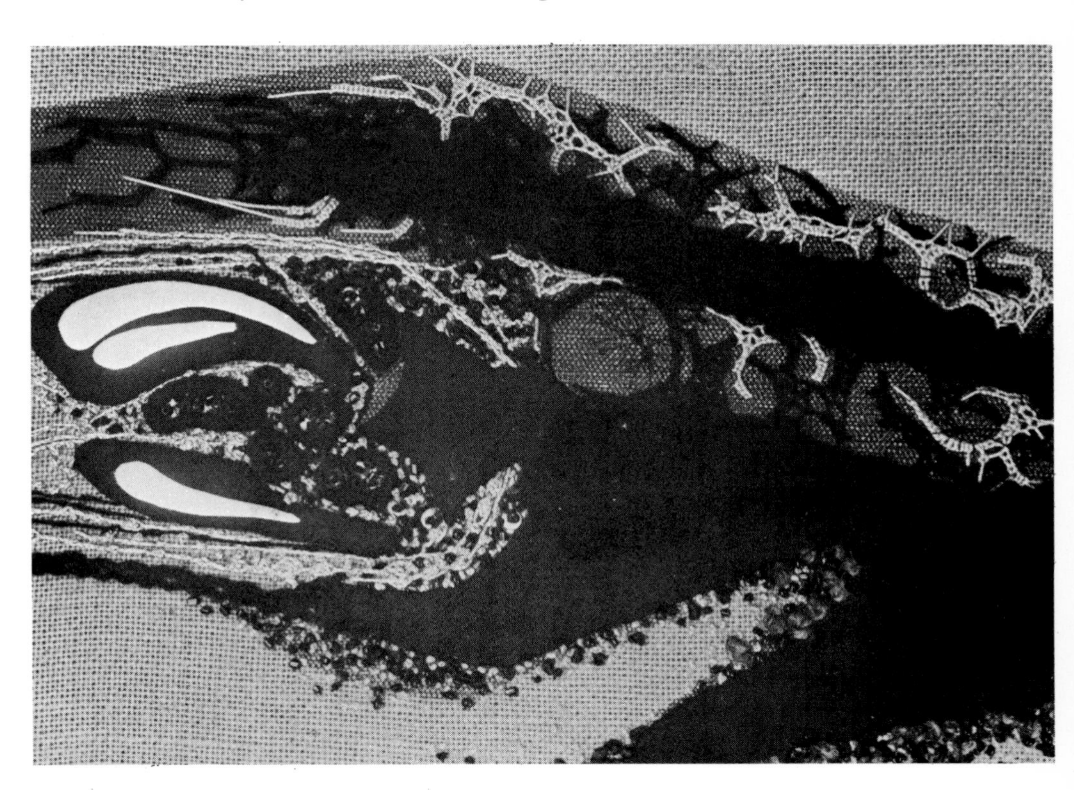

Stitchery can be used to emphasise the shape of applied fabric, by following it precisely, e.g. with couched thread. This gives a somewhat hard outline. Stitches can be used with varying intensity and thickness of thread to merge the shape gradually into the background (Figs. 100 and 101). Both methods have their place in creative embroidery.

Stitches massed together can give a rich, textured appearance. The French knots in Fig. 102 are made using a variety of thickness of thread.

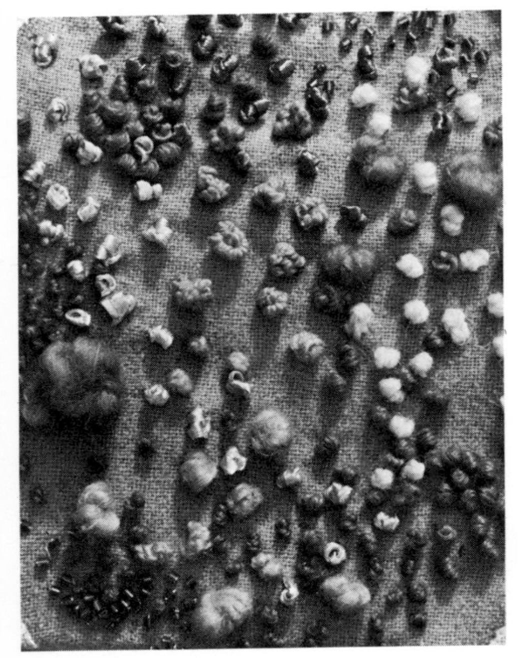

Fig. 102

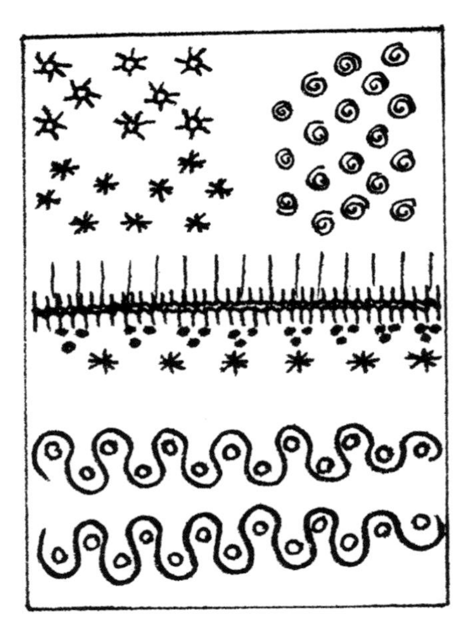

Fig. 103

Plain fabrics can be made textured with an irregular design or by planning the stitches in lines giving a striped or spotted effect (Fig. 103).

Check fabrics can be changed by blocking out light-toned areas with dark threads, making them tonally dark or the reverse; light threads may block out dark areas, giving a light-toned fabric (Fig. 104).

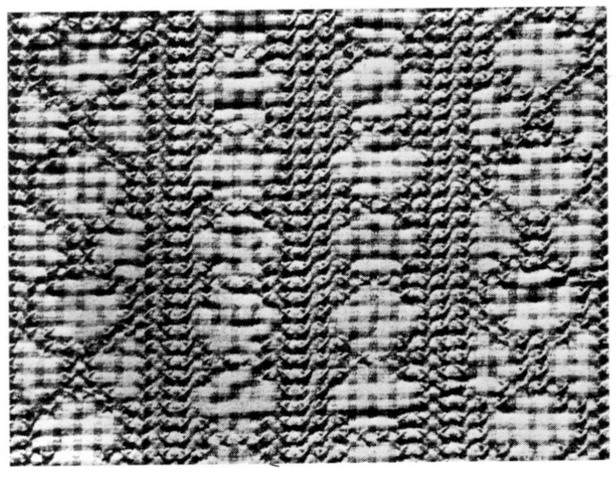

Fig. 104

TRADITIONAL EMBROIDERY

You will find all you wish to know about the types of traditional embroidery in many reference books. There is a vast store of information. Different craftswomen will find themselves interested in one of its many types. Take one particular example, discover the essence of it and use it.

Fig. 105 shows a piece of work by a student who became interested in Assisi work. Here she uses it for a place mat.

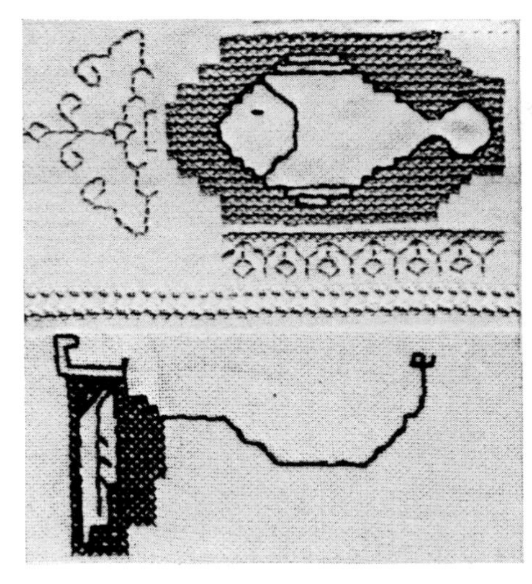

Fig. 105

She considered the design problem and decided to embroider the part of the mat where it could always be enjoyed and not covered when in use. Such work entails many hours of stitching, and it is essential that the cloth is of a quality worthy of the time that is spent in creation. An even-weave linen has been used in this example. The flat, secure stitchery, ensuring easy laundering, and the strong attractive edge finish are evidence of the thought that preceded the craft. A great deal of satisfaction is experienced in designing and working such a piece of embroidery. The hand stitching has a quality all its own. This standard of tension is achieved with experience.

Another example of using the background fabric to create something quite different is shown in Fig. 106. The effect is geometric, as one might expect. The different tones of thread used give an interesting effect. This could be developed further by stitchery and used as a decorative border on dress or soft furnishings.

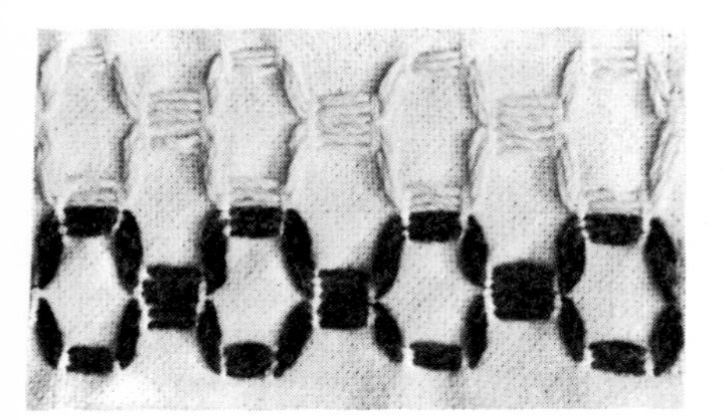

Fig. 106

Straight stitches radiating from a centre on tweed fabric are used with wooden beads for added texture in Fig. 107.

Fig. 107

Similar radiating stitchery, worked on different fabric, is shown in Fig. 108a. Fig. 108b shows experiments, which preceded this piece of work, using contrasts in texture.

Many examples of hand stitchery of an experimental nature may be seen in Chapter 6. The aim is to show up the best quality of each thread in use.

Fig. 108a

Fig. 108b

BEADS AND SEQUINS

A fine matching thread should be used to sew on beads and sequins in an inconspicuous way. Decorative effects can be achieved by allowing the thread to pass over the bead in radiating lines as shown in Fig. 109.

Fig. 109

It can be made more decorative by adding interlacing weaving as in Fig. 110.

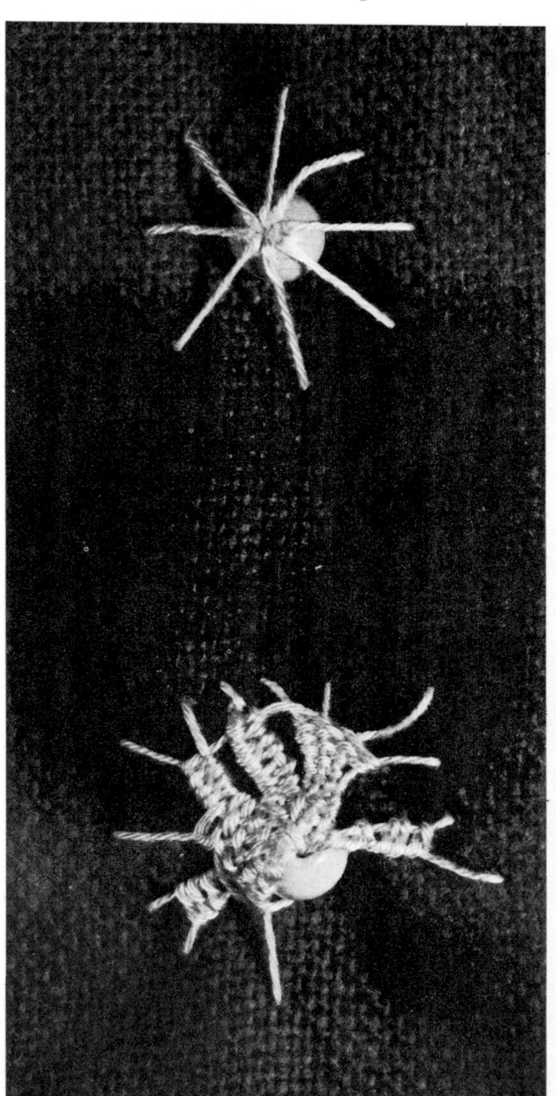

Fig. 110

MACHINE EMBROIDERY

Stitchery decoration can also be produced with the sewing machine. This work, like all machine work, is less individual, as the machine imposes a more severe discipline. The characteristic design for this is drawn with a continuous flowing line.

You must first discover what your machine is capable of doing and then start to use it in a creative way. This discovery involves sitting down and practising until you are absolutely in control. Building up linear pattern while practising with the machine can be fascinating. Try putting different threads in the bobbin, e.g. thicker threads, coton à broder, Sylko Perlé, or Lurex thread to give sheen. In so doing work on the wrong side of the fabric so that the thread in the bobbin appears on the right side. Figs. 111a and b show Lurex thread used with beads.

Fig. 111a

Care must be taken when winding Lurex thread onto the bobbin. Keep it flat. Allow the thread to pass through the thumb and forefinger just before it goes onto the bobbin. The stitch of the machine should be lengthened to show the beauty of the thread. It will be remembered that in any linear design combinations of thick and thin lines and variety of intervals between them will add to the interest.

All machines are capable of allowing thicker threads in the bobbin, but free embroidery is possible only on those that are treadle or electrically operated.

Fig. 111b

This is because both hands are needed to guide the embroidery frame under the needle. Relaxed and supple wrist movements and practice are required. Following a design is difficult until there is enough confidence to be in command of the situation and to direct the machine on the path it should take. Read the instructions in the machine manual for making the teeth inactive. Their function is to feed the fabric through the machine, but now it must be moved by hand.

Once control is established in hand movements and these co-ordinated with the pressure on the control knob of the electric machine or the foot movements of the treadle, progress is assured. It is a question of co-ordination of eye, hand, feet and the machine; all four must work as one, instinctively, without apparent thought. Some people are more able to solve this problem than others. Some will sit down and be able to work straight away, others will need to work at it.

Remember to:
1 Work in an embroidery frame.
2 Bind the inner frame with bias binding. It helps to grip the fabric better (see Fig. 90 on page 71) and protects it from rubbing against the pieces of wood. Let the fabric into the frame until it is really taut. Flick your finger on the stretched fabric: it should be taut like a drum.
3 At the start, experiment with fine cotton or organdie, using a fine machine needle and thread. Once confidence is attained, try a variety of fabrics and threads.
4 Keep the frame flat on the machine while moving it around.

The exercises in Fig. 112 show some ways in which a student experimented while learning to control the machine. She tried different exercises and textural effects.

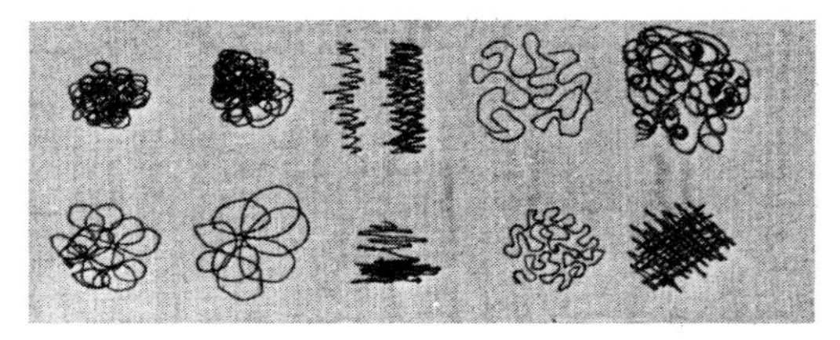

Fig. 112

The snowflake design in Fig. 113a was worked on organdie.

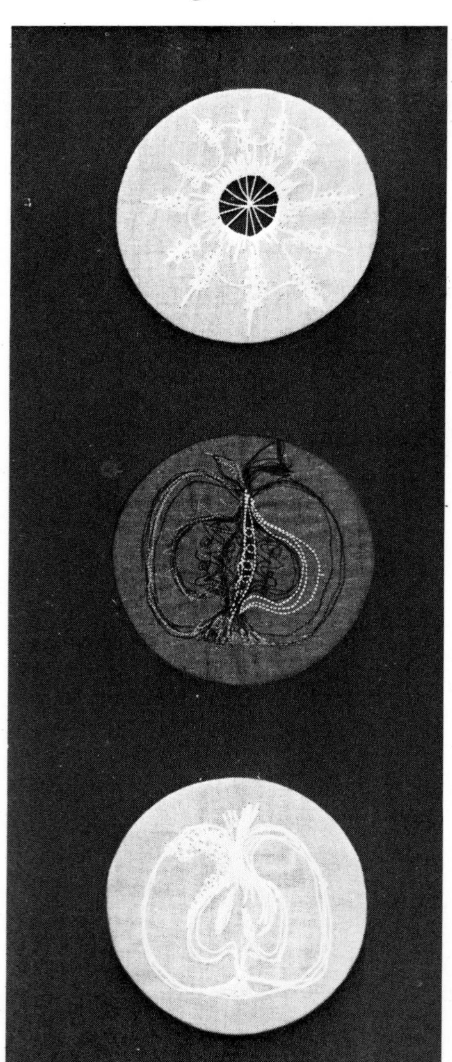

Fig. 113a

Fig. 113b

The designs in Fig. 113b were based on a cross-section through an apple and were worked with cable stitch and whipping.

Fig. 114

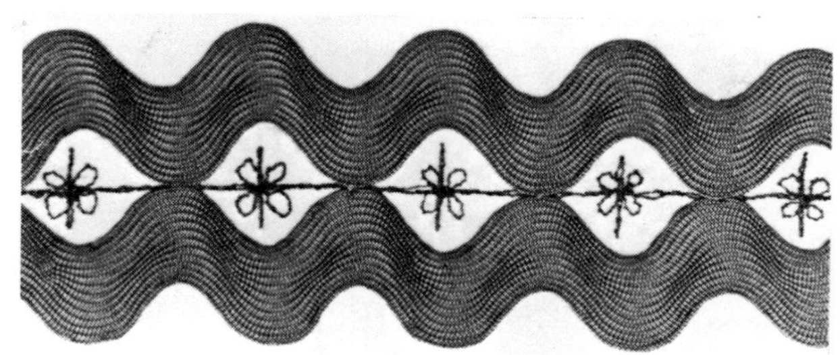

Fig. 115

Later the same student worked on a more ambitious group of figures and developed her technique further (Fig. 114). The student made wire and papier mâché figures, grouped them, made a drawing of the group, and then made this design for machine embroidery.

The attractive but simple combination of ricrac braid and free machine embroidery in Fig. 115 illustrates that simplicity has a great appeal.

The circular movements of the embroidery in Fig. 116 form a flower shape, which has been enriched with the texture of hand-worked French knots and tiny beads. (This can also be seen in Fig. 191 on page 136.)

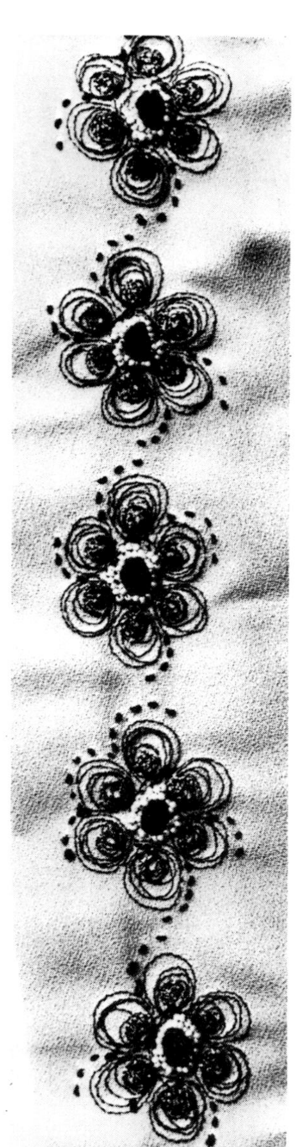

Fig. 116

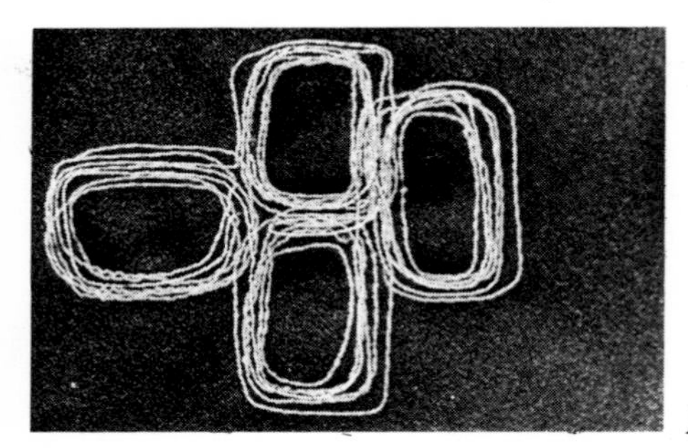

Fig. 117

The oblong linear shapes in Fig. 117 are built up to form an all-over pattern for a dress bodice. Texture and depth of colour are given by the addition of beads.

Whether you are working with a machine or using hand stitchery, certain problems of design need noting. You will be creating texture with line and spot. This is the moment to apply the theory in Chapters 3 and 4, where lines and dots were applied until the space surrounding them, the negative space, became a shape in its own right instead of being unconsidered space. These dots and lines forming textures were packed together at times and then relaxed. We called these tension and relaxation areas.

When you are practising with the machine line, you would be wise to aim for strong line that is never half-hearted in its character, and consciously to build up areas of tension and relaxation. The secret of successful textural effects lies in combining interesting textures and contrasting them with plain surfaces. Half-hearted attempts at texture look weak and insignificant, like spidery handwriting. Of course, to make a texture rich entails a great deal of work. It did not take long to make a successful spot exercise with a felt pen, but it is a much longer task to achieve a similar result in French knots. But it is the same problem, and if the aim is to make texture with a method such as French knots, they must be scattered just as generously as are the spots in an exercise with pen.

Do not be afraid to make a rich statement in fabric and thread. One learns by being adventurous in trying out many ways of working and then by assessing the results, by rationalising the reasons for failure or success.

THE ZIG-ZAG SEWING MACHINE

Simple zig-zag stitches are used to neaten the edges of hitherto problem fabrics and also to speed up appliqué in fabric collage. Stitches that are built into some zig-zag sewing machines can be varied by altering the width and length of the embroidery stitches, thus achieving a less mechanical effect. An imaginative use of different fabrics with stitches can produce an unusual result.

The fabric in Fig. 118 is a vegetable bag (turnips). This has been controlled with free machine embroidery, making shapes ready for additional embroidery.

Fig. 118

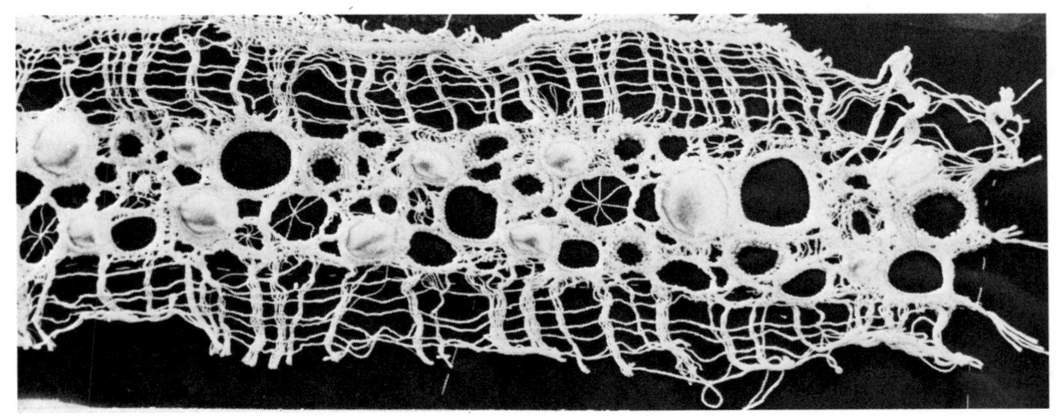

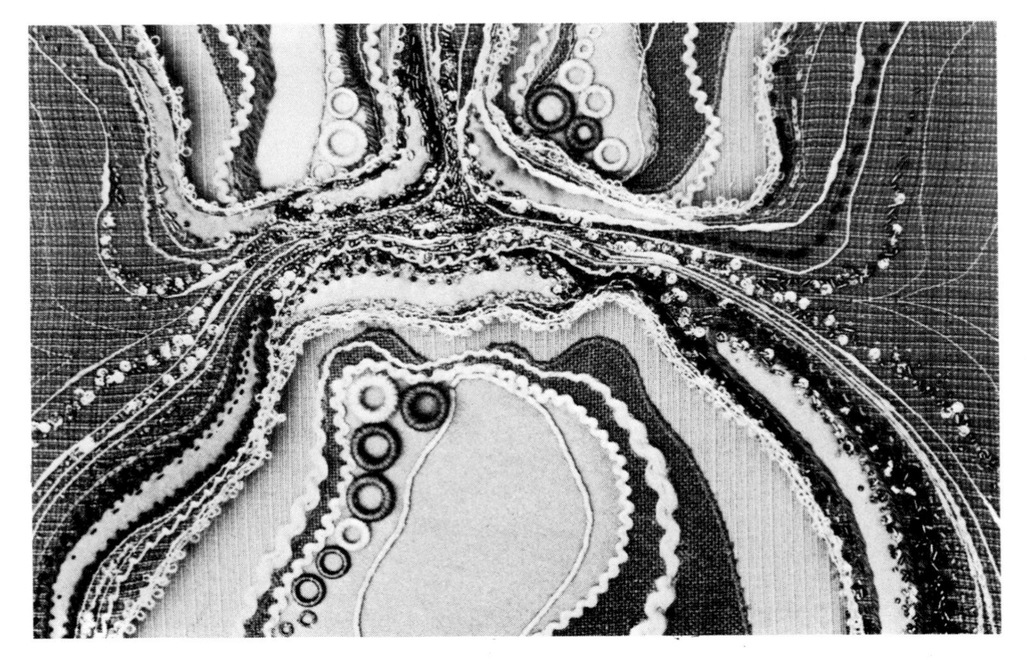

Fig. 119

It will be rewarding to look for examples such as the one above and to experiment on a variety of fabrics, transparent, opaque, shiny and dull.

Fig. 119 shows:

1 Fabrics applied and neatened by machine.

2 A combination of machine and hand stitchery.

3 Curtain rings with beads and sequins adding a rich textural quality.

Fig. 120

Fig. 120 shows:

1 The use of the machine for fabric appliqué.

2 Machine stitchery and beadwork.

3 Hand stitchery and applied gold kid.

JOINING FABRICS

Whether fabrics are joined by hand or machine, the thread used and the tension and size of stitch are all important. Decorative effects can be achieved by joining suede shapes with crochet, or patterned and plain shapes for patchwork. When two fabrics are joined together as seams and one is aiming at a strong seam of good clean appearance, the correct thread, needle size, machine tension and stitches per inch are of the utmost importance. Seams that support decorative work must be well constructed. Delightful creative work is often ruined by a clumsy approach to construction and detail.

Suggestions for threads and size of needles are provided by manufacturers of sewing machines and of fabrics, but we would urge everyone to find out for themselves by trying out any seaming on a piece of fabric, large enough to show a true picture, e.g. 6″ (15cm) long. Then adjustments may be made where necessary. The yarn of the fabric should always be matched by the sewing thread, i.e. synthetic thread is required for sewing synthetic fibres.

It was once said that experiment is the life-blood of creative work. All of us, however experienced, need to adopt an experimental attitude to the new fabrics and try to make every aspect of our work creative.

8

SOURCES OF INSPIRATION, EXPERIMENT & INVOLVEMENT

It may well seem to you that the cart has been put before the horse, in that inspiration, the source, comes in the eighth chapter. After all, it is necessary first to be inspired and then by experiment to become involved with the idea before designing anything. Through this involvement the creative process goes into action. It is necessary, therefore, to defend the placing of inspiration in this book. The reason is simply that rational thought is less easy once involvement has taken place. You can be clinical and clearheaded about the last seven chapters and prepare yourself for being truly creative. Then while researching and experimenting within your particular interest, you should endeavour to bear in mind the rudiments of design already studied and the characteristics and limitations – the possibilities – that the medium presents when it is used with freedom.

There was a temptation when writing about the elements of design and in particular composition, using the elements, to touch on the subject-matter for this chapter. It is all but impossible to separate the total design process into tidy chapters. However, there is a purpose in our attempting to do so for the sake of clarity in explaining the process of design. Our advice to you is to absorb as much as possible of the preceding chapters, then to start designing, making it the integrated task which, without a doubt, it is; return to the particular chapter concerned if one of the elements of design seems to be getting out of hand!

This is an immense subject to cover in one chapter. It could be the material for a whole book or books, in fact Constance Howard has written such a book, *Inspiration for Embroidery* (see bibliography) and we would strongly advise readers who have mastered the rudiments of design to read this book, which gives a wealth of ideas. Constance Howard is a contemporary embroiderer, a teacher of her craft who has had a great influence in the movement that has made embroidery an art form. Of necessity we must limit the information given here, although the choice for inspiration is limitless.

We would like above all to suggest ways of working with a limited number of subjects, which should start you developing your own particular interest and finding your own line of country.

It is easy, as a start, to become involved in natural objects, such as might be found on a walk in the country or along the seashore. The child's excitement in finding and looking needs to be recaptured. Whatever the environment, so long as the reader is 'tuned in' and 'seeing', there are possibilities for design.

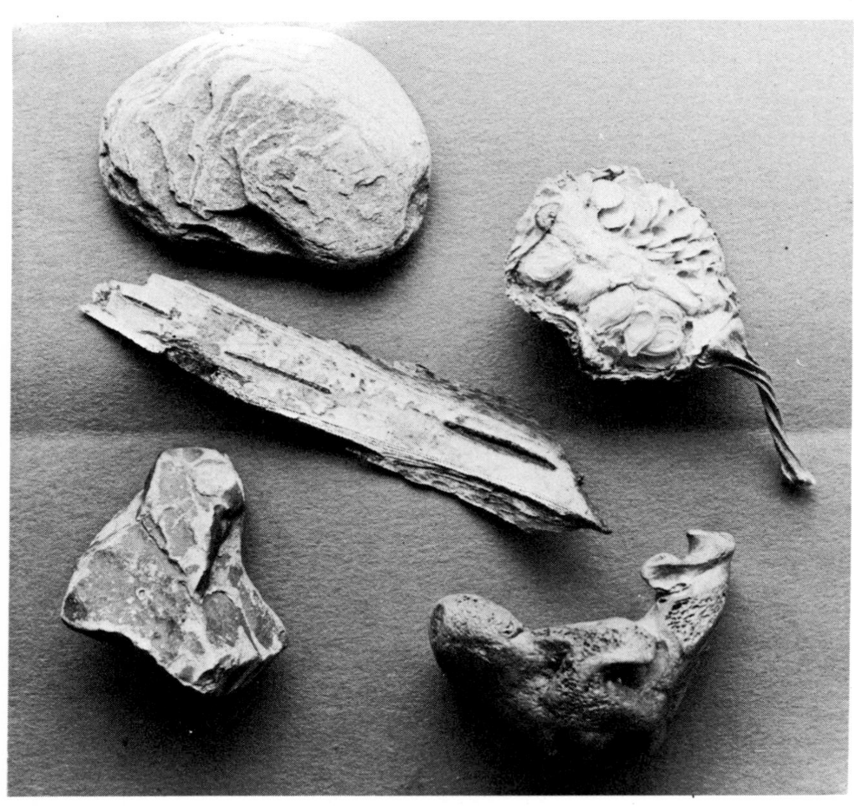

Fig. 121

THE TEXTURED, PATTERNED SURFACE

This could be a piece of bark, the grain in wood, the pattern on a piece of stone, the strata on a cliff, or a part of a larger design such as a shell. Fig. 121 shows an example of the sort of thing we mean.

All these natural objects in Fig. 121 were found easily, the most exotic being a gourd – other fruits would serve as well.

NON-FIGURATIVE DRAWING

At this point you begin to feel trapped! Here it comes, the need to draw, and maybe you have a built-in prejudice and belief that you cannot draw. We would like to allay such fears by saying that the skilled draughtsman often finds the process of designing from a natural object more difficult to do well than the novice who just observes and puts down a simple statement of what she sees.

We emphasised in the first chapter that no two artists would give the same interpretation of a subject. We would like to show three versions inspired by the same piece of bark. Fig. 122a is a drawing by a very able student. She was content to concentrate on a small part of the bark.

Fig. 122a

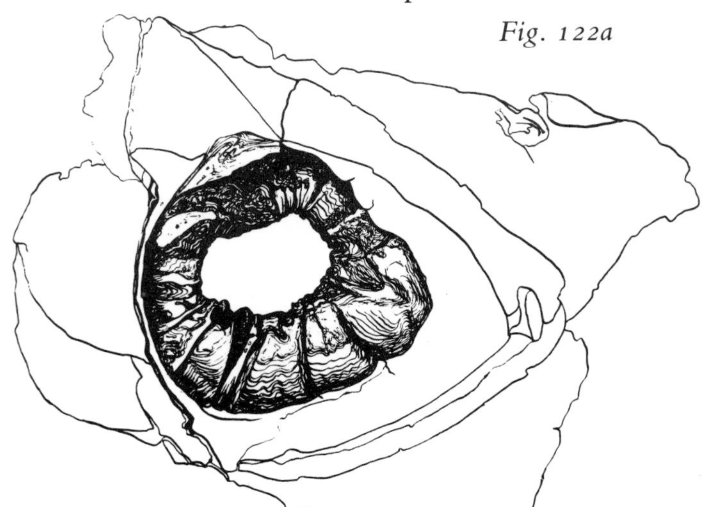

Figs. 122b and c show drawings by thirteen-year-olds, a boy and girl, respectively. The interpretations are very different; Tim emphasises the concentric design of the knot-hole whereas Deborah is fascinated by the rough textured surface and finds secondary interests outside the knot-hole.

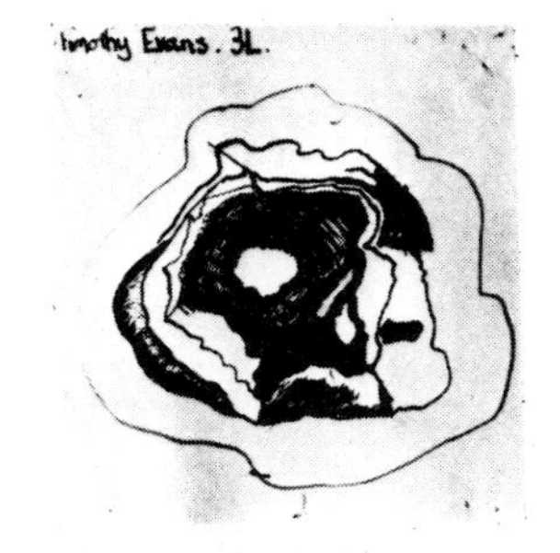

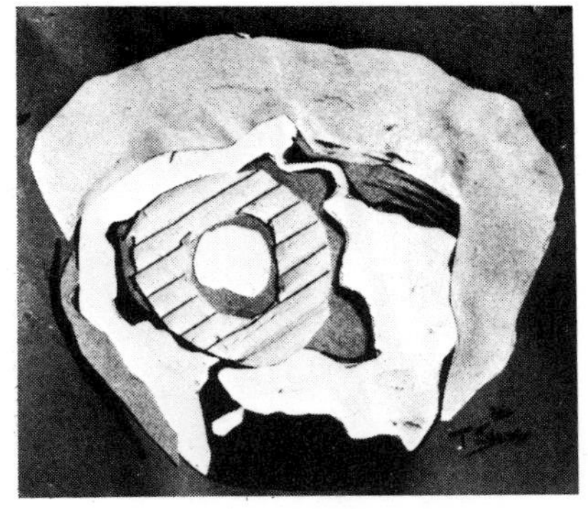

Fig. 122b

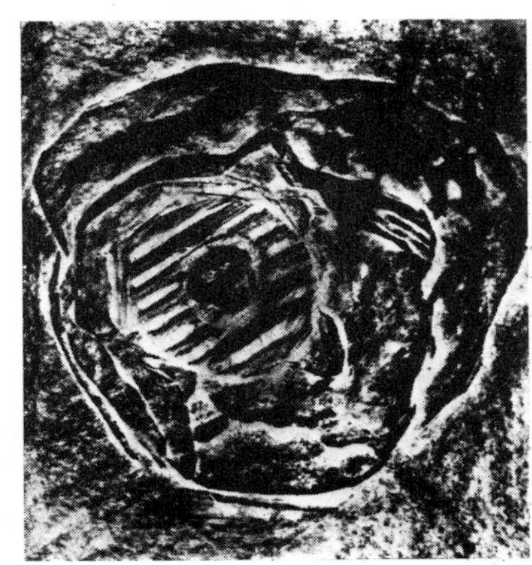

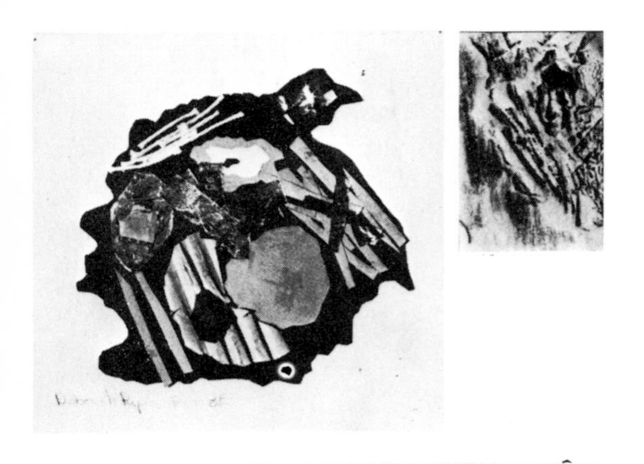

A look at the rest of the involvement on these sheets will reveal how the sketch was developed into paper collage, and the tendencies in the sketch are even more pronounced. Each has made a personal comment about that piece of bark. The rubbings show further involvement, and present the collage in a different way. Deborah explores further and finds a repeat border pattern.

Figs. 122d and e show studies (again by schoolchildren, two thirteen-year-old girls) of a peach stone and piece of bark. The development in Fig. 122d, Sheila's work, is as seen above – a repeat pattern emerging from the texture in the collage. Fig. 122e also shows this, but Kathy goes a stage further and designs a single unit by rubbing the collage and moving the paper.

Fig. 122c

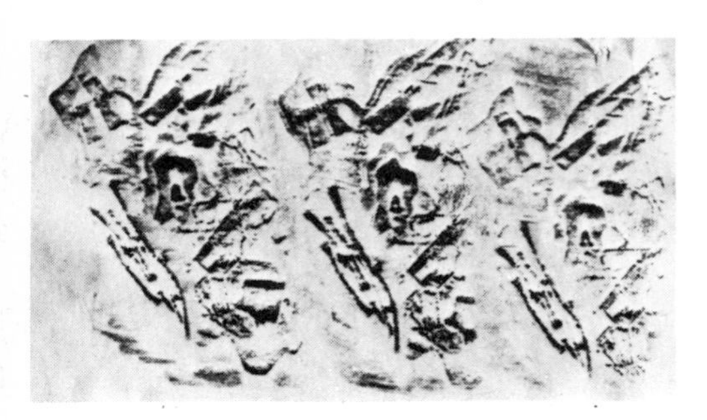

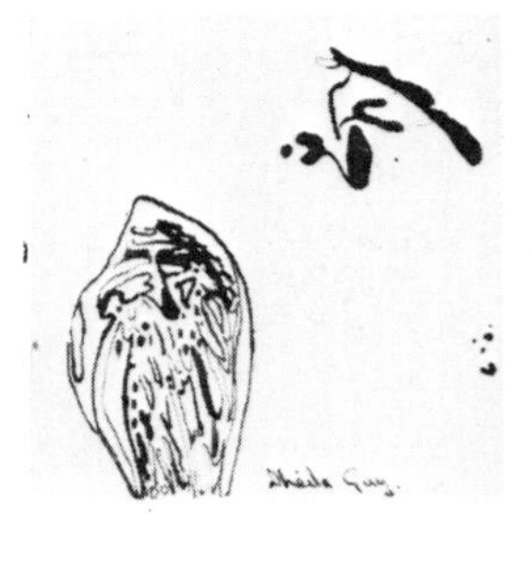

Fig. 122d

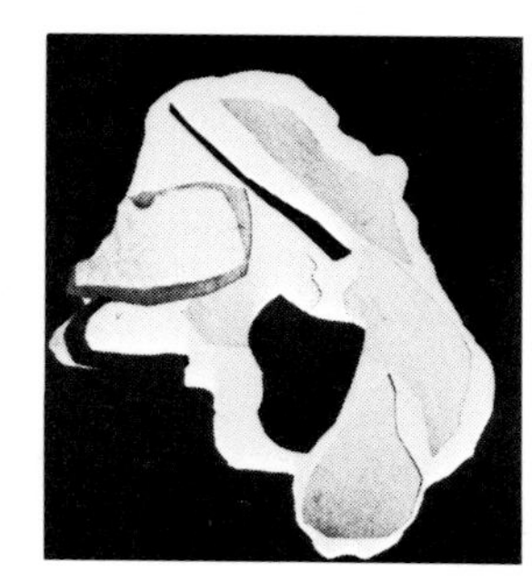

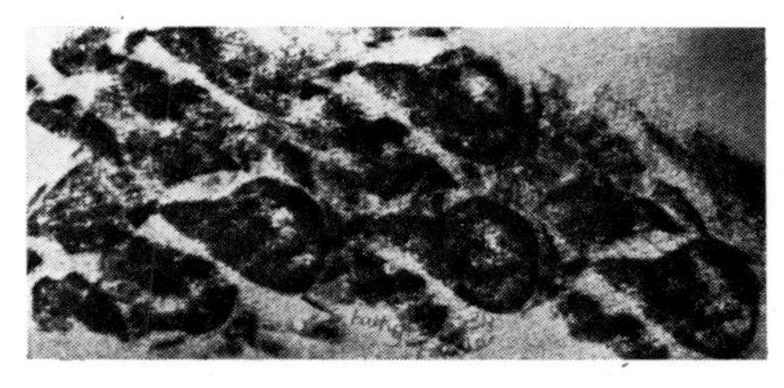

Fig. 122e

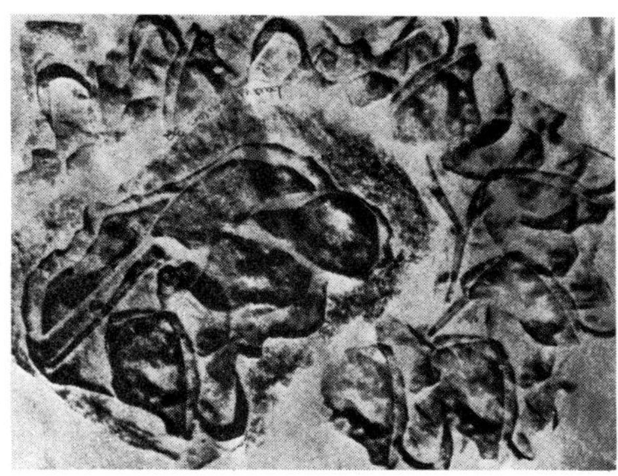

This work is shown firstly to point out that each person expresses his or her own feeling about an object in drawing and is not trying to make a 'likeness'. The point in making such a drawing is a search for information, to put down what is observed simply, if need be in diagram form. The drawing should show what the object is 'known' to be like, not a superficial, sketchy effect of light and shade, which is fleeting and forever changing with the sun, but shapes and lines observed in the structure.

Drawing should be careful and direct, allowing the freedom to emphasise the qualities that interest. A felt pen or pen and ink would be better for this than a pencil. Decisions should be made firmly, without a thought of rubbing out!

The drawing should be enlarged to at least double the size of the actual object. A magnifying glass will help. The frame may be passed over the object until a part that is arresting is found. The glass will frame the chosen part and separate it from the rest of the object, so removing any idea that a portrait of the object is being attempted. Once a selection is made of an area of interest, it is best to draw from it in all directions. We have discussed the focal point in composition, and this part which arrests interest may well form one in the design.

Fig. 123 shows a piece of bark as a starting point. Its silhouette is without interest, being arbitrarily broken from a tree and weathered by the elements. The pattern inside, however, is fascinating and has been drawn with pen and ink.

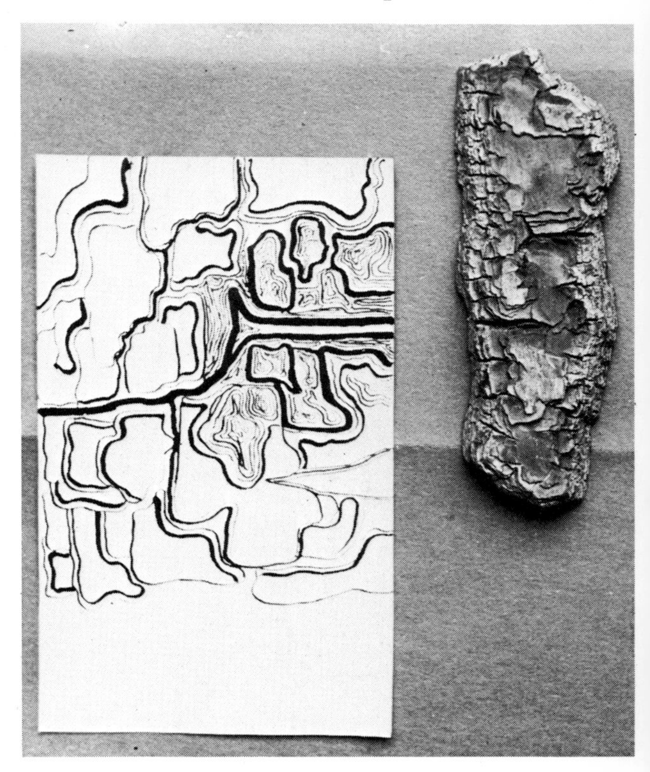

Fig. 123

The designer has selected a part, become involved and has drawn from that part.

The drawing may appear to be inaccurate. It is not a facsimile. It is unique, a student's drawing, a personal interpretation of this object. The process of designing has been both objective and subjective. The student is a needlewoman and already she is thinking in terms of shape and line, cloth and thread: the materials of her craft.

Fig. 124 shows two halves of shrivelled-up gourd. It sometimes pays to keep things like this. Like wine, they often become more interesting with age. The pen and ink drawings are by two student designers and the personality of these is revealed as much in drawing as in their handwriting. These drawings would also lend themselves to design for embroidery.

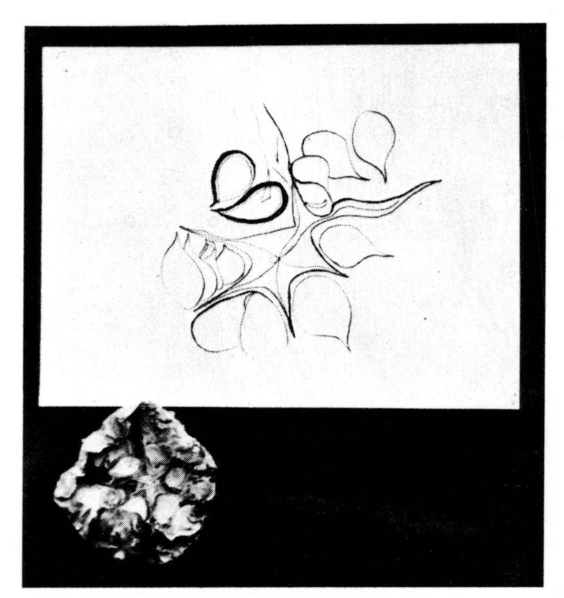

Fig. 124

Fig. 125 shows another piece of bark and two design attempts starting from the prominent knot-hole, which is a natural focal point. This student had previously done some exercises using a ball-nibbed pen as suggested in the chapters on shape and line and texture, and so she has interpreted the pattern on the bark into line and spot, which could easily be used for thread and stitches or beads.

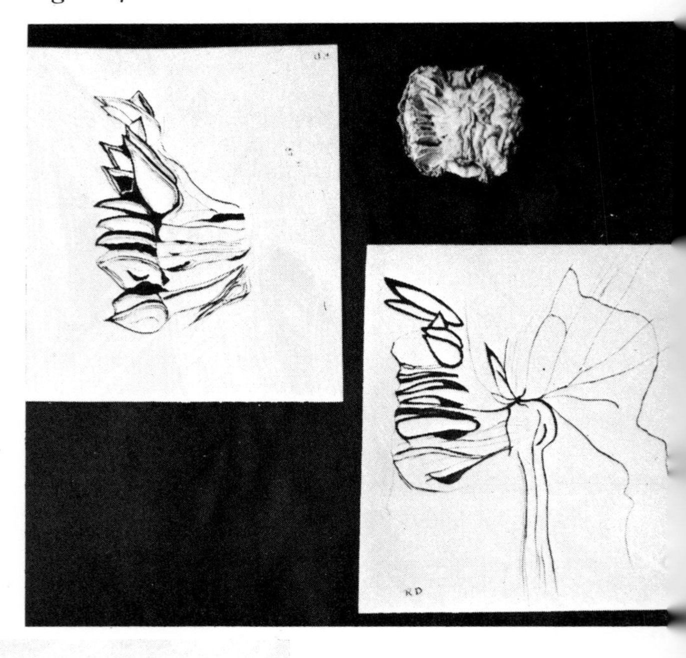

Fig. 125

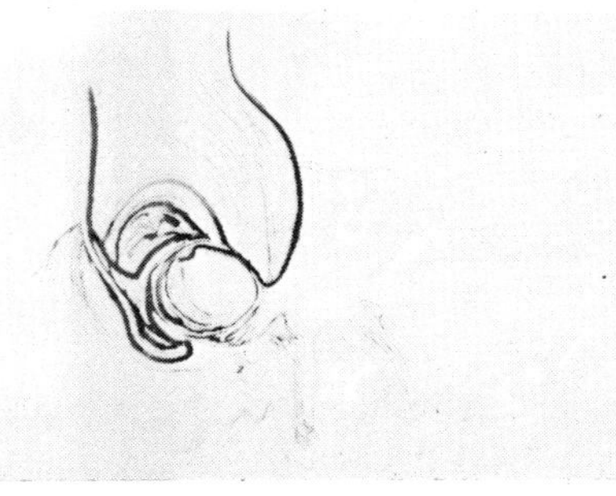

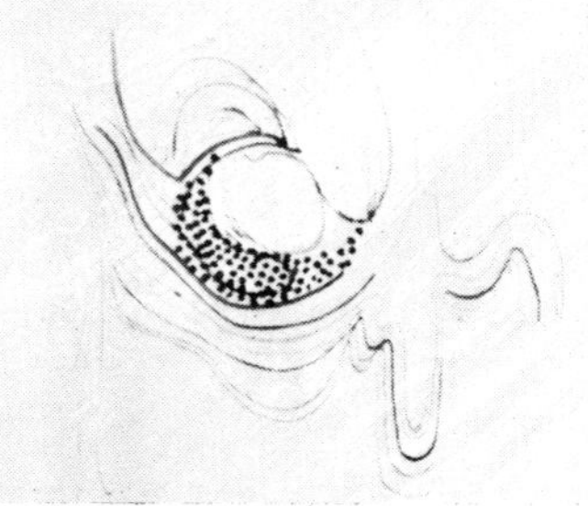

Fig. 126

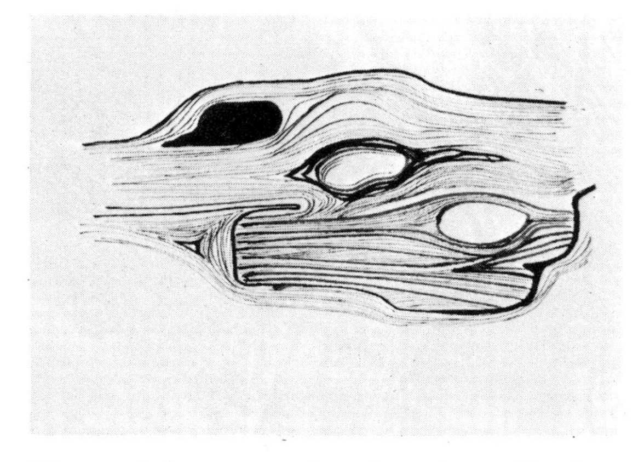

Fig. 126 shows another drawing of bark. What are in fact lumps on the bark appear as holes and might quite well encourage the designer to do a two-layer embroidery with a peep-show through the openings.

Sometimes a drawing from a natural object may contain conflicting interests, too many focal points, and it will be necessary to select the part to be used. It would be useful to project the drawing onto a wall. An old-fashioned epidiascope would do the job. Most older schools have one lying rejected in a cupboard, now out-moded by colour slides and film-strip projectors. A cheap projector that will project photographs onto a wall is often advertised in the press, and this would serve the purpose.

The enlarged image has several advantages. First the design is seen on a grand scale, which gives it dignity. It takes on the monumental scale of a wall-hanging instead of having book-illustration scale. It also is a means of enlarging a small sketch accurately.

The projector has only to be arranged at the right distance from the wall to ensure the right size image, and a tracing with charcoal can be made directly onto a piece of paper attached to the wall. This method can also be used as an aid in selecting from a drawing. A piece of paper of the size required for a panel can be taken and moved about over the image until a satisfactory arrangement is chosen. Parts of the drawing can be selected and the paper moved if it seems necessary.

This method has the virtue of showing results quickly. Freehand enlarging is not easy and the very quality admired in the small sketch can be lost in the process of enlarging. It is therefore very important to enlarge accurately. Using a projector is the easy way, and why not do it the easy way when we live in a technological age? If this method is not available there is an alternative.

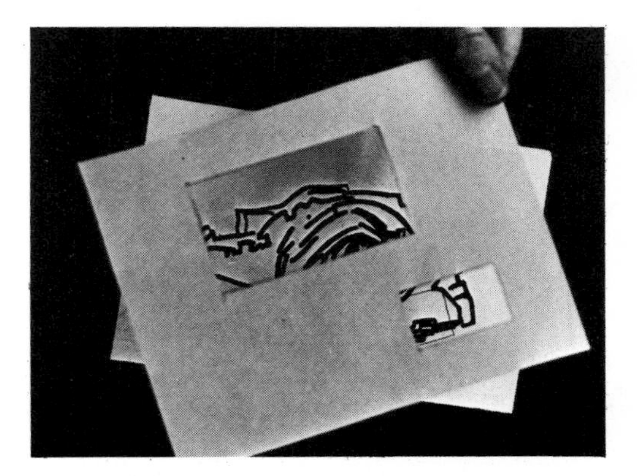

Fig. 127

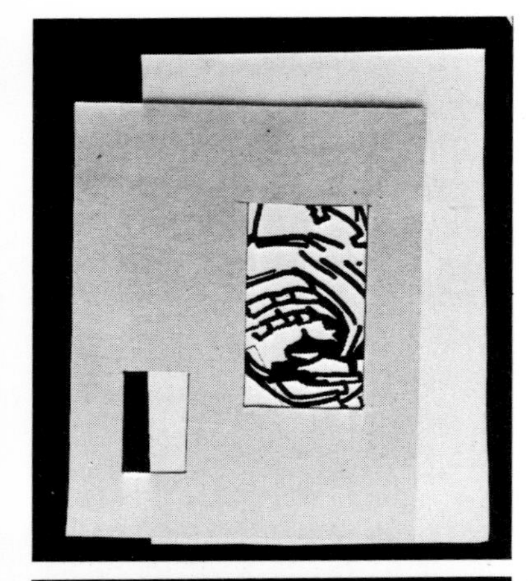

Fig. 128

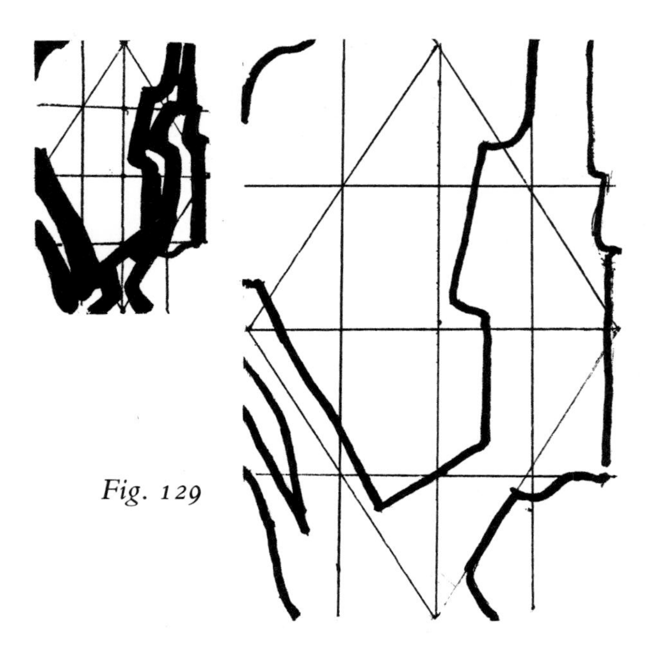

Fig. 129

Frames of card of various proportions and sizes can be cut (Figs. 127 and 128) and moved about over the drawing until a pleasing arrangement is within the frame. The rectangle of the frame should then be drawn onto the drawing.

You will need another sheet of paper of the same proportion as the frame selected and of the size required. Square up the rectangle on the drawing or on a tracing of the drawing by dividing it in half, then quarter it in each direction and finally join the centre points of each side of the rectangle to form a diamond.

The larger rectangle will be treated similarly, and it will be found that freehand enlarging is greatly aided by careful observing of these guide lines.

You may find it necessary to reduce the size of the design. Repeat patterns are easier to plan if they are on a larger scale than the finished embroidery. In such a case the reverse procedure would be followed.

Another use for a projector as inspiration for design is to use a modern slide projector with slides that have been made from pieces of paper, hair, cottons, leaves, seeds, string. Things that are slightly transparent or fine will give the best results. Plastics frames with two pieces of glass can be bought from photographic suppliers. To see small objects such as seeds blown up to the size of a wall gives a completely new outlook and suggests a starting point, not necessarily of the whole slide but of a selected area.

Modern life is complicated and busy. As a reaction to this we try to surround ourselves with simple shapes. Architecture is simple, in straight lines. The fine arts have always led the way in shape trends. We must try to bring simplicity of shape into embroidery designs to be in tune with the age. In the first chapter it was said that the designer selected and simplified. This is not easy to do, especially for the gifted draughtsman who sees all and has a gift of co-ordination of eye and hand making him capable of recording it all. We are going to try some ways of selecting and simplifying.

FIGURATIVE DRAWING

So far we have used natural and geometric forms to find 'abstract' – non-figurative – designs of shape and line. In recent years design has been non-figurative, non-representational, abstract, but there are signs that in painting, figurative work is appearing again and so it will follow in design. Whatever the subject matter, the problem remains the same. Figurative material also needs reducing to a simple statement of shape and line. It is more difficult to do. Let us see what can be done with a leaf shape, not taking a part of it but the whole of it. Leaves are interesting sources of design, the variety being enormous in the differing placing of the widest part and the distribution of veins.

Fig. 130 shows three students' interpretation of a selection of leaves. The first emphasises the vertical feeling by the arrangement of leaves on the page and the upright central vein. It is interesting to note the selected areas of pattern. The pattern would have extended all over the leaves, but a selection has been made: it has been used in parts, leaving areas of rest. The second sheet brings out movement, both in the arrangement of leaves, which gives a feeling that the wind blows, and in the lively way of drawing the veins and avoiding symmetry. The third page gives a more restrained, cooler look – more remote. The design is further removed from the original source with more control of line and delicate appreciation of shape. This student has succeeded in reducing the complexities to a very simple and pleasing statement.

RUBBINGS

There are ways of simplifying and selecting – other ways of seeing – which may prove of help. If a leaf is placed, back uppermost, under a sheet of white paper, it is possible, with a greasy crayon, to take a rubbing of the raised veins.

Fig. 130

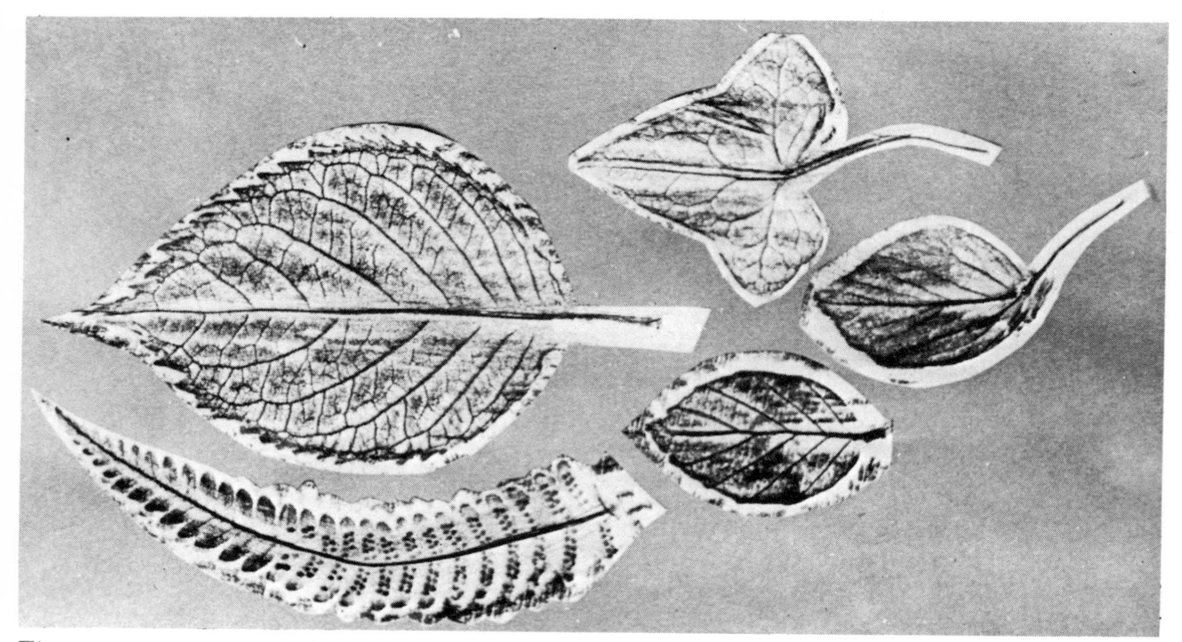

Fig. 131

In Fig. 131 you will recognise some of the same leaves. In taking a rubbing, already some of the complexities have been sorted out. In the fern, the seeds have shown up dark at the lower end against a light leaf, whereas when the seeds finish, the leaf becomes dark. This is counterchange of tone, which might never have been considered without taking this rubbing. It is one example of the rewards of experiment. In all the leaves there is some simplification to help the designer.

Fig. 132 shows further involvement with leaves. The hydrangea leaf has been cut on some of the veins and 'exploded'. These cut-paper shapes, in low relief, were then rubbed in their turn and the image repeated. This experiment worked out as a repeat pattern.

Figs. 133 and 134 were formed by repeats of selected parts of the cut-out leaf, to make a repeat pattern and a single unit design respectively.

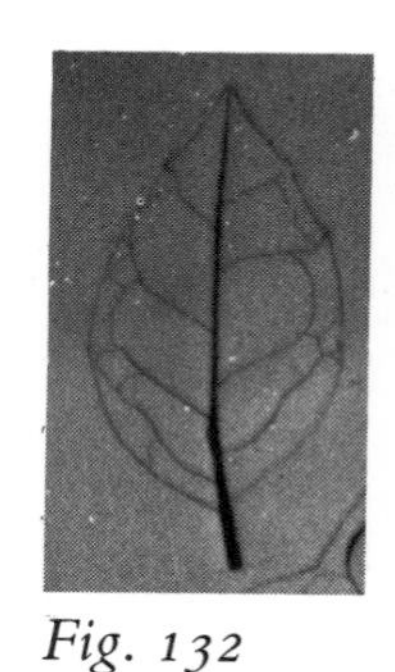

Fig. 132

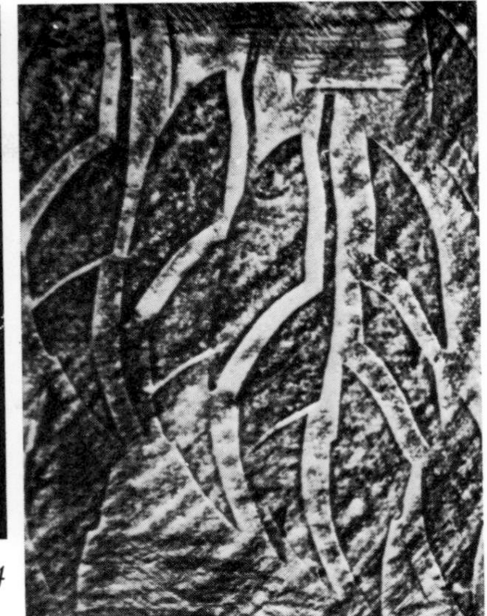

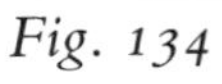

Fig. 134

Fig. 133

Fig. 135

Fig. 135 shows another cut-out leaf design with a rubbing alongside, which was made by combining this leaf with the one in the last drawing. This sort of experiment is absorbing and fascinating to do.

A further experiment could be to rub the designs or leaves on paper with candle wax and then run a watercolour wash over the rubbing. This would produce a different result again, a negative of the other rubbings, rather like a skeleton leaf. Other objects could be rubbed in the same way and something very useful might result. Such involvement is never wasted; even if the immediate gain is not obvious, it will sharpen the visual awareness to the possibilities in the environment, and enrich the visual vocabulary.

PRINTS

When looking at the first set of leaf pen drawings, Fig. 130, we commented on the fact that the designer had selected from a pattern that had covered the whole of the leaf and had chosen to show it in part, leaving welcome areas of rest. This is often effective in order to produce a satisfying design with a variety of size of shape and both textured and plain areas. In this case the selection works well. Is there a way to experiment with different areas of texture on the leaf?

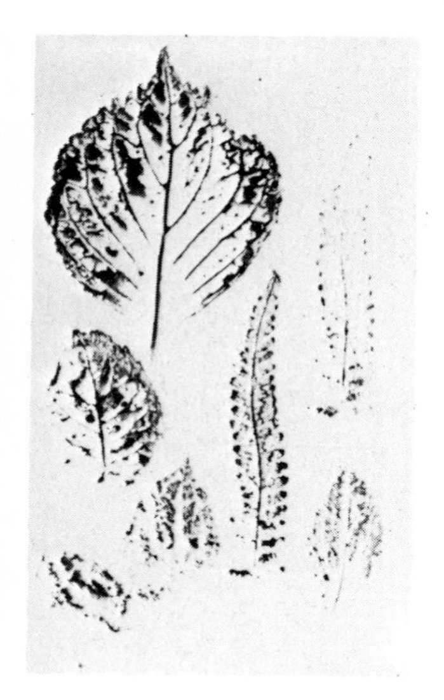

Fig. 136

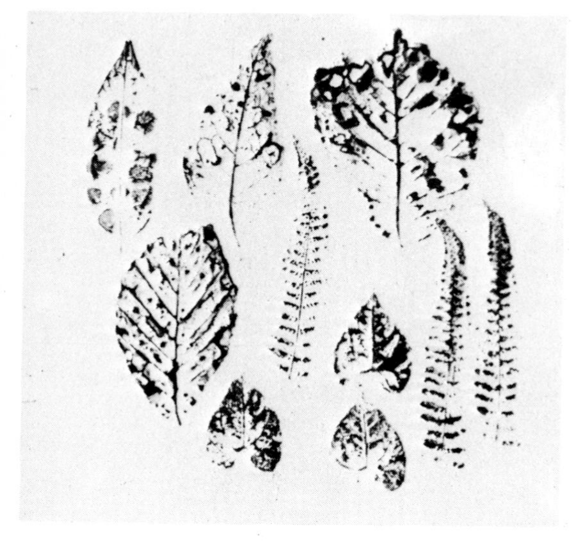

Fig. 136 shows some prints taken from the backs of leaves. The leaves are shiny and the paint (in this case powder paint) 'takes' badly. Hence the 'hit and miss' print. The rubbings gave a better appreciation of shape, but prints have their own charm. They give a concentration of detail and then an area of rest. Each print will be unique. Not all will be ready-made designs, but they will suggest designs, and several together may be consulted in making a design.

COUNTERCHANGE

The use of the leaf, a near-symmetrical shape, suggests another treatment, counterchange. Fruits and vegetables with a centre line could be used similarly. Half a tomato, a lemon, onion etc.

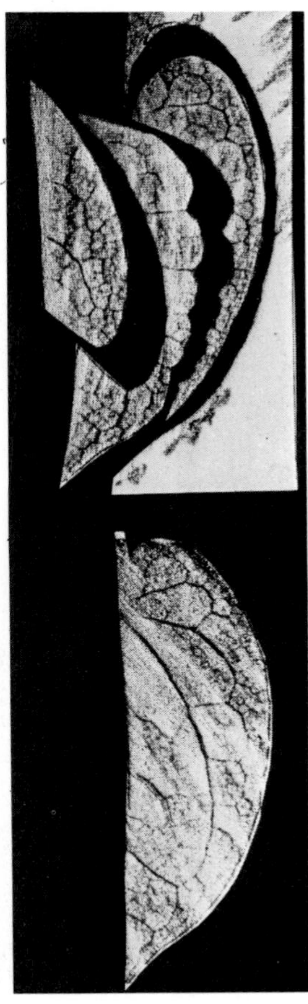

137

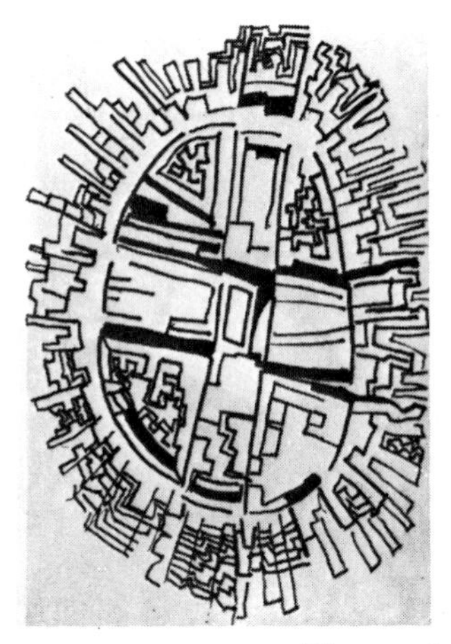

Fig. 138

Fig. 139

Fig. 137 shows the simple method of counterchange, where one half of the design has been used and alternate pieces are turned over. Paper which has been used for rubbing on one side and typing on the other will make clear when the paper is turned.

USING SOURCES OF INSPIRATION

We have shown designs in line and shape. One source of inspiration may be interpreted in both ways, sometimes line, sometimes shape, sometimes positive, sometimes negative. Interests are varied and can lead to fascinating designs.

The design in Fig. 138 was suggested by an aerial view of an ancient South American town.

It is surprising what can be done from supposedly unpromising material, with real involvement. Fig. 139 shows a sketch of a tombstone in the graveyard of Llandaff Cathedral. The drawing shows more detail than was actually used. The student became involved with cut-out shapes and found the negative ones more interesting than the positive ones which she cut. (See Figs. 140 and 141.)

Further shapes have been formed with the negative shape. The outcome of the involvement was a length of printed cloth, but each of these try-out screen prints could have been starting points for embroidery. It matters little what is the initial inspiration, but it matters much that the student experiments and becomes involved in the idea.

Fig. 140

Fig. 141

The idea for Figs. 142 and 143 came from a study of Tudor architecture, 'magpie' houses, the dark line patterns of half-timbered walls. Fig. 142 shows a block print of four straightforward repeats. Fig. 143 shows the same block twisted around and overprinting the first print. This could equally well be the foundation for embroidery. It could be treated as a symmetrical design, as it appears in Fig. 144a, giving each of the four repeats similar treatment. It would also be possible to choose one area as the focal point and break the symmetry, as in Fig. 144b. It would be interesting to see the variety of ways that different needlewomen would treat it. Fig. 144a gives some idea of the variation of tonal effects possible.

Fig. 142 *Fig. 143*

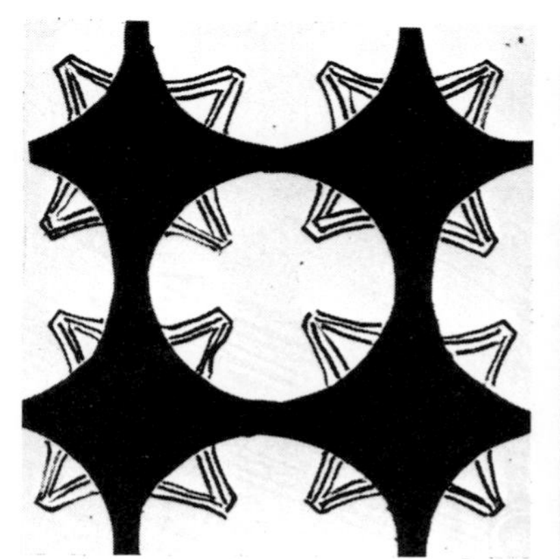

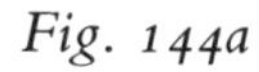

Fig. 144a

Fig. 144b

TIE-DYE AND BATIK

Simple tie-dye and batik designs could also be used as a start for embroidery. Single colour dyes would work best. When part of the ground is already coloured with a nucleus for design, you may be inspired to develop this with fabric and thread. This may be a single unit panel or a repeat dyed pattern. Colour plate 17 shows a piece of free weaving, which was suggested by a tie-dyed circle in colour plate 16. The weaving was carried out over the tie-dye and all but covers it. Rich work could also be done by reinforcing the original dye pattern with fabric and thread. (See bibliography for books on tie-dye and batik.)

Fig. 145

REGULAR MODULE PATTERNS

Sculptors, painters and fabric designers have used the theme of a regular module pattern, the monotony of which is broken by variation of colour, shape, texture or tone within the regular pattern. Some sculptors have made constructions, which are repeated units like honeycomb or egg boxes, through which lights play in a changing sequence, giving the sculpture a focal point and constant interest and variety. The 'magpie' design gives scope for such a treatment in embroidery. Cut-paper and tie-dye designs could also lead to this way of working.

Involvement with cut paper in this way produces repeat patterns (Fig. 145). By treating the similar shapes differently, it could become a single unit for a wall-hanging. It would be necessary to create a focal point and secondary interest as explained in Chapter 5.

In Chapter 3 we examined 'exploded' shapes, related shape. Fig. 146 will recall how we cut up squares and circles and parted the shapes.

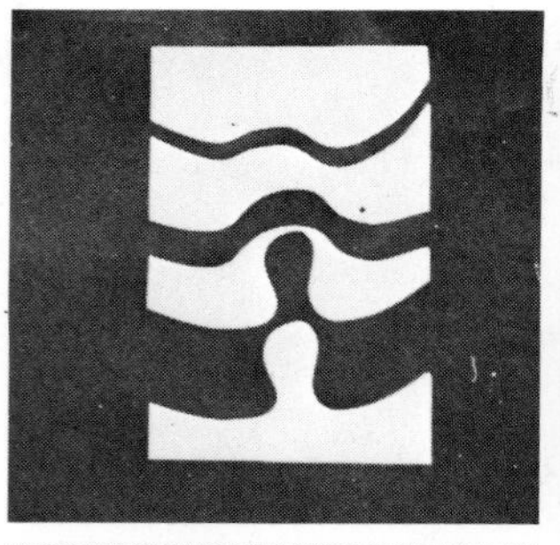

Fig. 146

Fig. 147 shows how such designs may be developed by rubbings. Certain forms may be rubbed more strongly than others; a selection may be made of which forms to rub. Again, at this stage selective and creative powers are used to form a larger design of related forms.

Fig. 147

Fig. 148

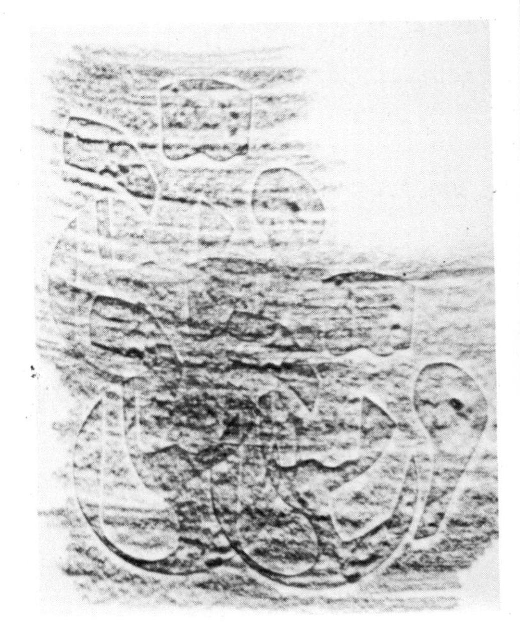

Given single-mindedness and involvement, the creative side will develop. You should set yourself a problem with limitations. When such a problem is set there is no single solution but dozens, this is the fascinating part about it. Limitations are a help, not a hindrance.

Fig. 148, another variation on the square and circle, is an example of such limitation. It looks as though it could be a development of the 'magpie' design, but in fact it is the work of someone absorbed with design in mathematics.

This chapter has tried to give you a way of approaching design. Each of you will choose your own area in which to work. A study of designed objects will stimulate an appreciation of shape. Browsing through books on ancient civilisations will prove rewarding. The older they are, the more likely to be in tune with today. Relief carving, sculptured forms in stone and ivory, may show distortion to fit the shape of the material and may be studied as design problems.

The immediate environment should provide material. Modern office blocks at night, making rectangular patterns of light and dark shapes, car lights seen as spot pattern, perhaps combined with line as they appear in photographs taken with a time exposure, rubbings of worn paving stones, tombstones, Georgian and

Victorian coal hole covers, museum exhibits, all of these might inspire the city dweller.

Country and seashore folk have a wealth of natural form. The museum will bring the country and the seashore to the town. The National Museum of Wales is the authors' closest one and provides a fund of ideas; machinery, fungi, fossils, pattern in animals, birds, bones, wood, minerals, crystal forms, Celtic crosses, plants, insects – to mention a few from an embarrassment of choice.

Once you are visually aware, life becomes of continual interest. You will be constantly delighted by the mundane, which many *look* at but do not really *see*.

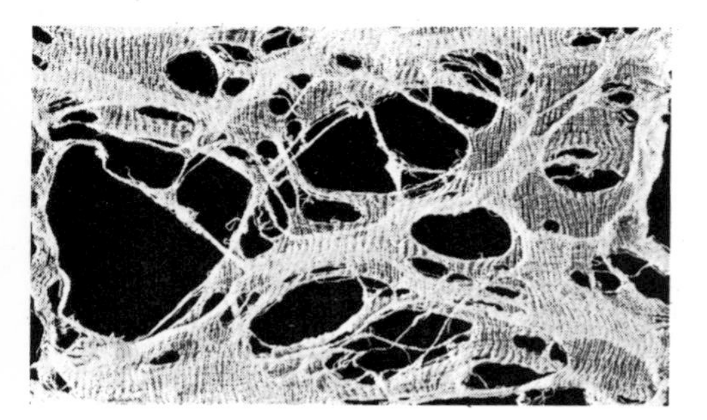

Fig. 149a

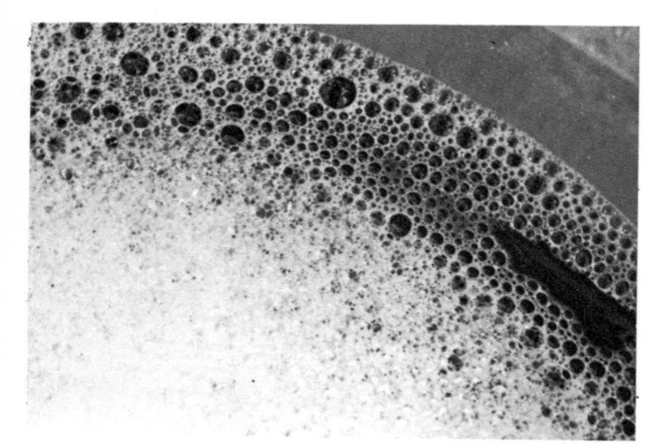

Fig. 149b

The bubbles in the washing machine (Fig. 149b) make a common task the easier, and an old dishcloth, which was a piece of circular knitted fabric wrapped around a carcass in the butcher's shop, now worn into a fascinating pattern of holes (Fig. 149a), is yet another inspiration. This is all the more interesting because, being a tube, it has two layers and sets our mind working on two-layered embroideries with further interest seen through a peep-hole.

The daily paper, a magazine, these may provide photographs. Selection is the important thing because not everything is suitable. The sketches that follow were taken from a series in our local press of aerial views of a new road from Cardiff up into the Merthyr Valley. It alerted us to look for other possibilities in landscape. As has already been said Fig. 138 (page 103) was taken from an ancient South American town, which was planned as a symmetrical shape and which we interpreted in both shape and line. Colour plate 30 shows a further development of this in fabric and thread.

Little planning took place, however, in the architecture of the Welsh valley towns. Cottages were thrown up quickly to house the workers in the nineteenth century Industrial Revolution, but the builders still had to contend with the beautiful natural contours of the landscape. This results in *related* form, which is fascinating for the artist. (See Figs. 150a and b.)

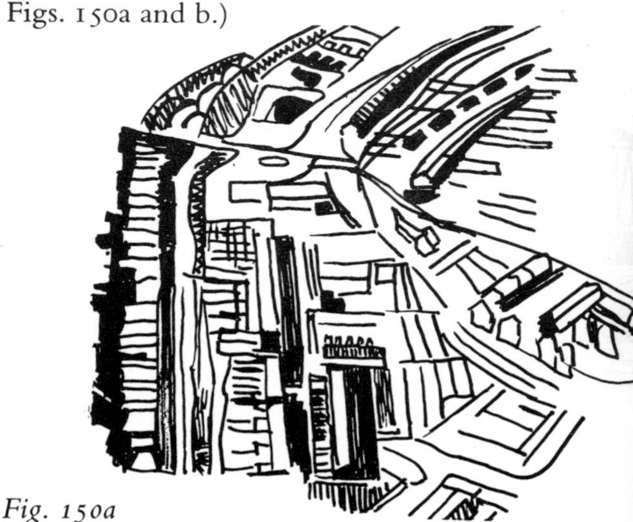

Fig. 150a

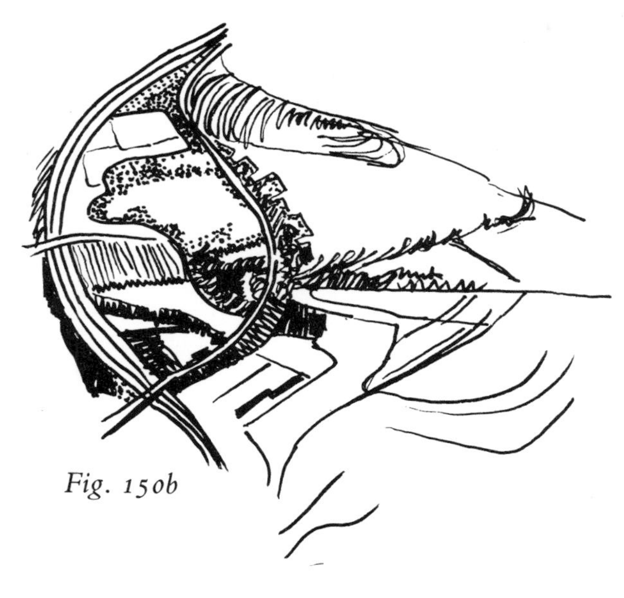

Fig. 150b

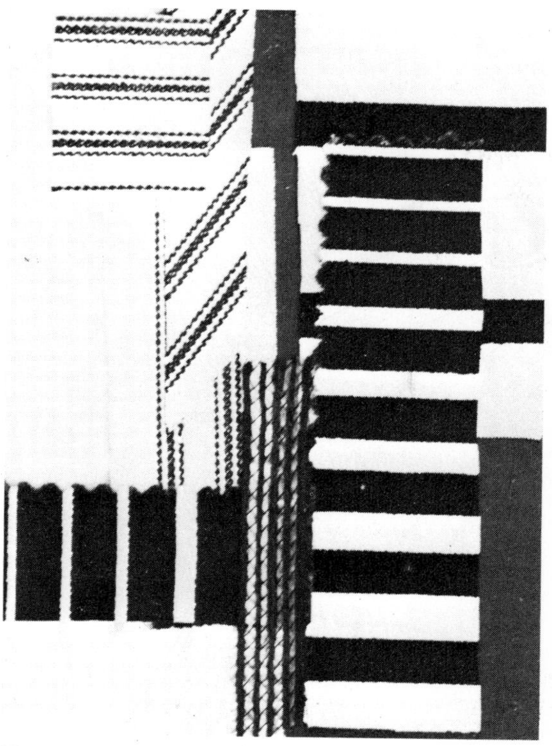

Fig. 153

Fig. 151

Fig. 151 shows a bird's-eye view of another town, designed to border each side of a river, and Fig. 152 is another landscape study with related form. This becomes a stripe pattern, but was derived from a landscape of wooded hills, mists and water between mountain ranges.

Fig. 153 shows fabric that could be used to interpret this last landscape. Stitches too could give this effect.

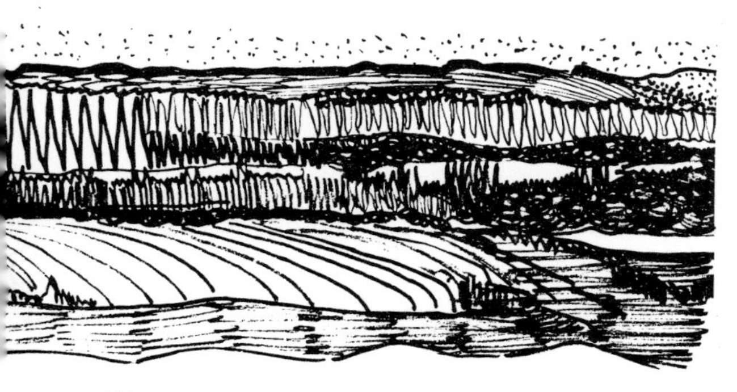

Fig. 152

We have shown related forms in landscape when the roads and houses were built 'in sympathy' with the features that already existed. This is one of the chief points we have made in composition. We have also used 'exploded shape' as a means of arriving at related form.

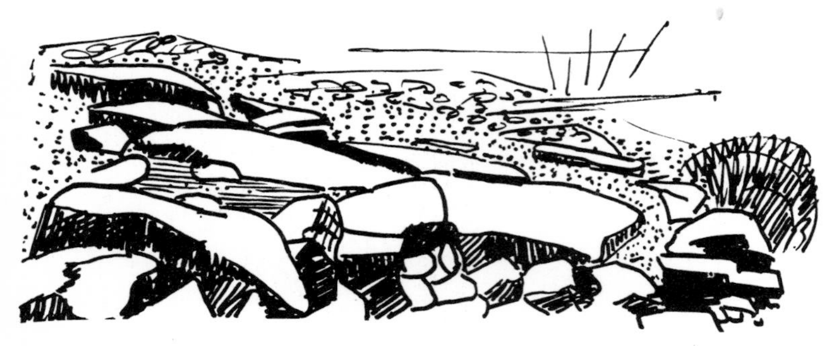

Fig. 154

Fig. 154 shows a drawing of a field in Ardèche covered with a layer of limestone rock, which has cracked like crazy paving and separated. Some has been removed to make dry stone walls. The whole is a fascinating textured landscape of related shapes.

All of these might serve as starting points for creation with fabric and thread, not taking them in total but in part. Once an interest has been found, there is great satisfaction in sticking with it and worrying it. Many artists work on themes. We think of Monet's series of haystacks and Rouen Cathedral. Involvement is the key.

The design on paper is the mere germ of an idea, a skeleton plan with which to become involved with materials and to interpret in terms of fabric and thread. You may miss opportunities the materials present if you adhere too rigidly to the plan. It is impossible to visualise the whole process at this stage and work with a creative spirit. Better to start hopefully with an open mind and be willing to change course if the materials suggest a different approach.

Interpretation is an attitude of mind. The more the craft is truly understood, the more possibilities are seen. Involvement may lead to the exploration of many avenues in order to be satisfied. If the materials are available to encourage experiment and the technical knowledge is varied, the interpretation will be as inspired as the imagination allows.

Stripes may be the current interest. We have seen them in landscape. They might also be suggested by a stone, strata in rock, a tiger skin, skyscape or seascape. The rock in Fig. 155 can be interpreted into fabric in a number of ways apart from using striped fabric, as Fig. 156 shows.

1 Plain fabric with flat braid and sequins added in stripes.
2 Threads have been withdrawn from a loosely woven fabric and textured ones have been substituted.
3 Rows of machine stitches, thick and thin, have been worked on plain fabric.
4 Strips of felt and net have been added to plain fabric.
5 Plain fabric has been tie-dyed in a striped pattern.

Often the effects achieved will spark off an involvement with the materials themselves, and the source of inspiration becomes unrecognisable and momentarily forgotten.

Shapes can be interpreted in many ways. The circle, the age-old favourite in design, appears many times in natural form and geometric designs. It may appear as:

1 A continuous line of stitchery.
2 A circle of flat or raised stitchery.

Fig. 155

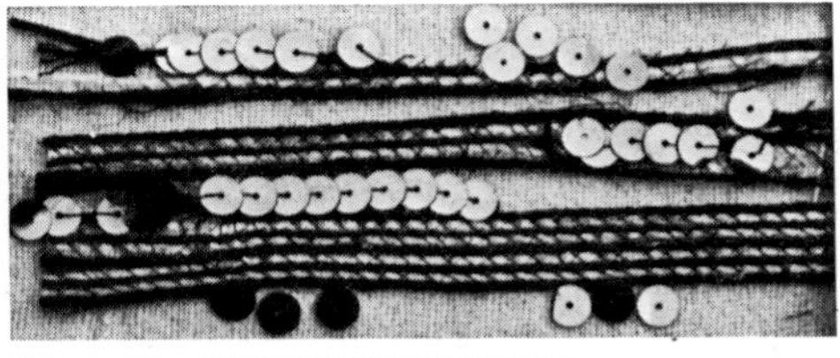

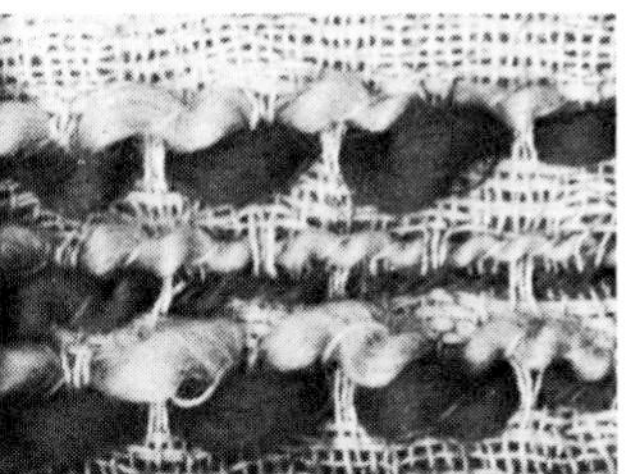

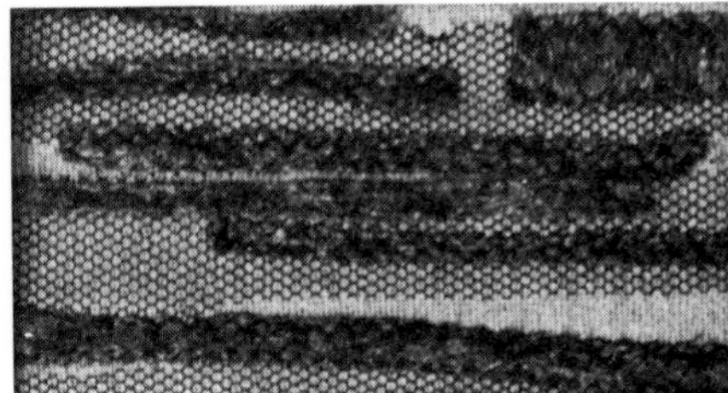

Fig. 156

3 An applied shape of fabric – transparent, opaque, shiny, dull, flat or padded.
4 A hole through which one looks.
5 The top of a cylinder.
6 A curtain ring.
7 Felt scrolls.
8 Circular weaving.
9 A cluster of beads, sequins, French knots.

The drawings of towns and landscapes in Figs. 150–2 on the previous pages can be interpreted this way. The simple plan could be block or screen printed as Fig. 142 with the addition of appliqué rectangular sequins, stitchery etc. The spotted areas might become: stitches,

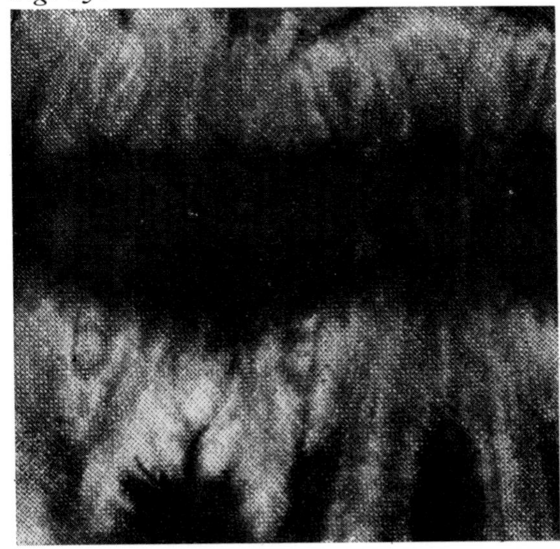

beads, fine wire, lace, rolls of felt or more printing. This is the age of mixed media in art, and you should not be afraid to try anything that will give the desired effect.

The way in which shapes are interpreted will often depend on the materials by which you are inspired. Thus with sensitivity and experience the work develops as a whole. Fabrics and threads subtly take over. What one will visualise in hessian and organdie, another will develop in PVC and velvet. Some will want to explore stitchery and find unity in colour while being adventurous in texture and scale. The greater your tenacity and adventurous spirit the greater are your chances of finding personal satisfaction and building up a reserve vocabulary of first-hand information. It takes a human being years to learn to express itself in words, and learning expression in any medium has no quick, ready solution. It is long rather than short term.

Finally, we hope you will be helped towards this self-expression by seeing how some needlecraft students attempted their first interpretation of a personal interest. In all cases natural form was their choice.

Fig. 157 shows a drawing of seaweed, which was followed up by an experiment with weaving. A piece of card was cut to a shape similar to that of the general shape of the drawing. The edges of the card were serrated and a warp was set up into which weft threads of a highly textured nature were woven. The weaving was taken from the card and mounted on a hessian ground.

It is easy to see how this leads on to the further expression in appliqué and stitchery. The outline which was warp is now seen as a grey shape and the design becomes controlled and serene, the

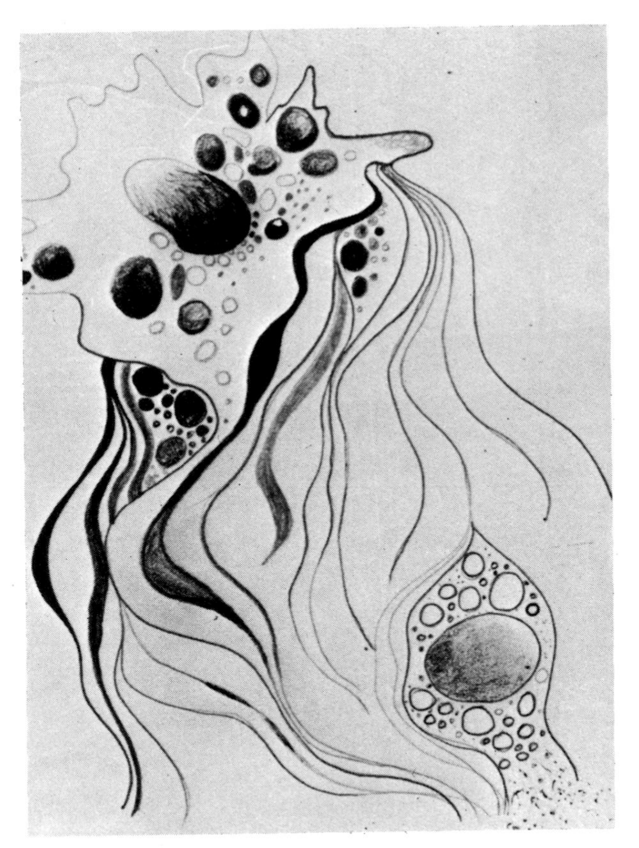

Fig. 157

materials being used with more confidence and mature thought. The design is more abstract – further removed from the original through involvement with materials. (See colour plate 19.)

Fig. 158 shows a drawing of a stone – limestone – riddled with holes, and also a simplification of this. Colour plate 18 shows a subsequent experiment in interpretation. Felt has been used, parts of which are padded and part left flat to give the pitted effect.

Fig. 159 is a drawing of driftwood. Further involvement is shown in colour plate 6.

A 'pebble' picked up on the beach at Porthcawl inspired Fig. 160. In fact it is a collection of many pebbles embedded in some binding substance, perhaps concrete,

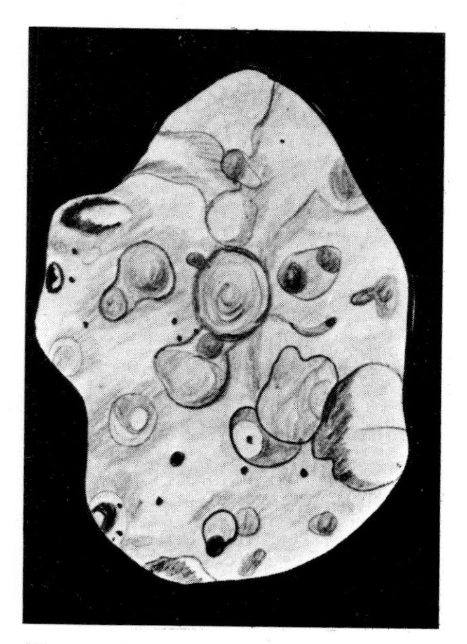

Fig. 158

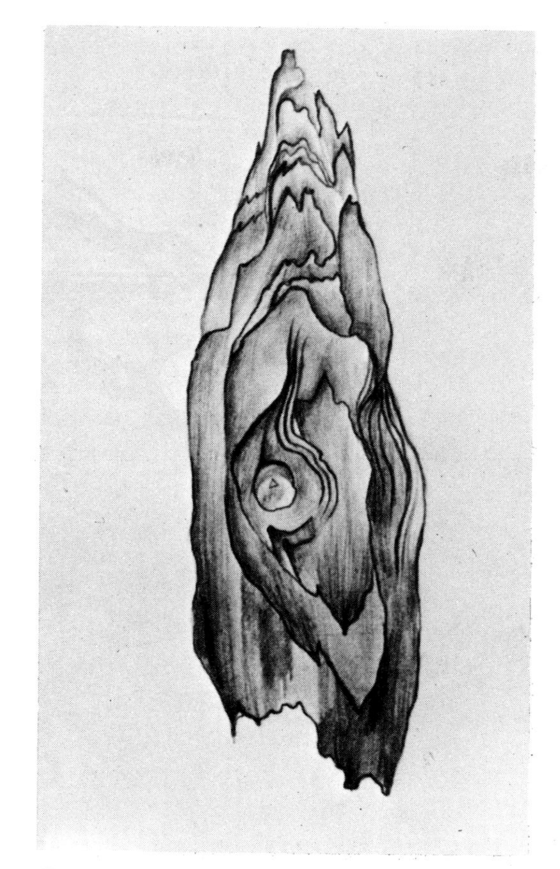

Fig. 159

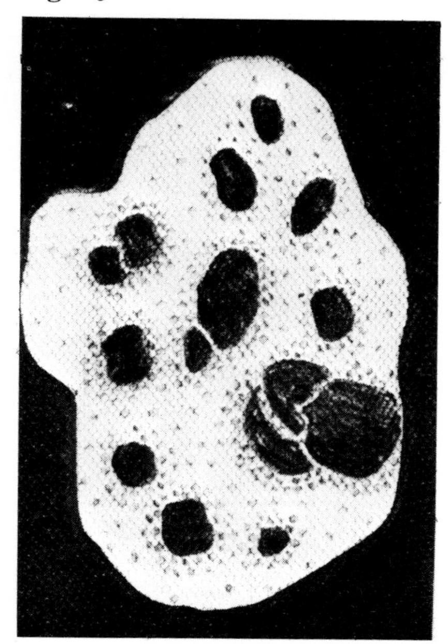

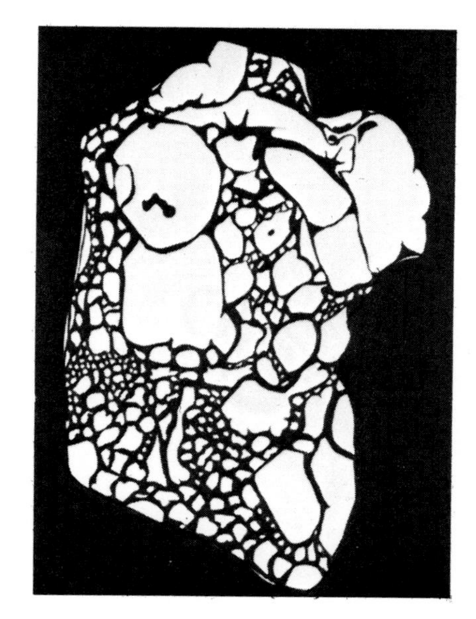

Fig. 160

and buffeted by the tide into a shape of its own. Colour plates 20 and 21 show experimental weaving interpretations. Curtain rings have been introduced into the warp, suggested by the separate stones. The linear quality in the drawing is expressed by the dark warp which is left exposed and the same dark thread which covers the rings. The complexity of rich weaving is an interpretation of the complex nature of the inspiration.

So we reach the stage where needlecraft students are beginning to work as artists; selecting, drawing with analysis, and interpreting with the materials of their craft. This voyage of discovery is leading up to the more complicated task of carrying out a major work with fabric and thread, which is the subject of our next chapter.

9

EMBROIDERY 'COLLAGE'— THE WHOLE PROCESS

We use the term 'collage' for decorative fabric panels in which the fabric may have been stuck down (as the word suggests), but also when it has been stitched and developed with embroidery. At its most profound level embroidery collage is an art form, and consequently requires, as do any of the arts, a long apprenticeship, both in theory and practice. The preceding chapters are an introduction to that apprenticeship. But you must remember that although it is necessary to understand the theory to be articulate in thought while working, nothing can replace the practice you will need in designing and experimenting with materials.

A successful embroidery collage is difficult to accomplish because it involves so much time-consuming detail. This often results in a tendency to put together a collection of unrelated items. We know from past chapters that mass shapes must be placed before detail, and that while considering detail a firm grasp must be kept on the design as a whole. Time must be allowed 'to stand and stare'; no snap decisions can be made with such a medium.

We have tried to lead you up to this pinnacle in the craft by gentle slopes and we will now show you collages that are the first attempts by students of needlecraft. Analyse what has been done in them, then find your own theme and work in your own way, calling on your past experience of experiment.

Colour plate 23 is by Susan Rogers. Does it call to mind anything that we have already seen? It stems from her line drawing in Chapter 8, Fig. 123 (page 95). A Y shape seemed the natural focal point in the bark and she drew from that area. The next stage was to enlarge it by projecting the image onto a wall and to trace the enlargement onto paper. She realised the value of the space at the bottom of the drawing, an area of rest that raised up the interest, and decided to make it 'work' in the collage. Then a colour scheme was worked out by painting on the enlarged drawing. The line drawing was changed first by paint and then by the materials into shape that was positive, the line becomes the negative space between these shapes.

The ground chosen was a knobbly wool that would provide textural interest in the shape at the bottom. The focal point became a warm colour with neutral stone acting as a foil. It became apparent in the course of planning that some plain surfaced fabric was needed over the textured ground in order to make the negative space clearcut, and this was all that was required to make this large area at the top of textural interest without colour distraction. We show stages in this work.

Colour plate 22 shows the collage
1 In its early moments when the thought is for simple shape: padded focal point with flat stone-coloured appliqué supporting it.
2 The finished collage is seen in colour plate 23. It has become a highly textured surface, reflecting the complicated texture of the bark of the tree. Gold kid and French knots give texture to the focal point and secondary interests.

The collage is a very rich piece of work, which depends upon contrasts for its effect – contrast of intensity of colour, contrast of tension and relaxation, contrast of dull and shiny materials and plain and textured areas. Fig. 161 shows its tonal effect.

Fig. 162 shows a paper collage made up from practice screen prints; the chief shapes are those of cockle shells, which had been rubbed with candle grease onto the organdie screen. Kara Doyle, the designer of the collage, lives in Swansea, where cockles abound.

Fig. 163 shows further experiment in cutting the screen print and adding two tones of plain areas, which enhance the pattern. The whole is then mounted on striped texture.

Fig. 161

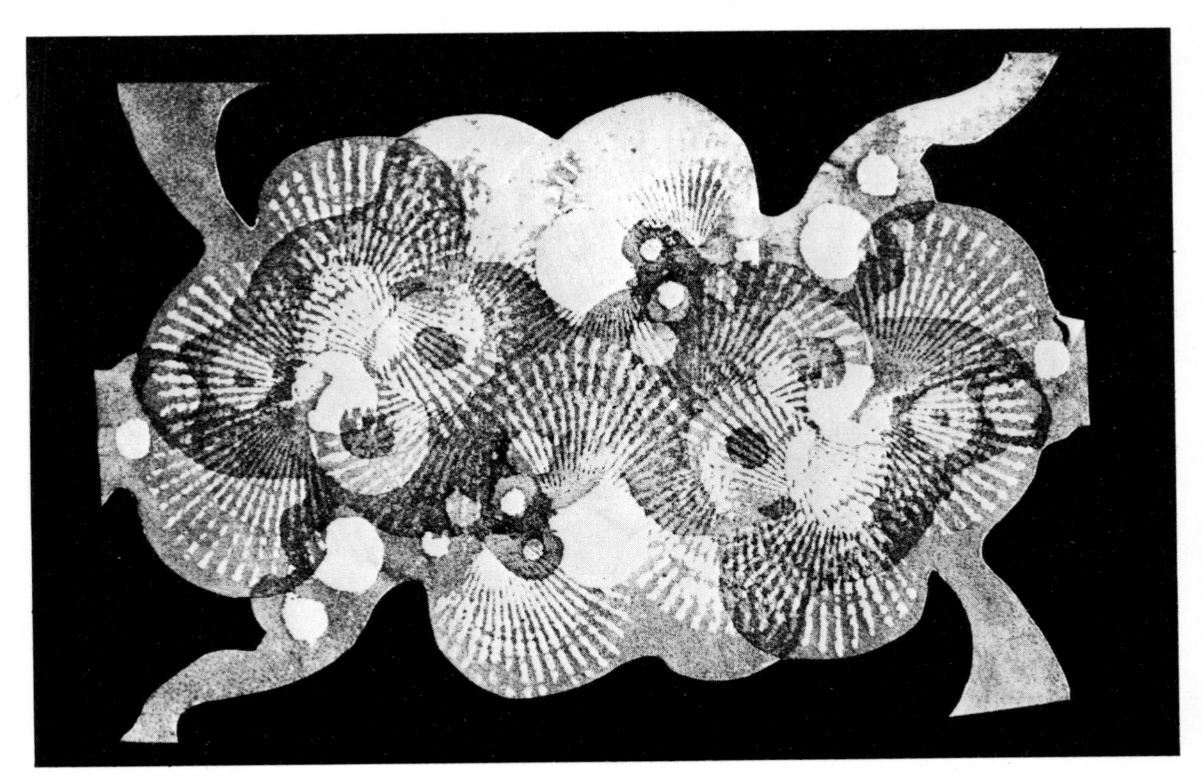

Fig. 162

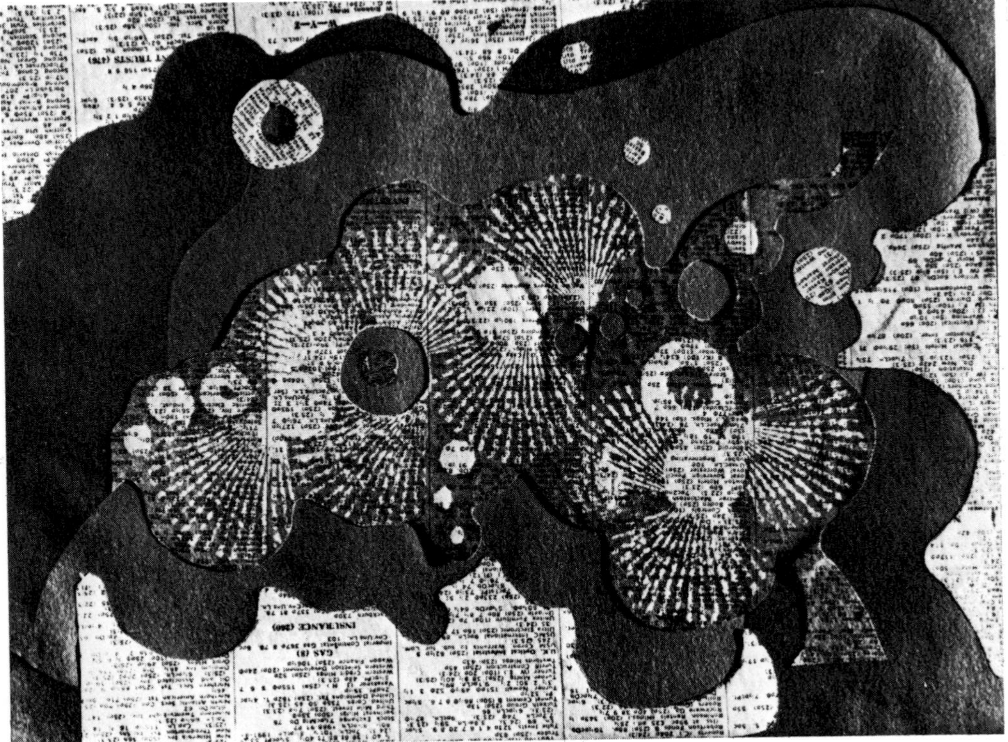

Fig. 163

Fig. 164

Fig. 164 shows the finished article in tone. A print-patterned ground fabric was chosen and the first task was to relate the design to it. The change of tone links up the shapes well. The cut paper shapes were translated into grey fabric, raised with trapunto method and machined around to form pebble-like shapes. The edges were softened and broken by small beads and French knots, giving the impression of a sandy cove surrounded on three sides by tiny pebbles and bigger ones – a lovely frame in which to put something really dramatic. The drama comes in the pompons, which are placed at the round hinge of the shells. Long, strong threads suggested by the ribs of the shells form warp for weaving and beads. Notice the linear effect in the design, which is strong but never restless, being steadied by the flat, plain areas.

In Chapter 4 we looked at line and the way in which it reinforced shape in the section of an onion. The next collage started from a pen line pattern exercise, Fig. 165, in which two lines opposed each other a third of the way in from one side, then other lines were added in sympathy with these and extending to the shape's edge. From this simple beginning stems a long train of thought by Sue James.

1 Fig. 166 is an experimental screen print.

2 Fig. 167 is a further involvement with the print; cutting out paper shapes and inserting those of more brilliant colour.

3 Fig. 168 shows a first attempt at embroidery collage using black and white only.

165

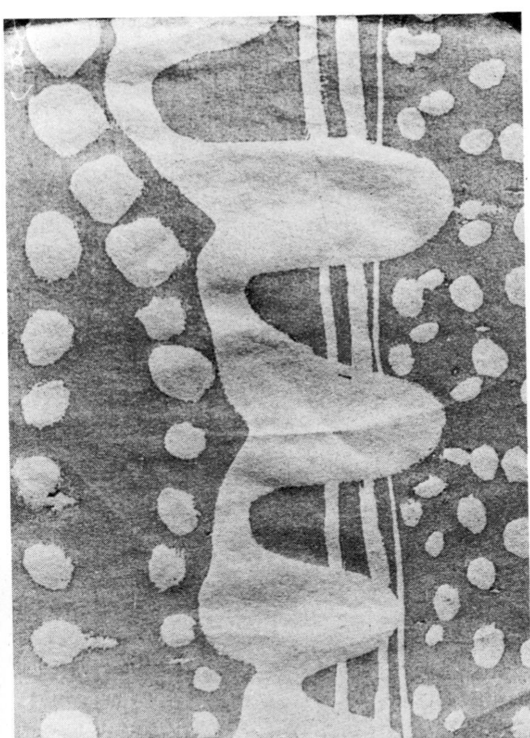

Fig. 166

Fig. 167

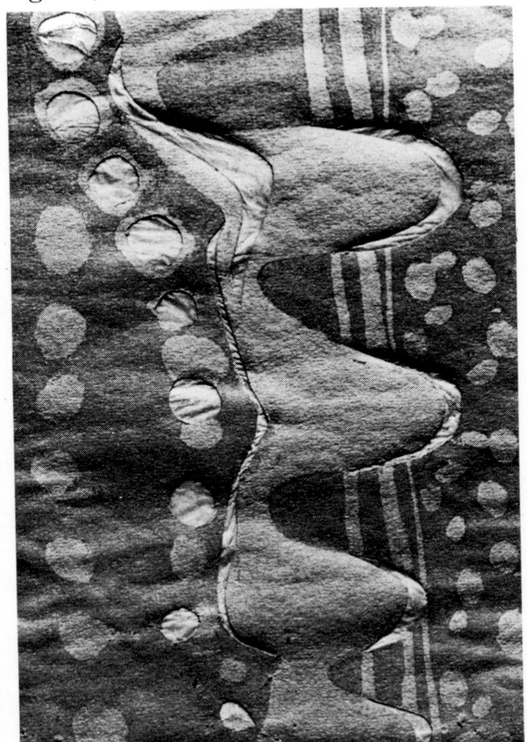

Fig. 168

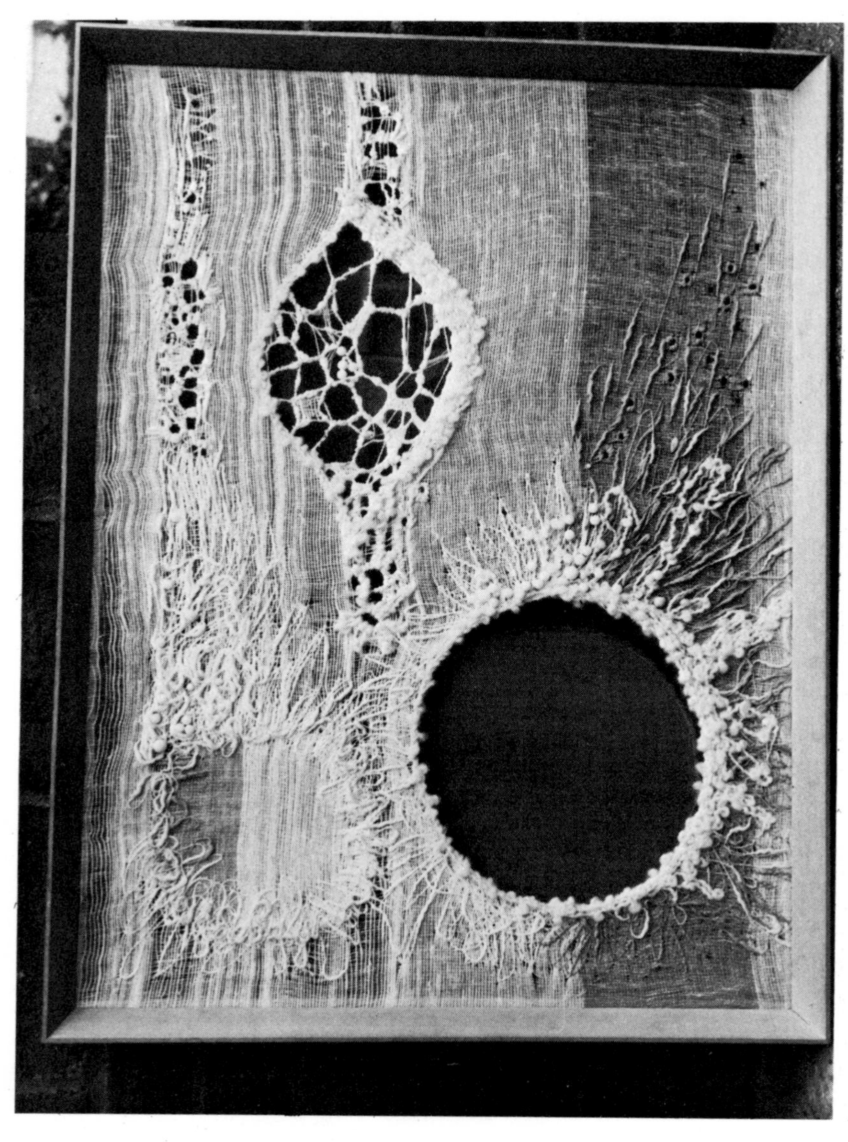

Fig. 169

The collage by Shân Humphrey Thomas in colour plate 24 has already been used to illustrate the limitation of working with circles and the rectangle from which they were cut. It owes its success to its exploiting of limitations. Black and white is used with interesting textured tonal effects of grey. A tweedy ground is complemented by a shiny black leather, and white felt appliqué. The sharp, clearcut design is a foil for the subtle disintegrating circle, which seems to be growing mould, in counterchange.

Fig. 169 is a two-layer collage by Dwynwen Jones. For the top layer she chose to work on an off-white loosely woven fabric (Dralon) embroidered in self-colour to a rich textural intensity. This she contrasted vividly by placing an orange circle on the lower layer. The design was suggested by pen exercises of water negotiating stepping stones.

Jennifer Ash works with quiet precision, delicacy and elegance in the collage of three related shapes derived from natural

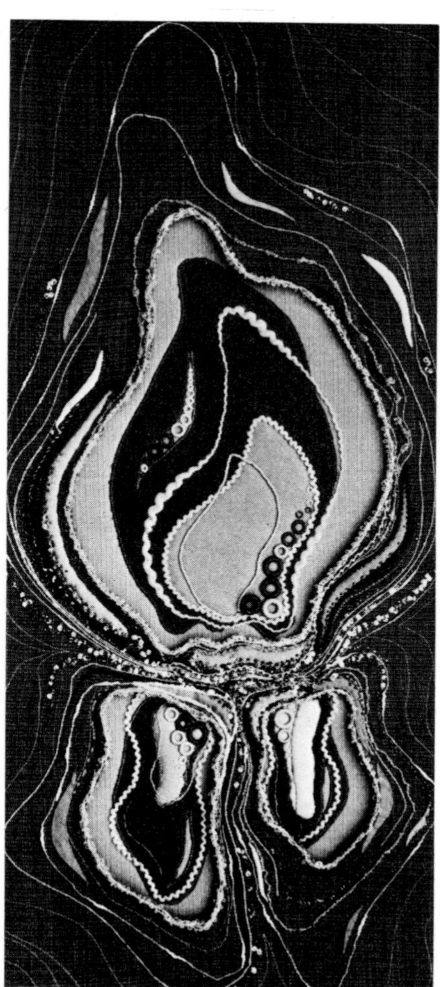

Fig. 170

form shown in Fig. 170. The shapes are like islands seen in clear water. The mass is contrasted by lovely fine line. The focal point, a natural one, is the channel between the appliqué shapes, with couched thread, beadwork and hand stitchery at the core of interest. The appliqué reaches out to the background in a gentle tentative way.

In complete contrast, Christine Perry's collage, colour plate 26, uses a section through a gourd (Fig. 171) and shows vigorous business, the whole giving a sense of vitality. The subject of pips and pith has inspired good shapes and we like especially the creative weaving, which is very sensitive.

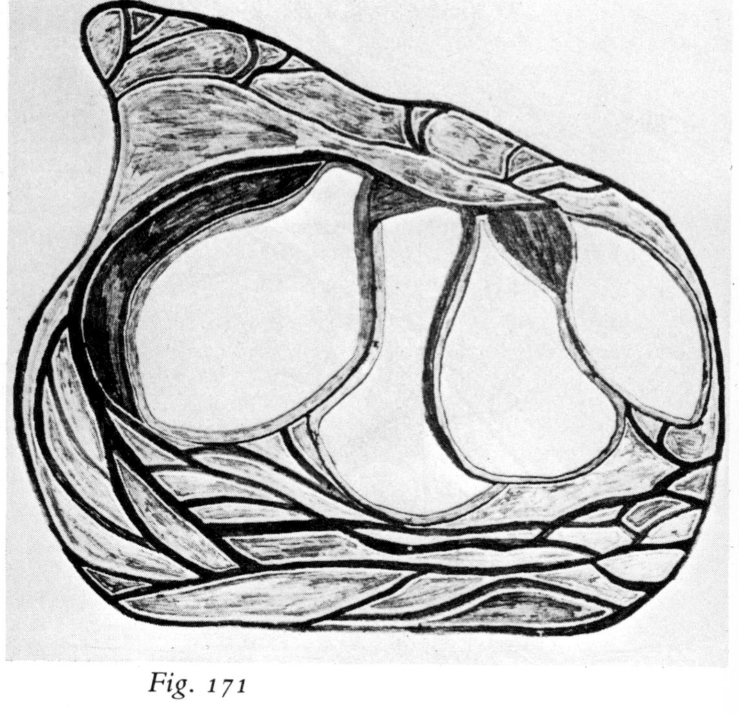

Fig. 171

Colour plate 25, a design of simplicity and serenity, shows contrast again. This started as an exercise in applying different fabrics. Sandra James found those that covered a third of the colour circle and arranged them in the natural order. Surrounded with machine-stitched Lurex thread, they look like semi-precious stones in a setting. This very simple idea with self-imposed limitations worked well and she went to work on developing her theme in a more sophisticated embroidery.

A waterfall inspired the highly textured work by Hilary Humphrey in Fig. 172. Appliqué fabric is superimposed by experimental weaving in the central area, representing the bubbling and fall of water in textured white and silver threads, crochet, beadwork and stitchery. A cool piece of work in the subtle colours of nature.

Colour plate 27 shows Irene Clarke's study from a stone. Fabric appliqué was

Fig. 172

carefully and systematically superimposed by beadwork, and couched thread. This is a two-layer panel. The focal point is padded out from the lower level.

Colour plate 28, an ambitious trio by Angela Burt, consists of cellular shape interpreted in three different ways, but unified by the colour scheme. The idea to work in this way was conceived when visiting an exhibition of Barbara Hepworth sculpture.

Stephanie Groves, colour plate 29, shows the experimental approach that we have tried to foster. She chose a checked ground, which she endeavoured to change into a textured fabric using chicken wire, partly covered with wool and felt scrolls. We show a detail of the right side. The colour is stirring and the attempt adventurous.

Have we seen the design in colour plate 30 before? It is a fabric and thread interpretation of the symmetrical plan of a town seen in Fig. 138. It was quickly and effectively carried out by applying fabric in an oval with turret-shaped edges on a strongly contrasted ground – purple. Further appliqué in orange and red was machined down; black net, placed partly over this brilliant colour, changes it to shades, giving much to the colour scheme. Stitchery, beadwork and shapes of discordant pink off-centre completed the embroidery, with the pink echoed in the surrounding area.

An interesting involvement with the human figure, with a very original point of view, is shown in colour plate 31 by Elaine Davies. She was interested in distortion in art and through studying this came to consider how in the modern world human beings suffer distortion.

Hunger was an obvious example when the body is swollen. This led to the temporary distortion of pregnancy. The colouring suggests the transitory nature of this distortion, while the backbone and embryo remain strong; the latter cushioned in white satin. This is a completely individual outlook from an intellectual student who thought deeply and expressed her ideas with conviction.

Fig. 173, a drawing of a piece of bark, inspired Joan Smith to make an embroidery collage that evoked coral reefs and under-sea discovery. It is not illustrated in this book, but it is a very accomplished piece of work; it has a striking focal point of gold thread weaving, supported by a bracelet set at an angle and further enhanced by covered

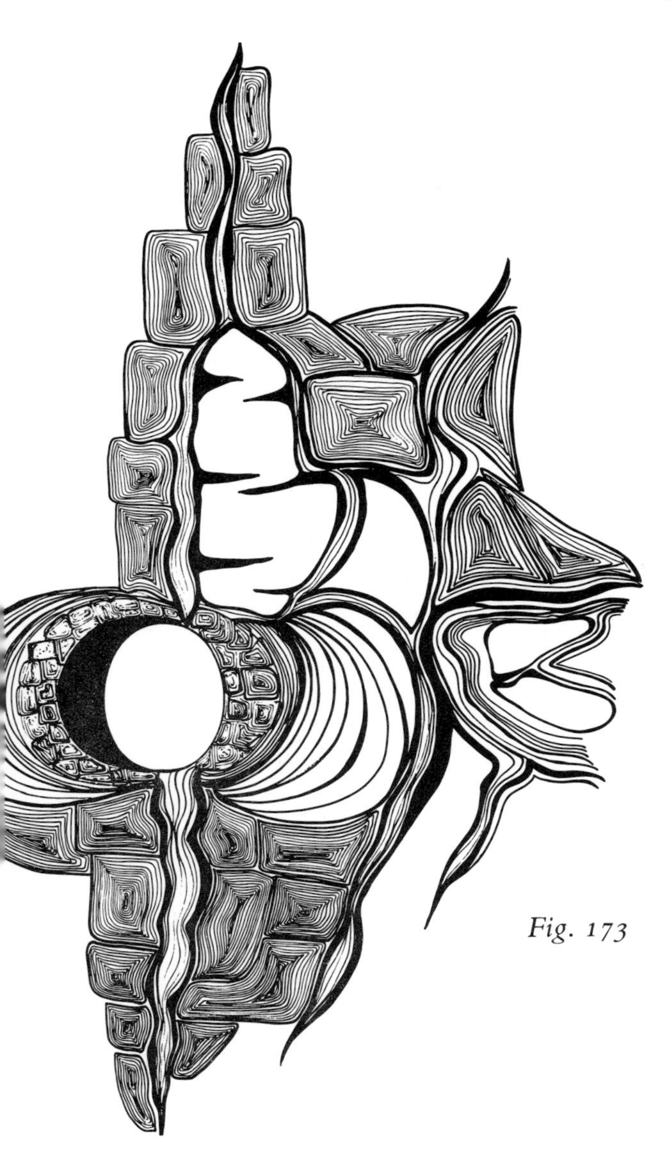

Fig. 173

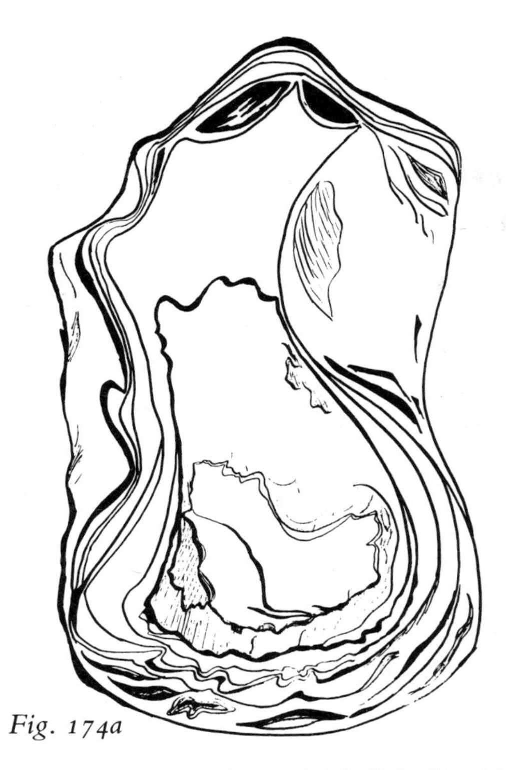

Fig. 174a

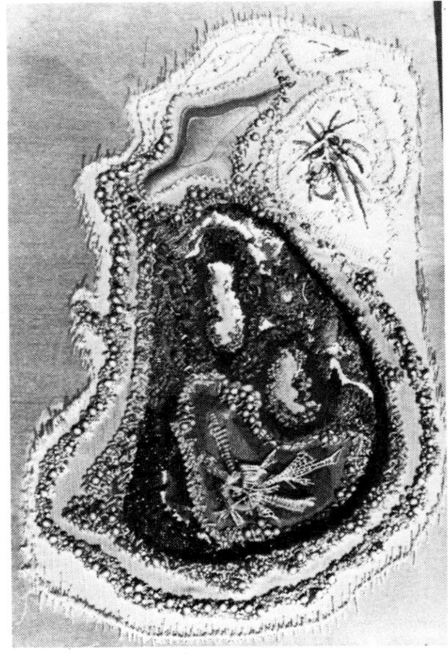

Fig. 174b

curtain rings, beadwork and sequins. Padded-out areas move from this centre of interest in warm green through the colour circle to cool blue at the edge on the right.

In Fig. 174b Merlith Watts shows a two-layered collage inspired by a limestone pebble (Fig. 174a) from Barry, Cold Knap. Her interpretation of the layered effect of the pebble is achieved by combining stitchery, couched thread and beadwork on two layers. Padded appliqué is used on the upper and lower section. We look from the light into darkness. Complementary colours, blue and orange, are blended into a rich colour scheme by the use of black. The hard outline of the stone was skilfully broken by long and short stitches.

When teaching any subject there is always the danger of having too much influence over the students/pupils in the class, especially if the teacher is an enthusiast. It would be possible to have an hypnotic effect and to produce through others replicas of one's own work. This must be avoided at all costs. Each student/designer, after being guided through a basic course of experiment, must develop in her own way even though she may still have guidance. In the selection of collages we have shown you we feel sure that the personality of each student is very clearly expressed in her creative embroidery.

10

A CREATIVE APPROACH TO DRESS

The popularity of embroidery in fashion fluctuates. When in vogue it is often used to emphasise a particular line, because by the very nature of its enrichment it attracts attention. The haute couture designer who studies carefully the shape of his client and extracts from current fashion those aspects that will flatter and draw attention to her best features is treating dress as a design problem. We should follow his example. One element remains, that of choice of fabric. The more experience one has in handling and experimenting with a wide variety of fabrics, the more one develops a sensitivity for apt fabric usage.

Much of the inspiration for dress springs from the fabrics themselves, so that their properties are exploited for creating line and embellishment. A garment should fulfil its function as well as be flattering. For example, day wear is practical in shape and any enrichment should be as launderable as the garment on which it is placed. This applies particularly to children's garments and sportswear. Special occasion garments can take a more exotic approach.

There is a need then to:

1 Be aware of current fashion. There are plenty of advertising media including magazines and television. These can act as a warning as well as a guide.

2 Look as objectively as possible at the shape of the wearer. Most people have something special about them that is worthy of extra attention, e.g.

(i) Good facial features and neck call for dramatic necklines, collars or scarves.
(ii) Attractive bust – bodice detail.
(iii) Small waist – belts accentuate the area from bust to waist.
(iv) Well-shaped hands – interesting detail on cuffs or sleeves.
(v) Well-shaped arms – short sleeve detail.
(vi) Slim hips – style line enhanced by embroidery.
(vii) Shapely legs – interest at hem level on short skirts, slit on long skirts.

3 Have an experimental approach to a wide range of fabrics.

(a) Some fabrics with a clearly defined weave can have this characteristic exploited decoratively, the direction of the grain being dependent on the cut of the garment. The weave can be used as a guide line for decoration or withdrawn for decorative purposes (see Fig. 175).
(b) Patterned fabrics may be exploited for further embellishment following the pattern (colour plate 32).
(c) Firm fabrics have the property of holding a shape well and can take the addition of surface stitches, other applied fabrics or bead work.
(d) Softer fabrics with good draping qualities may have the folds enriched with surface stitches, e.g. smocking (see colour plate 33).
(e) Transparent fabrics give shadowy effects and can be used in a delicate way with stitches or appliqué.
(f) Non-fraying fabrics, e.g. suede, felt, or very closely woven fabrics, e.g. fine linen and mixtures of linen, can have

Fig. 175

shapes cut out of them.

All three things – fashion, the wearer and the fabric – have to be considered. We realise that this is oversimplifying the design problem, but it is a start. The chapter on colour and texture should give guidance here.

Fabrics are frequently used together, either for their contrast in textural qualities, e.g. surface and patterns, or because one makes up for the deficiency of the other in certain circumstances, e.g. an embroidered cuff or belt on chiffon, backed with a firmer lining to hold the shape required and to accept the embroidery. It is not our aim here to explain in detail the different types of embroidery you can try – there are many good reference books available – but rather to encourage interesting and individual explorations.

Whatever fabric is ultimately selected for embroidery, the quality should be in direct relationship to the time and effort spent on it. Our advice is to buy as good a quality as possible. It has to withstand a fair amount of handling as well as wear. The interpretation of a design will relate to the fabric and the function of the garment. The experimental pieces should suggest alternatives, and the experience thus gained should influence the final selection.

Additional surface stitchery and bead work often stiffens the area that is embroidered and sometimes adds extra weight. Ensure that the weight and stiffness are where you want them.

PLANNING EMBROIDERY FOR DRESS

Consider the areas to be embroidered – detachable parts, e.g. belts, panels, scarves, boleros, hoods, collars, cuffs. These are more easily handled and more manageable areas on which to work as well as making the garment more adaptable.

The areas to be decorated on a garment either have to fall over a curved shape or travel around, e.g. cuffs, belts, collars. If you are in any doubt about the fitness of scale (see Chapter 5) or the general effect, you would be wise to stick, pin or paint the design on to the full-scale pattern piece and look at it in a mirror against the area of the body it is to cover. Time used in observing effects is well spent and little in comparison with the ultimate work involved.

The positioning of the embroidery is all-important. In our experience, designs that seem reasonable when placed on the flat can look disastrous on the body shape. This may seem obvious, but star-like shapes have appeared on the bust point before now, when the embroiderer had no intention of emulating the Folies Bergère!

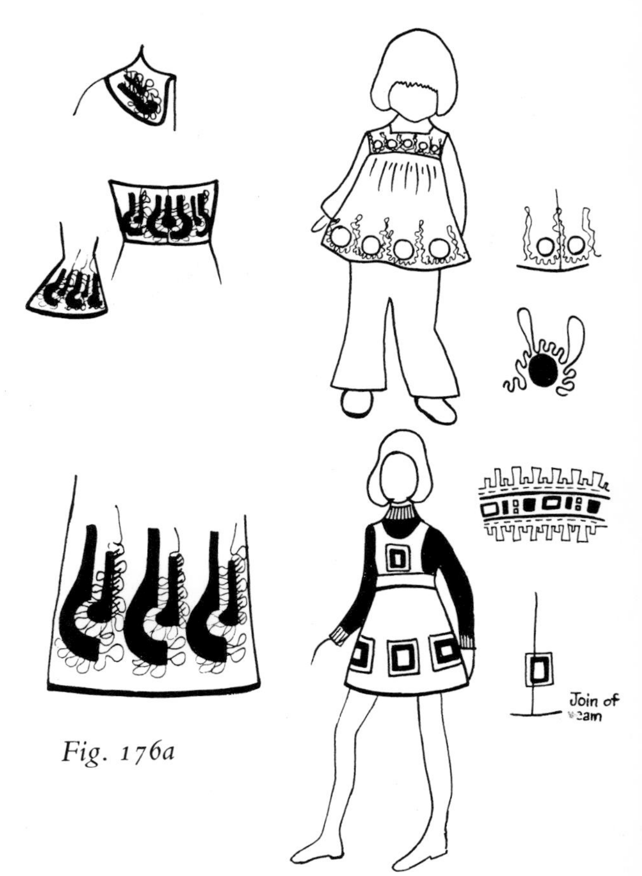

Fig. 176a

SCALE

Border designs may be repeated on different areas with a change of scale relative to the area covered, e.g. small around sleeves and larger at the hemline. It is essential to see that the design joins at the seam line (see Fig. 176a). Dramatic effects on hemlines can be used when the design is planned to be appreciated within the fall of the skirt (small-scale patterns could be lost in the folds of a gathered skirt). If the design is all over the garment it is much more flattering to vary the scale, making bold the areas you wish to emphasise and reducing the scale of the areas you want to diminish.

Machine stitchery forming a textured background is better if roughly planned on the full-scale pattern. The 'flow' exercises in Chapter 4 (page 32) are a great help in developing a sense of balance and promoting confidence (Fig. 176b).

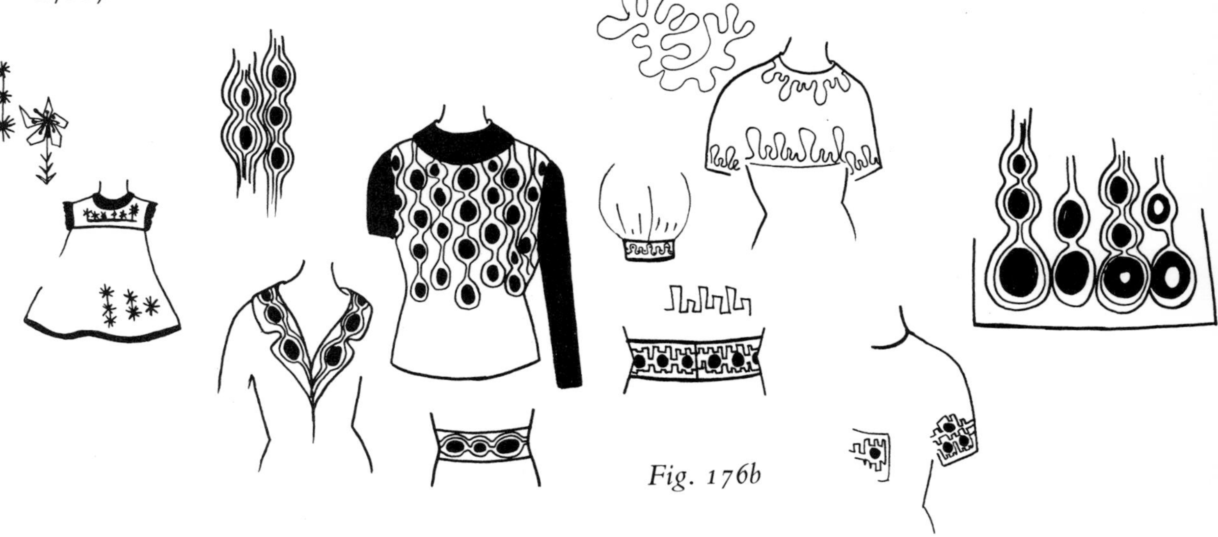

Fig. 176b

Fig. 177

Any design that involves appliqué should indicate the direction of the grain line on the parts to be applied once the position has been decided, because the appliqué is always cut with the weft and warp parallel to the ground material. Consider the area to be embroidered before cutting out the fabric. And remember to allow for darts (Fig. 177).

Place the pattern on the fabric and leave a generous allowance of at least $2\frac{1}{2}''$ (6cm) around the pattern-cut edge – better still to cut out a block. Mark in the fitting lines and other relevant markings, e.g. dart positions, pockets, etc. These markings allow for work within the area to be embroidered, and the extra surrounding fabric safeguards fraying and distortion of the fabric while it is being handled. On completion of embroidery, replace the pattern, check on the position of the markings (sometimes the embroidery 'takes up' the fabric and this affects the fit). Cut out when you are ready to assemble the garment.

Special occasion garments can be fitted by replacing the embroidered section with another fabric – keeping the original fresh and allowing the embroiderer to have a change of activity in making up the garment. Never underestimate the possible effects of stiffness and weight in the embroidery.

TRANSFERENCE OF DESIGN

Some people have sufficient confidence to draw their designs straight on to the fabric using white pencil or chalk. For those who are less adventurous, the majority, the following suggestions will help:

1 Pin the paper pattern on to the background fabric, and chalk or tack around the shape.

2 Trace the pattern on to thin paper, tack this on to the background and either:

(a) tack through the main design lines; or

(b) prick holes around the design and press powdered tailor's chalk through. This will show clearly without discolouring fragile fabrics; or

(c) insert carbon paper before tacking the paper to the background and outline the design with a tracing wheel.

Transfer the design on to a thin fabric that is sympathetic to the background, e.g. muslin, organdie or organza. Tack carefully from the centre out to the wrong side of the fabric. This will also act as an interfacing.

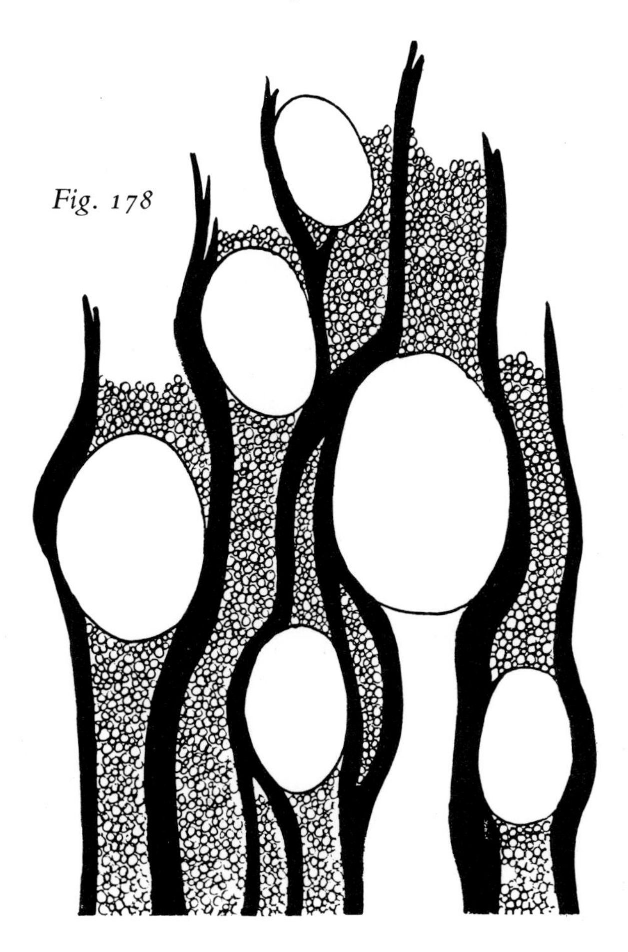

Fig. 178

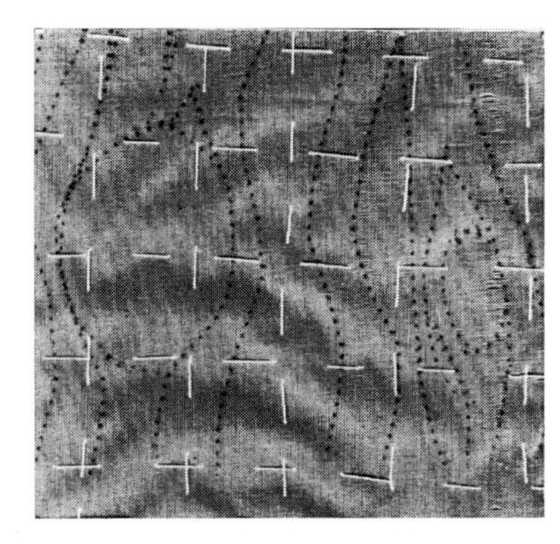

Fig. 179

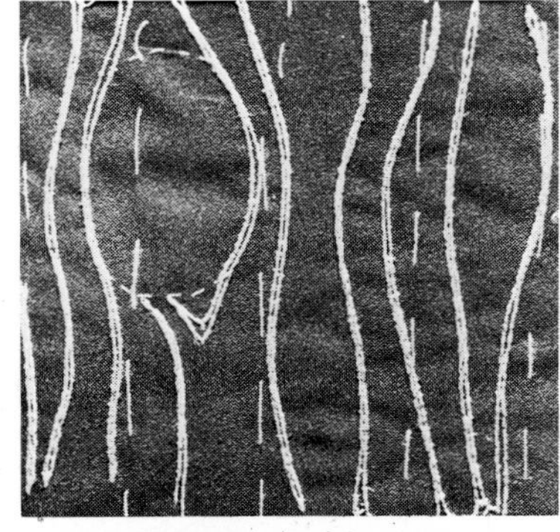

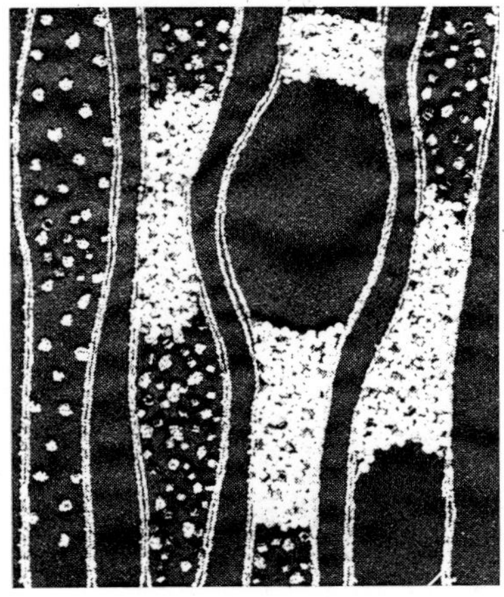

Fig. 180

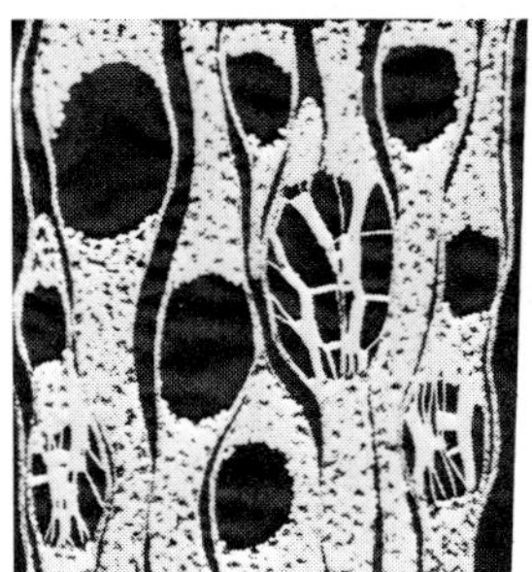

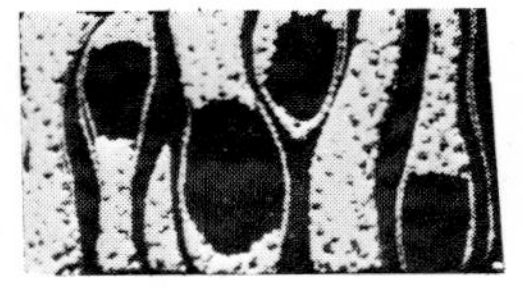

Figs. 179–180 show the development from the design in Fig. 178, which was inspired by cell structure, to the completed embroidery. Fig. 179 shows an example where the design has been transferred by means of a carbon paper and tracing wheel on to organdie.

Fig. 180 shows the embroidery developing in two stages, and the final pieces that were used on the bodice and sleeve of an evening dress.

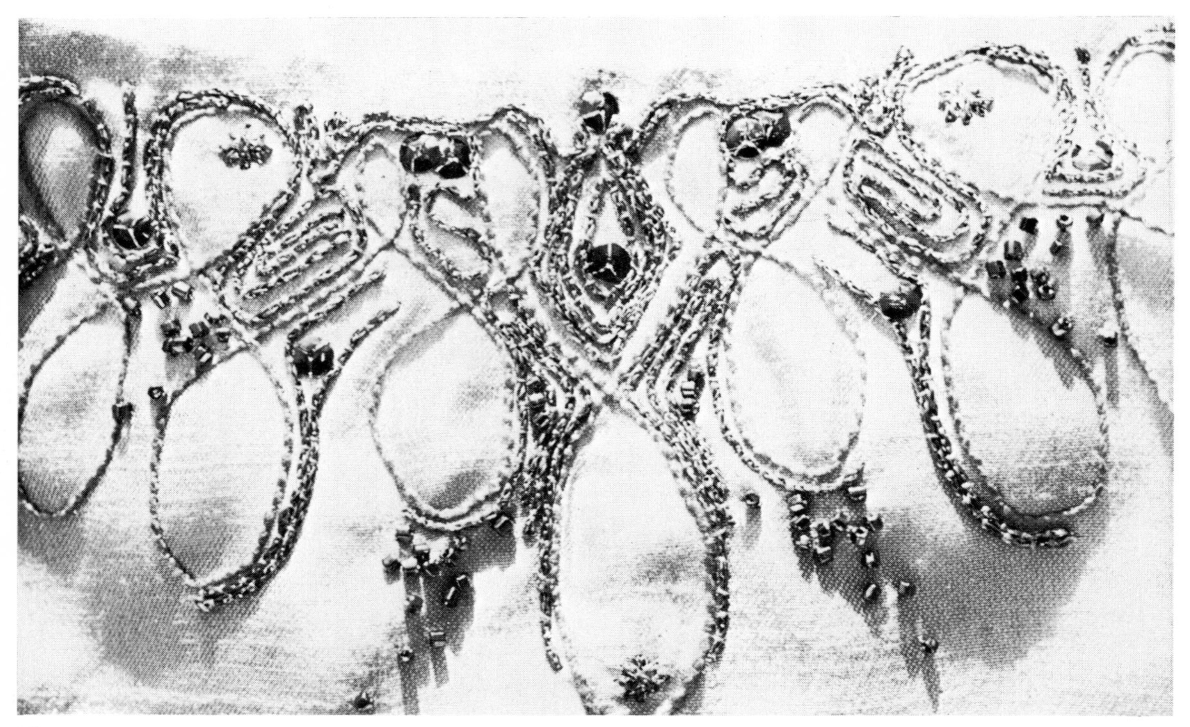

Fig. 181

Some ways in which students tackled the relationship between their choice of fabric and the areas they wanted to embroider are shown below. The first three have one technique in common, machine cable stitch, but each student has used it in a different way.

Fig. 181 shows part of a scooped neckline. The threads were initially allowed to fall in loops around the neckline, and once a reasonable flow was established this was recorded by drawing it on paper. The line was improved and transferred to organdie. The organdie was tacked to the wrong side of the fabric and the lines machined from the wrong side. Additional lines of couching by hand using a thicker thread and extra beadwork added depth and texture.

Fig. 182 shows part of a bodice and the rough plan of the bodice covered with overlapping geometric shapes, so arranged that they are more concentrated

Fig. 182

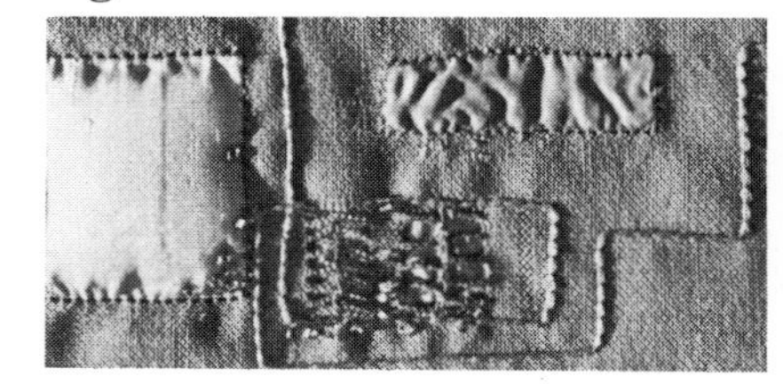

on the lower edge of the bodice, thus drawing attention to the band of applied shapes and drawn fabric work. Here a whole area of the plain wool worsted fabric has been given a textured effect by the machine work.

Fig. 183

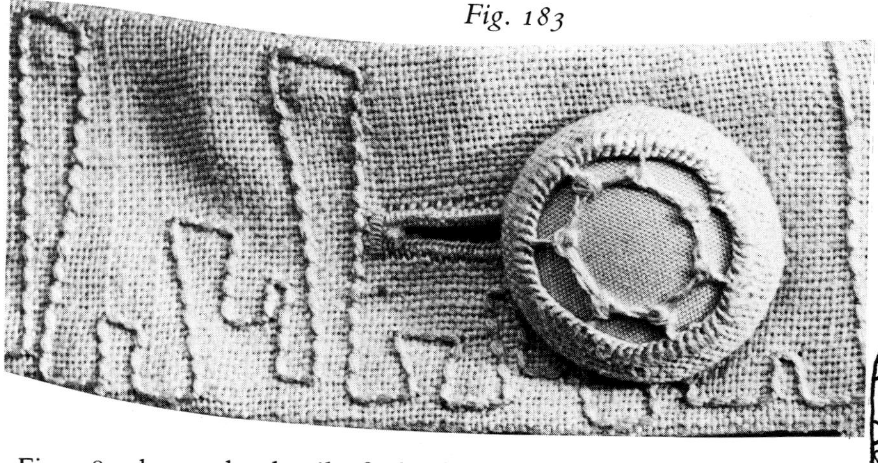

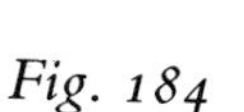

Fig. 183 shows the detail of a half-belt in a mixture of linen and Terylene. The sleeves (see drawing) have circles cut out, designed to reduce in size as they reach the head of the sleeve. The bottom row of circles has additional decorative filling and a line of machine cable that takes a journey around them. This idea is repeated on the half-belt, which is slightly curved to meet neatly at the back. Note button fastening.

The next two illustrations show different ways of tackling circles as shapes. Fig. 184 shows how the circular motif has had to be planned carefully to fit into the bodice shape. The continuous design was tried in a darker pink thread, which proved to be unsatisfactory, so silver Lurex threads with added beadwork and sequins were finally decided upon in order to give added texture and interest. Note the join of the design in the dart line – foreseen in the planning stage.

Fig. 184

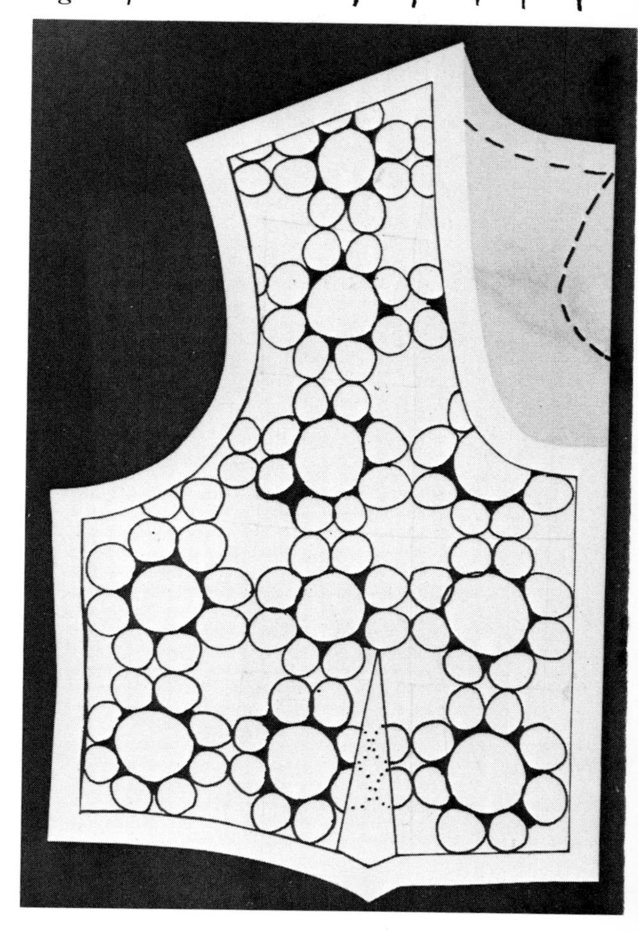

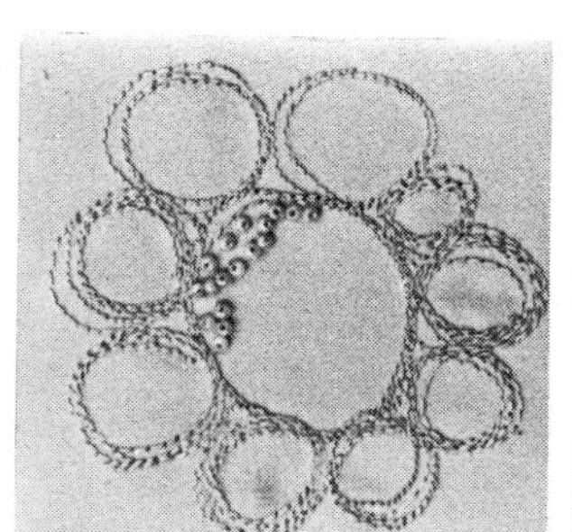

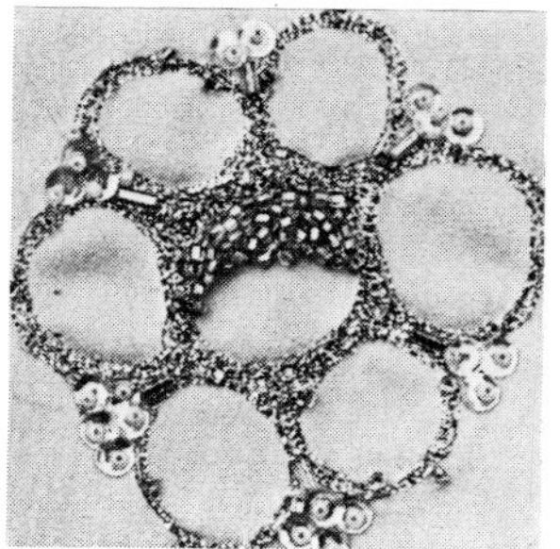

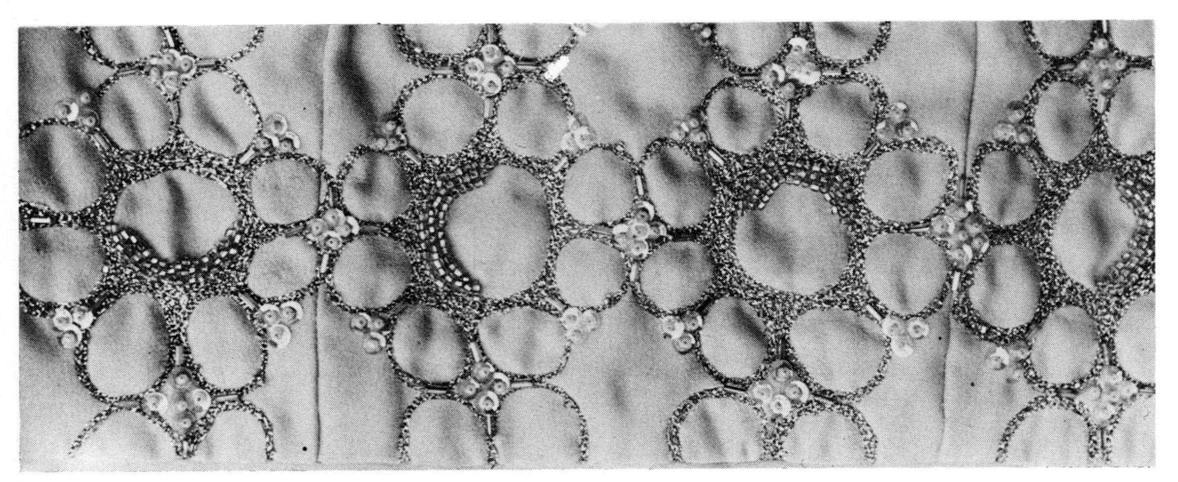

Fig. 184

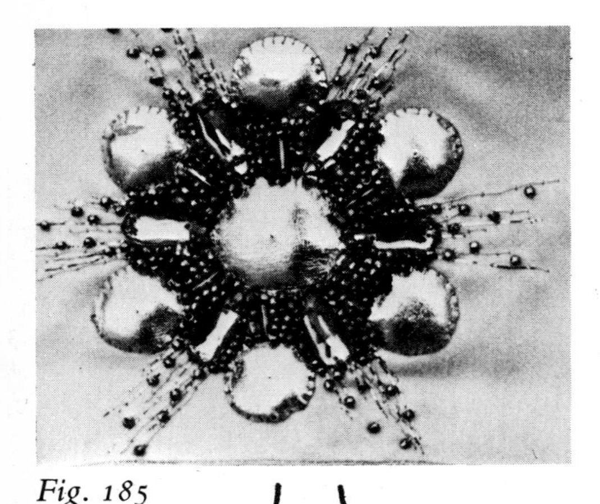

Fig. 185

Fig. 185 shows a similar shape designed to be used as a unit for an inset band. The gold kid has been padded and attached to the silk background with small, fine hand stitches. A rich, textured appearance is achieved by the addition of large topaz-coloured beads that pick out the colour of the rest of the garment. The scatter of bronze beads adds a variety of scale and texture.

A very different approach is seen in Fig. 186. Here the student originally designed the motif for a repeat pattern, but used it as a single unit on a sleeve, adding stitches by hand to give additional texture. The wool shantung fabric used for the main part of the garment and the sleeve was dyed together with some silk organza for the appliqué.

We showed in Figs. 181–184 examples of planning within the main part of a garment. Now let us see some examples of planning within a smaller area.

Fig. 187 shows an example of the line of the basque being emphasised. The chequered effect is emphasised in colour (blue and jade green). This was achieved by tacking one fabric very carefully on top of the other and machining in the main shapes. Some areas were cut away

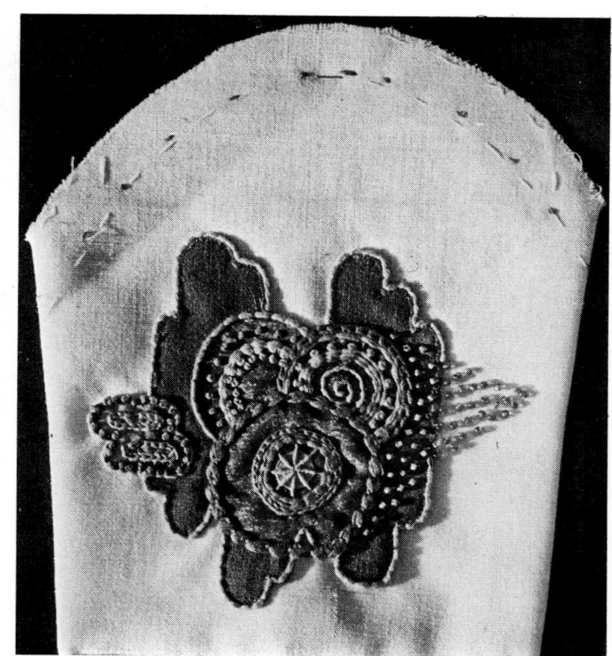

Fig. 186

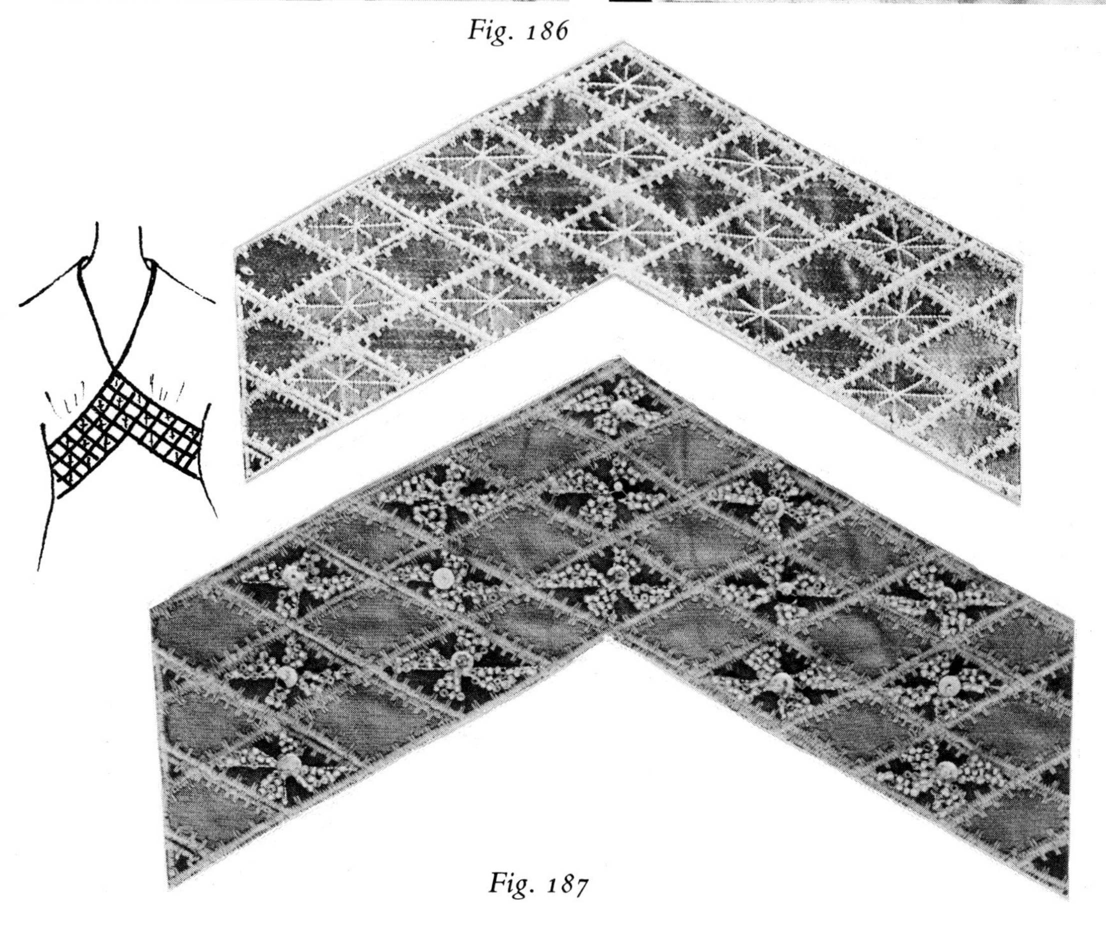

Fig. 187

to expose the underlying fabric. The shapes were then strengthened and made decorative by machine embroidery stitching on the right side. Beadwork and sequins added richness and texture.

The four bands illustrated in Fig. 188 are all different ways of treating a similar shape – but all using different materials. Fig. 188a appeared at an earlier stage in Chapter 6, but now the shapes are more controlled. Silver kid and beadwork have been added for enrichment.

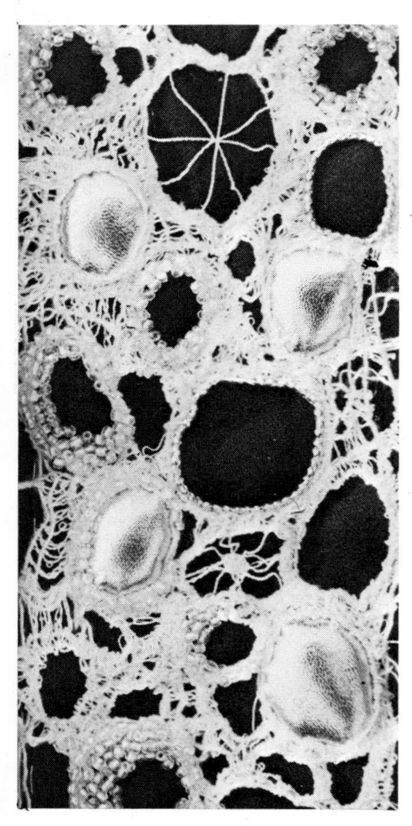

Fig. 188a

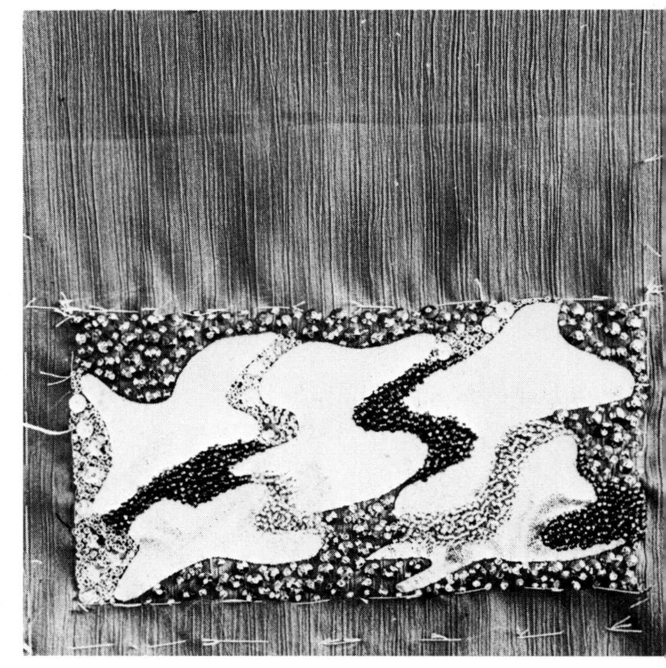

Fig. 188b

In Fig. 188b the shapes fit like a jigsaw into the belt. The pieces of silver kid are attached by hand with invisible thread. The silver French knots, vivid blue and green beads add texture and interest. Note the tacked area showing the 'fitting line' and the cutting line. Fig. 188c is a belt in cream wild silk; it has alternate squares in gold kid appliqué and is padded with cut-out square shapes exposing brown silk georgette. The couched gold thread is enriched with bronze and cream beads.

Fig. 188c

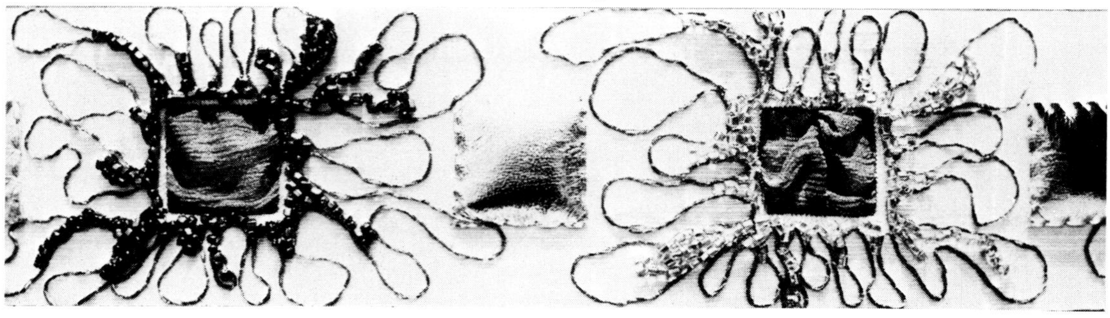

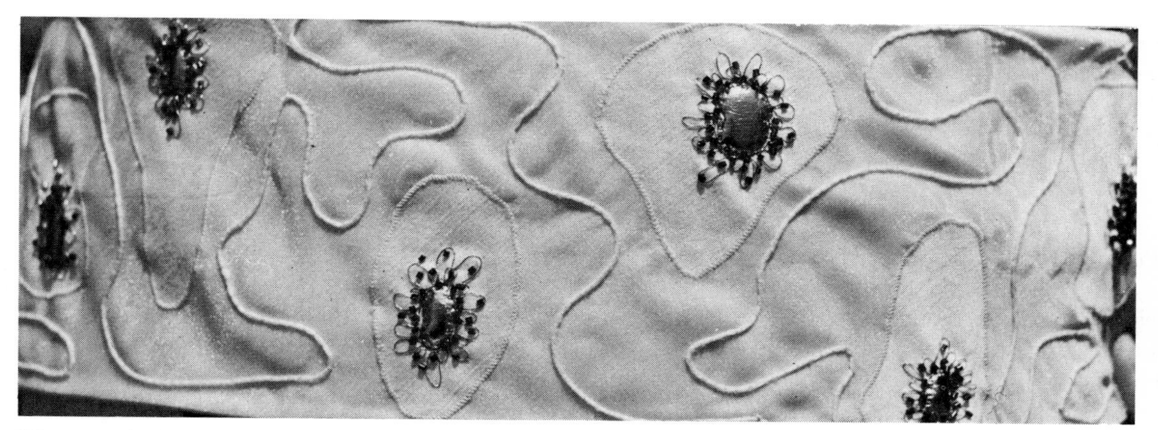

Fig. 188d

Fig. 188d is a belt cut on the true cross of the fabric with pieces applied following the grain; these islands are enriched with gold padded shapes, fine gold thread and beadwork.

The section of the bodice in colour plate 34 is richly textured with applied padded shapes, beadwork and French knots. The planning for this was done by cutting a paper shape and dividing it up into shapes that were sympathetic to the original and moving them apart, so that channels were formed for beadwork and stitches.

The border design in colour plate 35 was planned to form a band around a hood, framing the face and linking with the colour of the lining that would show when the hood was dropped. The basic outline of the border was made by machine cable stitch. This was then used as a basis for satin stitch and French knots.

Fig. 189

THE DESIGN PROCESS FOR DRESS EMBROIDERY

The following illustrations indicate the whole design process of the embroiderer. We would like to emphasise, as will be shown here, the need to select and reject throughout the work, both at the drawing stage and after trying small samples of embroidery on cloth, which alone gives the real idea of the weight and effect of the finished work.

The positioning of embroidery is shown in Fig. 189.

Figs. 190a, b and c show some ideas roughed out on paper; b and c were selected for experiment on fabric and the results are shown in d and e.

Fig. 190a

Fig. 190b

Fig. 190c

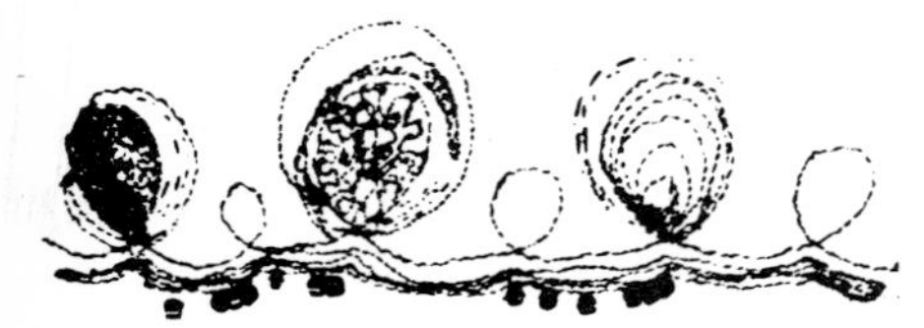

Fig. 190d

Fig. 190e

Fig. 191

Fig. 191 shows the final selection carried out on the garment. Note the way in which the motif joins at the dart line.

Fig. 192 shows a small waistcoat which Mary James wished to make. It could be worn over a variety of dresses as it was detachable. She chose a rich, beaded treatment on pink.

The preliminary sketches in Fig. 193 show possibilities for the all-over design upon which she had decided. She designed in line on paper but was envisaging the finished product in cloth, thread and beads.

Fig. 192

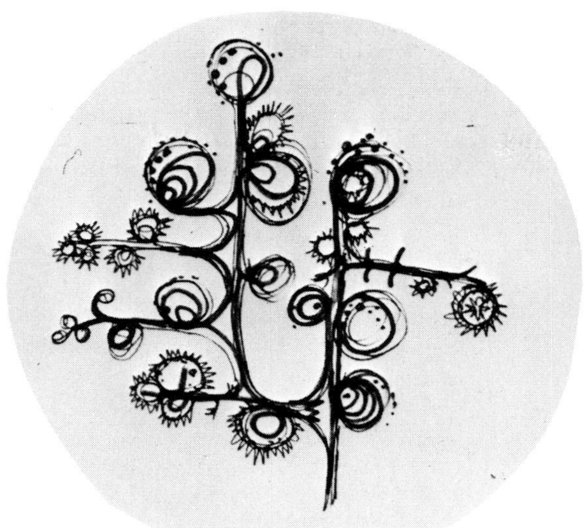

Fig. 193a

(a) Machine embroidery in a variety of threads, the tension being loosened to create whipping. Embroidery in white and with the addition of beads.
(b) Flower shapes worked on machine embroidery using No. 60 Sylko and couching in Sylko Perlé. A variety of shapes and sizes to be worked all over the waistcoat and beads added.
(c) Flower shapes worked in machine embroidery over organdie mounted on polyester. The organdie to be cut away at the centre of the flowers and threads drawn across. Varied weights of threads to be used and beads added.
(d) Embroidered shapes in machine embroidery connected with vermicelli pattern in No. 60 Sylko. Some parts are to be padded and a variety of white threads used.
(e) All-over design using different weights of threads to create a three-dimensional effect.

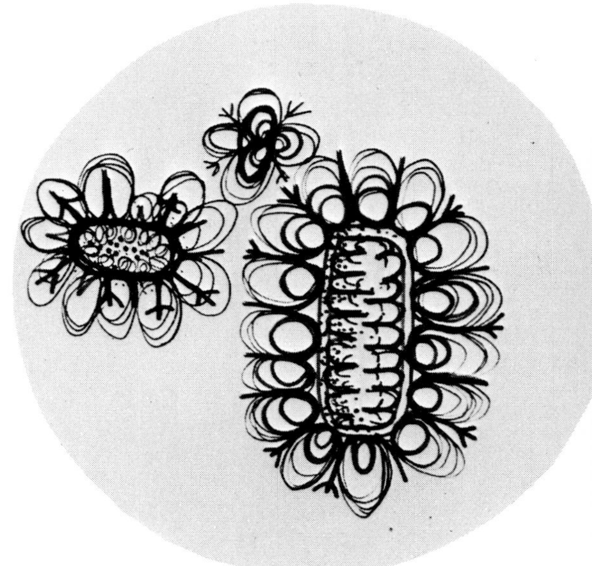

Fig. 193b

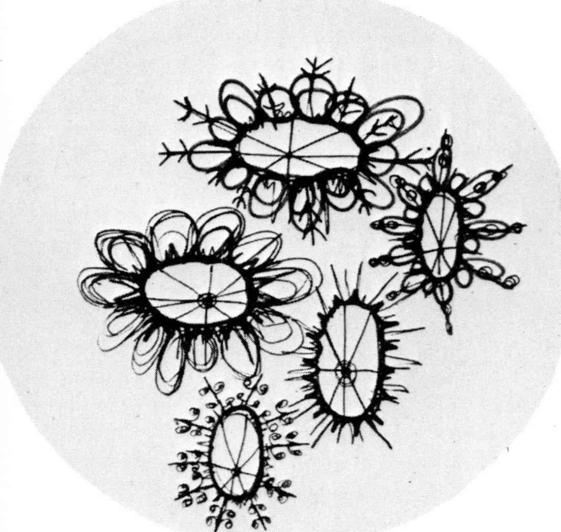

Fig. 193c

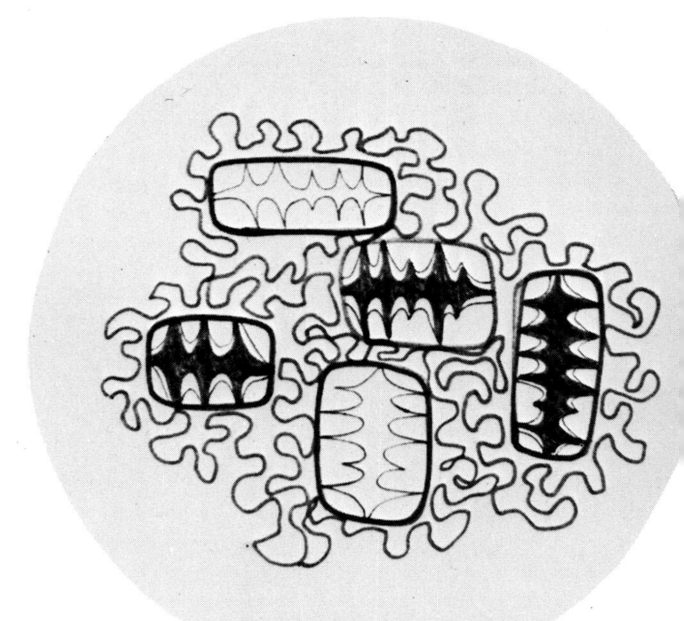

Fig. 193d

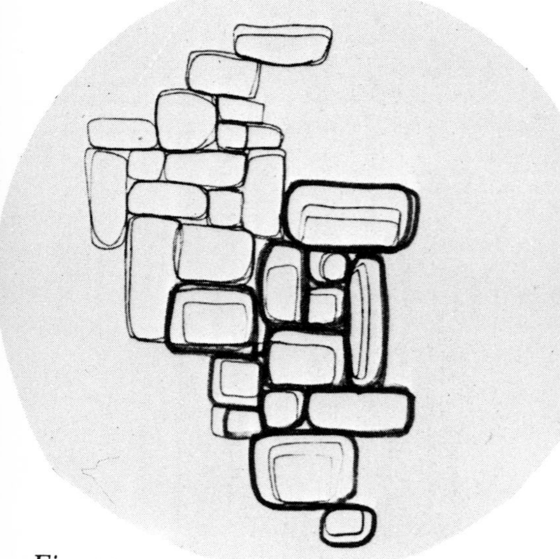

Fig. 193e

After trying out one of these designs in fabric, she rejected it because 'the flowers intertangle and so create a confused design. It would be better if the flowers were isolated', i.e. with surrounding negative shape (Fig. 194).

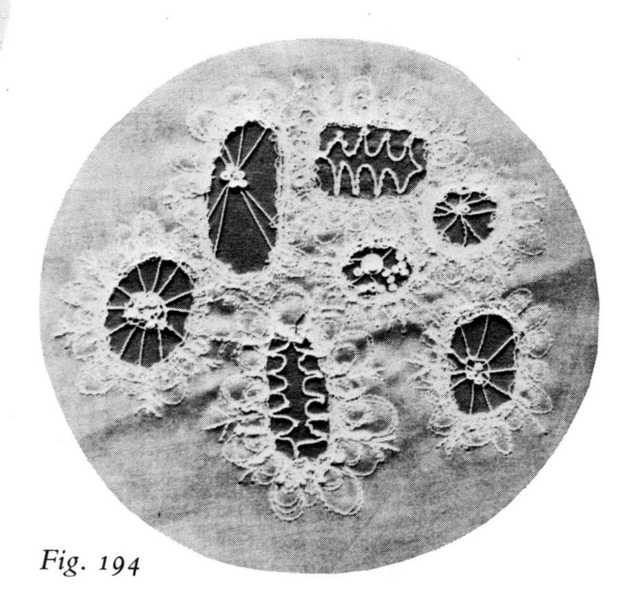

Fig. 194

Fig. 195a

Fig. 195b

Fig. 195 shows the final design choice (Fig. 195a) and a try-out (Fig. 195b) in sample form. The plan when designing was to work triangular motifs in free machine embroidery, using No. 60 Sylko and Sylko Perlé couching. A variety of shapes, including flowers, were to be worked within the triangles and the spaces between these filled in with sequins, different-sized round beads, bugle beads and French knots, worked in Sylko Perlé and coton à broder. Sections would be padded using the trapunto quilting method. White threads, beads and mother-of-pearl sequins would be used. This plan was followed almost as first conceived, as can be seen in the sample embroidery (Fig. 195b) and the close-up of the finished textured work (Fig. 196). Fig. 197a shows the join on the side of the waistcoat and Fig. 197b on the shoulder seams.

Fig. 196

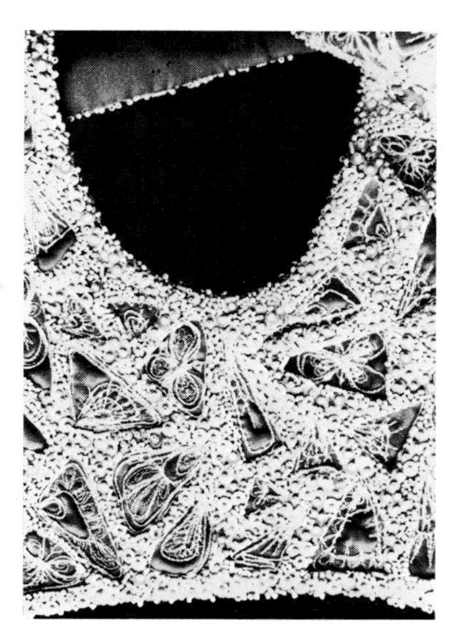

Fig. 197a

Fig. 197b

An experimental approach to dress embroidery, such as we have seen in the above photographs, will pay dividends. The ability to see what is good and reject what is bad or less pleasing will increase with practice and experience. Dress embroidery, as all other aspects of design, is a personal comment, perhaps the most personal of all, because no two people have the same problems of figure to solve any more than two people have the same personality to express.

CONCLUSION

We are aware that we have not been able to cover everything in this book, but what seemed more important was to try to instil an attitude that the learning, experimenting process never stops. This is especially true with creative work that is living and always changing with the times. We already see a changing influence on needlecraft now that men and boys are studying the textile arts and producing collages of a less detailed, more robust nature.

Living as we do in a busy technological age, we must not scorn its benefits. A piece of work carried out quickly by machine may well be a gem, while the work of a lifetime can be of no value. There is no virtue in drudgery. Joy should be our aim. There must be room for all ways of working.

More than ever today people want to find themselves – to 'do their own thing', the current way of saying 'to thine own self be true'. All creative work is an expression of the individual personality and it is no good bluffing and trying to be like another. One person may find real satisfaction in painstakingly covering a large area with French knots to achieve a textured effect; another, with the same aim and less effort, might use a textured wriggling couched thread. Well-considered detail and accuracy of technique are qualities that give pleasure to the beholder, in the same way as certain qualities in the use of oil paint show the joy of the artist in his materials, which he communicates to all who view his work. Whichever way one works, the essential is to have a largeness of vision, to see the design as a whole and to ensure that it remains a unified whole throughout the working.

Because creative work is living and changing all the time, what is done today will not be 'in tune' with the spirit of ten years hence. The illustrations in this book may date therefore, but the advice will not. Basic design and technique principles do not change with fashion or style. All art is an expression of the age in which we live, and we must keep abreast of the times and cultivate a sense of contemporary design as well as being alive to new materials and tools (machines).

The world grows smaller and in the twentieth century national styles have all but disappeared. There is, however, an international style that is simple and functional. We referred, when considering composition, to the amount of space that is permissible in different eras. At the moment, a space that is considered can be large and very valuable in effect. In interior decoration a feature may be given splendid isolation in order that it may be viewed and appreciated. Imagine the Victorians allowing such a thing! If we think of the Victorian and Georgian eras, we could talk of them as 'cluttered' and 'elegant' respectively. Because of our liking for simplicity, we are nearer in spirit to the Georgians and similarly more in sympathy with prehistoric and primitive art than with the artists of the Renaissance. To foster this contemporary feeling for design, we, today, would advise constant looking at what is going on in the fine arts – contemporary architecture, sculpture and painting – in order to accustom the eye to the artistic trends, in much the same way as one studies the changing lengths of hemlines shown by the couturiers and eventually becomes a conditioned disciple of whatever fashion dictates!

Architects, sculptors and painters, like couturiers, are avant garde, but in the fullness of time their influence is seen in our dress and our furnishing textiles. Looking at fabrics is a natural pursuit for the needlewoman, and a study of the most modern printed fabrics available will help to keep her in touch with the contemporary movement.

New materials, as yet undreamt of, will be appearing. Use them adventurously and explore them, as we have done the more traditional ones and those at present available, for their limitations and characteristics.

It may seem, looking back over the chapters, that there are many rules for designing when in fact there are none – only a few guide lines. Anyone who makes a rule will find that a genius will break it successfully. Witness Gainsborough's 'Blue Boy', which was painted in defiance of Reynolds' theory that the main interest should always be painted in warm colours! We are not writing for geniuses, and so we hope that the grammar for creative work will prove helpful. Once fluency is achieved and expression comes easily, grammar is no longer a concern, yet the grounding was essential and its effect will always remain evident.

A young child's fancy soars instinctively to create in blissful ignorance of his limitations, like the bumble bee which flies unaware of aero-technical tests that prove his wings unequal to the task in the relation of their span to the weight and shape of his body. The adult, however, is all too mindful of shortcomings and becomes inhibited by them to the point of not getting off the ground at all unless he can see a reasoned way of working creatively. We have tried to give a logical sequence, which should aid the craftswoman to have a pattern of working. Our aim has been to destroy the mystique surrounding creativity, to show that there is much that one can learn about designing without having a flair for it.

At the very end of the book, however, we admit something that we would not have dared to mention earlier for fear of discouraging. There is something beyond mere reason in creativity, which those who practise it, those who have come to a full understanding of what it is about, will recognise. There are moments of exhilaration when it is no longer reason that urges one on to create something that one never imagined possible. Call it inspiration, the Muse, whatever you will, it is some power that takes over once confidence and involvement are completely established. Something beyond explanation, when one thing leads to another.

We asked one of our students to tell us how she had gone about working one of her embroidery collages. After telling us that the source of inspiration was a group of ceramic figures and that she had wanted to incorporate certain techniques that she had enjoyed in earlier exercises, she added, 'and then one thing leads to another'. Not very helpful advice if she were teaching others, but a remark that was absolutely true in her experience because she had reached a stage of knowing how to get going by finding an idea for the design, how to become completely involved with the materials, using techniques previously practised in experiment, how to continue working without inhibition, a spirit of adventure and, very important, when to stop. Although she would not say it herself, she had a sense of power, that special exhilaration that told her that she was capable of succeeding.

You may feel that all that is very fine for one who has without doubt a real flair for the job, but it all grew from very small beginnings, and we are sure (because we know the progress she made in three years' study) that she would be the first to admit this. Our hope is that you will similarly feel that you are being helped, stage by stage, encouraged, finally gaining the confidence to work creatively with rewarding enjoyment.

BIBLIOGRAPHY

Ash, Beryl, and Dyson, Anthony. *Introducing Dyeing and Printing,* Batsford 1970.
Gale, Elizabeth. *From Fibres to Fabrics,* Mills & Boon 1968.
Giltsoff, Natalie. *Fashion Bead Embroidery,* Batsford 1971.
Howard, Constance. *Inspiration for Embroidery,* Batsford 1966.
Jameson, Norman. *Batik for Beginners,* Studio Vista 1970.
John, Edith. *Needleweaving,* Batsford 1973.
McNeill, Moyra. *Quilting for Today,* Mills & Boon 1975.
Maile, Anne. *Tie and Dye as a Present-day Craft,* Mills & Boon 1969.
Mason, Enid. *Embroidery Design,* Mills & Boon 1970.
Nea, Sara. *Batik,* Van Nostrand Reinhold 1970.
Nield, Dorothea. *Adventures in Patchwork,* Mills & Boon 1975.
Palmer, Dennis. *Introducing Pattern, its Development and Application,* Batsford 1970.
Pfannschmidt, E. E., *Twentieth-Century Lace,* Mills & Boon 1975.
Pilcher, Ann Mary. *Macramé for Beginners,* Bell 1972.
Rottger, Ernst. *Creative Paper Craft,* Batsford 1973.
Rottger, Ernst, and Klante, Dieter. *Creative Drawing–Point and Line,* Batsford 1964.
Rowland, Kurt. *Looking and Seeing,* 1-4, Ginn 1964-6.
Searle, Valerie, and Clayson, Roberta. *Screen Printing on Fabric,* Studio Vista 1968.

SUPPLIERS

Pens, batik wax, lino blocks and cutters, rollers, screen print frames, squeegees, tjantings:

Dryad Handicrafts
Northgates
Leicester

Terylene gauze for screens, cotton and dyes for printing:

Polyprint
815 Lisburn Road
Belfast BT9 7GX

Dyes for printing:

Skilbeck Bros.
55-7 Glengall Road
London SE15

Dyes, hot and cold:

Dylon International
Lower Sydenham
London SE26 5HD

Dyes, acid, reactive direct:

Basil Hollobon
67 Skipton Road
Ilkley, Yorks.

Embroidery fabrics, thread, church embroidery, metallic threads, gold and silver kid:

Mace & Nairn
89 Crane Street
Salisbury, Wilts.

Beads and sequins:

Ells & Farrier
5 Princes Street
London W1 8PH